SCIENCE FICTION AND FANTASY

SCIENCE FICTION AND FANTASY

26 CLASSIC AND CONTEMPORARY STORIES

Fred Obrecht
Member, Department of English
Los Angeles Mission College

BARRON'S EDUCATIONAL SERIES, INC./WOODBURY N.Y.

© Copyright 1977 by Barron's Educational Series, Inc.

All rights reserved.
No part of this book may be reproduced
in any form, by photostat, microfilm, xerography,
or any other means, or incorporated into any
information retrieval system, electronic or
mechanical, without the written permission
of the copyright owner.

All inquiries should be addressed to:
Barron's Educational Series, Inc.
113 Crossways Park Drive
Woodbury, New York 11797

Library of Congress Catalog Card No. 75-34067

International Standard Book No. 0-8120-0651-8

Library of Congress Cataloging in Publication Data
Main entry under title:
Science Fiction and Fantasy
   Bibliography: p. 253
   SUMMARY: Includes short stories and selections
from larger science fiction works. Suggestions for
discussion and writing follow some stories.
   1. Science fiction. 2. Short stories.
[1. Science fiction. 2. Short stories] I. Obrecht, Fred.
PZ5.157   [Fic]   75-34067
ISBN 0-8120-0651-8

PRINTED IN THE UNITED STATES OF AMERICA

Preface

The purpose of this anthology is to provide a comprehensive survey of science fiction by presenting some of the most intriguing examples of the form ever assembled in one volume. A parallel objective is to help elevate science fiction in the critical estimation of students, to give them reason to delve further into this rich and unique literary resource, and to demonstrate that science fiction, far from the insignificant latecomer it is sometimes held to be, is, rather, a distinguished and vital part of our literary tradition.

In the introduction, as do most editors of science fiction anthologies, we attempt to define the term science fiction, favoring a more liberal definition which allows inclusion of derivational works like Edward Bellamy's *Looking Backward*, Sir Thomas More's *Utopia* or Mary Shelley's *Frankenstein*. But we mean our definition to be temporary; by the time students have finished this short course, we hope they will be at least inspired to form their own definitions of the term. *Science fiction* is truly that elusive; its scope is so outreaching, and so unbounded, that only personal and individual definition, based on what each of us has read, can be held valid.

To clarify the form somewhat, we have divided our selections into six broad categories:

(1) The Early Challenge of Space and Time
(2) Tampering with Human Nature
(3) Going a Step Further—Robots
(4) Traffic with the Planets
(5) Changing the World for Better or Worse
(6) Extension? Prediction? Fantasy?

Needless to say, this arrangement of stories is not the only logical one. As many teachers prefer to teach by short story elements, an alternate *Suggestions for Discussion and Writing* following many stories are designed to highlight such attributes of the stories as their main themes, their social implications (surprisingly important in many cases), or their artistic forms. Often they require more careful preparation than mere discussion will allow, although as initial stages in essay planning, such discussions can be an important class activity. The vocabulary exercises, of course, should be just part of the vocabulary building that goes on in every class, at any hour. It is our feeling that students who take the trouble to learn the contextual words should be rewarded, at least by means of a summary test.

While the selection of stories in this book will give the student many hours of fascinating reading, we must emphasize the fact that it is intended only as a sampler, as an appetizer-prelude to further pursuits. In keeping to practical size limits, it was not possible to include stories by *all* major contemporary writers. We leave it to the reader to seek our omissions, and to enjoy the thrill of happy discoveries.

Introduction

Ask any two persons—anytime, anywhere—to give you their definitions of *science fiction* and you will have two different answers. Read any six books on the subject and you will have six more versions of what the term means.

It is not our intention to impose upon you, or even to suggest, our choice in this matter; rather, it is our hope that this book will enable you to formulate a definition of your own. When you can explain clearly what science fiction means *to you*, this book will have served its purpose.

In the past, this form of literature—whether in books or magazines—was published under such titles as *Travel Adventures, Wonder Stories, Fantastic Tales, Mysteries of the Universe,* etc. It took such garish "headlines" to draw public attention to the nature of the books' contents.

Hugo Gernsback, a New York magazine publisher and one of the great pioneers in the field we are exploring here, provided the much needed common denominator by coining the magic name *Science Fiction* in 1929.

Instantly and universally, science fiction was defined and accepted as a form of literature distinct and apart from all others; a form which imposed on the writer none of those shackles that confine traditional writing to the limits of so many rules and precedents.

Comfortably settled under the aegis of its brand-new generic name, science fiction prospered in spite of a world-wide depression and World War II. Other media of entertainment contributed their shares: the movies gave us Boris Karloff as Frankenstein's monster and Fredric March as Dr. Jekyll. In 1938 a science fiction radio program threw the east coast of the United States into a panic . . . (more about that in Chapter 4).

Now that we have a rough sketch of its present structural form, what of the basic elements of science fiction; how and when did it begin?

All creatures in the animal kingdom have the instincts of curiosity and fear. Man alone was endowed with imagination, a fact which was bound to complicate matters for him: whereas a fox, let us say, was able to shrug off the mysteries of the heavens and such whims of nature as lightning and earthquakes, Man demanded an explanation . . . .

And so began the myths, the ancient creeds, witchcraft, astrology, the fantastic tales of wanderings into the unknown reaches of space and time, the distortions of the mental and physical capabilities of Man himself. Evidently, "explanations" were not enough: Man developed a thirst for something *beyond* the ever growing knowledge brought to him by concrete scientific research. The French call this thirst *le culte du merveilleux*. We call it science fiction.

To keep ahead of reality as he must, the science fiction writer has had to do some fast thinking: in the span of about thirty years, true science has given us the atomic and hydrogen bombs, coast-to-coast television, the jet engine, intercontinental ballistic missiles, Sputnik I, two Navy submarines under the North Pole, John Glenn in orbit, the first human heart transplant, Neil Armstrong and Ed Aldrin on the moon.

You will determine, in the course of your study, how well contemporary science fiction has met the challenge of reality. Somewhat to your surprise, you will learn that it could not have done so without your help. We are referring to the tacit understanding between the writer and you, the reader: your willingness to accept the unbelievable if, by doing so, you are entertained, surprised, mystified, even frightened. There will be other, more lasting rewards. You will gather much valid technological information; your imagination will be challenged by the presentation of actual problems of which you were not aware, and you may be tempted to help solve them. Now and then, a story will lead you to serious thoughts about the future—yours, and that of all of us. And who knows? . . . *You* may find some of the answers.

Acknowledgements

The author gratefully acknowledges the following sources for granting permission to reprint the stories included in this book,

"A Bad Day for Sales." Copyright by Fritz Leiber, Reprinted by permission of the author and the author's agent, Robert P. Mills, Ltd.

"August 2026: There Will Come Soft Rains." Copyright © 1950 by Ray Bradbury. Reprinted by permission of The Harold Matson Company, Inc.

"There Will Come Soft Rains," a poem by Sara Teasdale. Copyright © 1920 by Macmillan Publishing Co., Inc.; renewed 1948 by Mamie T. Wheless. Reprinted by permission.

Chapter Two from *Brave New World* by Aldous Huxley. Copyright © 1932, 1960 by Aldous Huxley. Reprinted by permission of Harper & Row, Publishers, Inc., and Chatto and Windus Ltd.

"Eat, Drink, and Be Merry," by Dian Crayne. Copyright © 1974 by Jerry Pournelle. Reprinted by permission of the author; from *2020 Vision*.

"Erem" by Gleb Anfilov from *The Ultimate Threshold: A Collection of the Finest in Soviet Science Fiction.* Translated and edited by Mirra Ginsburg. Copyright © 1970 by Mirra Ginsburg. Reprinted by permission of Holt, Rinehart and Winston, Inc.

"Fondly Fahrenheit" by Alfred Bester. Reprinted by permission by the author's agent, Lurton Blassingame. Copyright © 1954 by Mercury Press, Inc.

"The Fun They Had" by Isaac Asimov. Copyright © 1951 by NEA Service, Inc. Reprinted by permission of the author.

"The Great Nebraska Sea" by Allan Danzig. Reprinted by permission of the author.

"Helen O'Loy" by Lester del Rey. Reprinted by permission of the author and the author's agents, Scott Meredith Literary Agency, Inc., 580 Fifth Avenue, New York, New York 10036.

"In the Matter of the Assassin Merefirs" by Ken W. Purdy. Reprinted by permission of the author's estate and its agents, Scott Meredith Literary Agency, Inc., 580 Fifth Avenue, New York, New York 10036.

"The Man Inside" by Bruce McAllister. Originally appeared in *Galaxy* (1969) and *Best Science Fiction: 1969,* ed. Harry Harrison and Brian Aldiss (Putnam, 1970).

"Men are Different" by Alan Bloch. Copyright © 1954 by Groff Conklin. Reprinted from *Science Fiction Thinking Machines* by permission of Groff Conklin, editor, and the author.

A selection from *Nineteen Eighty Four* by George Orwell. Copyright © 1949 by Harcourt, Brace & World, Inc. Reprinted by permission of Brandt & Brandt.

"Of Course" by Chad Oliver. Reprinted by permission of the author and Collins-Knowlton-Wing, Inc.

"Report from the Planet Proteus" by Lawrence Sail. From *Opposite Views.* Reprinted by permission of J. M. Dent & Sons, Ltd.

The first act of *R.U.R.* by Karel Capek; English version by Paul Selver and Nigel Playfair. Reprinted by permission of the author's agent, Samuel French, Inc.

A selection from *The Time Machine* by H. G. Wells. Reprinted by permission of the estate of H. G. Wells.

A selection from *Utopia* by Thomas More. From Thomas More's *Utopia,* translated and edited by H.V.S. Ogden. Copyright © 1949 by AHM Publishing Corporation. Reprinted by permission of AHM Publishing Corporation.

A selection from *The War of the Worlds* by H. G. Wells. Reprinted by permission of the estate of H. G. Wells.

CHAPTER 1

The Early Challenge of Space and Time

Introduction 1

From the Earth to the Moon *(Selections from the novel)* 3
   JULES VERNE

Twenty-Thousand Leagues Under the Sea 13
(Selections from the novel)
   JULES VERNE

The Time Machine *(Selections from the novel)* 23
   H. G. WELLS

Christmas 200,000 B.C. 31
   STANLEY WATERLOO

In the Year Ten Thousand 39
   WILLIAM HARBEN

CHAPTER 2

TAMPERING WITH HUMAN NATURE

Introduction 49

Frankenstein *(Selections from the novel)* 51
   MARY W. SHELLEY

The Strange Case of Doctor Jekyll and Mister Hyde and
   Other Famous Stories *(A selection from the novel)* 57
   ROBERT LOUIS STEVENSON

Fondly Fahrenheit 65
   ALFRED BESTER

The Man Inside 83
   BRUCE McALLISTER

CHAPTER 3

Going A Step Further- ROBOTS

Introduction 89

R.U.R. *(A selection from the play)*...................... 91
   KAREL CAPEK

Helen O'Loy 103
   LESTER DEL REY

A Bad Day for Sales 113
   FRITZ LEIBER

Men Are Different 119
   ALAN BLOCH

Some Fun With Space Jargon 121

CHAPTER 4
TRAFFIC WITH THE PLANETS

Introduction 127

War of the Worlds *(Selections from the novel)* 129
   H. G. WELLS

Of Course 139
   CHAD OLIVER

CHAPTER 5
Changing the World for Better or Worse

Introduction 155

Utopia *(A selection from the novel)* 157
   SIR THOMAS MORE

Looking Backward *(A selection from the novel)* 161
   EDWARD BELLAMY

Brave New World *(A selection from the novel)* 171
   ALDOUS HUXLEY

Nineteen Eighty-Four *(A selection from the novel)* 179
   GEORGE ORWELL

August 2026: There Will Come Soft Rains 189
   RAY BRADBURY

The Fun They Had 197
ISAAC ASIMOV

CHAPTER 6
EXTENSION? PREDICTION? FANTASY?

Introduction 203
The Great Nebraska Sea 213
ALAN DANZIG

Erem 219
GLEB ANFILOV

Report from the Planet Proteus 225
LAWRENCE SAIL

In the Matter of the Assassin Merefirs 227
KEN W. PURDY

Eat, Drink, and Be Merry 239
DIAN CRAYNE

Alternate Arrangements of Contents 249
Appendix I: Short Story Structure and Point of View 251
Bibliography 253
Some Recommended Reading 255

In this great crucible of life we call the world—in the vaster one we call the universe—the mysteries lie close packed, uncountable as grains of sand on ocean's shores. They thread gigantic the star-flung spaces; they creep, atomic, beneath the microscope's peering eye. They walk beside us, unseen and unheard, calling out to us, asking why we are deaf to their crying, blind to their wonder.

A. Merritt
in "The Metal Monster"

Chapter 1

THE EARLY CHALLENGE OF SPACE AND TIME

The title of this opening chapter deserves an explanation, an answer to the obvious question the reader will ask: "Why do you link Space with Time, and were there not *earlier* challenges to both which predate your selections?"

Time and Space are equal entities in the laws of the Universe and, moreover, you will find that they often parallel each other in science fiction; we dwell at some length in the general introduction on our option for a beginning. We can but urge inquisitive students to search for earlier works at their public libraries—and assure them that their efforts will be richly rewarded.

We are setting as a foundation for modern science fiction these four books: *From the Earth to the Moon* (1865), and *Twenty Thousand Leagues Under the Sea* (1869), both by Jules Verne; *The Time Machine* (1895), and *The War of the Worlds* (1898), both by H. G. Wells.

The two Jules Verne stories hold the unique distinction of having passed from "fiction" to "reality" in your lifetime. That removes much of the suspense intended: you will make mental notes of the differences and similarities between what you are reading and what you know to be "the facts." But that, in itself, is a rare literary treat.

The winged creatures of ancient mythologies and folklores traveled through Time by means of locomotion varying from the supernatural to the ridiculous. *The Time Machine* was the first man-made, mechanical conveyance designed specifically for Time Travel; it worked so well that we suggest you read the entire story and share with "The Time Traveller" some of his discoveries.

The time lapse between "Christmas 20,000 B.C." and "In the Year Ten Thousand" might well be the life span granted to man upon this earth . . . Both stories were written before 1900.

Illustration from the 1874 publication of Verne's *From the Earth to the Moon*.

Selections from

From the Earth to the Moon

JULES VERNE

fire!

THE FIRST of December had arrived! the fatal day! for, if the projectile were not discharged that very night at 10h. 46m. 40s. p.m., more than eighteen years must roll by before the moon would again present herself under the same conditions of zenith and perigree.

The weather was magnificent. Despite the approach of winter, the sun shone brightly, and bathed in its radiant light that earth which three of its denizens were about to abandon for a new world.

How many persons lost their sleep on the night which preceded this long-expected day! All hearts beat with anxiety, save only the heart of Michel Ardan. That imperturbable personage came and went with his habitual business-like air, while nothing whatever denoted that any unusual matter preoccupied his mind.

After dawn, an enormous crowd covered the fields which extend, as far as the eye can reach, round Stones Hill. Every quarter of an hour the railway brought additional numbers of sightseers; and, according to the statement of the Tampa *Town Observer*, not less than five million spectators thronged the soil of Florida.

For a whole month previously, the mass of these persons had camped in the enclosure, and laid the foundations for a town which afterward was called "Ardan's Town." The whole plain was covered with huts, cottages, and tents. Every nation under the sun was represented there; and every language might be heard spoken at the same time. It was a perfect Babel reenacted. All the various classes of American society were mingled together in terms of absolute equality. Bankers, farmers, sailors, cotton-planters, brokers, merchants, boatmen, magistrates elbowed each other in the most free-and-easy way. Louisiana Creoles fraternized with farmers from Indiana; Kentucky and Tennessee gentlemen and haughty Virginians conversed with trappers and the half-savages of the lakes and butchers from Chicago. Broad-brimmed white hats and Panamas, blue cotton trousers, light-colored stockings, cambric frills were all here displayed; while upon shirt-fronts, wristbands, and neckties, upon every finger, even upon the very ears, they wore an assortment of rings, shirt-pins, brooches, and trinkets, of which the value only equaled the execrable taste. Women children, and servants in equally expensive dress, surrounded their husbands, fathers, or masters, who resembled the patriarchs of tribes in the midst of their immense households.

At meal-times all fell to work upon the dishes peculiar to the Southern States, and consumed with an appetite that threatened speedy exhaustion of the food resources of Florida, fricasseed frogs, stuffed monkeys, fish chowder, underdone 'possum, and raccoon steaks. And as to the liquors which accompanied this indigestible repast! The shouts, the vociferations that resounded through the bars and taverns decorated with glasses, tankards, and bottles of marvelous shape, mortars for pounding sugar, and bundles of straws! "Mint-julep!" roars one of the barmen; "Claret sangaree!" shouts another; "Cocktail!" "Brandy-smash!" "Real mint-julep in the new style!" All these cries intermingled produced a bewildering and deafening hubbub.

But on this day, 1st of December, such sounds were rare. No one thought of eating or drinking, and at four p.m. there were vast numbers of spectators who had not even taken their customary lunch! And, a still more significant fact, even the national passion for play seemed quelled for the time under the general excitement of the hour.

Up till nightfall, a dull, noiseless agitation, such as precedes great catastrophes, ran through the anxious multitude. An indescribable uneasiness pervaded all minds, an indefinable sensation which oppressed the heart. Everyone wished it was over.

However, about seven o'clock, the heavy silence was dissipated. The moon rose above the horizon. Millions of hurrahs hailed her appearance. She was punctual to the rendezvous, and shouts of welcome greeted her on all sides, as her pale beams shone gracefully in the clear heavens. At this moment the three intrepid travelers appeared. This was the signal for renewed cries of still greater intensity. Instantly the vast assemblage, as with one accord, struck up the national hymn of the United States, and "Yankee Doodle," sung by five million hearty throats, rose like a roaring tempest to the farthest limits of the atmosphere. Then a profound silence reigned throughout the crowd.

The Frenchman and the two Americans had by this time entered the enclosure reserved in the center of the multitude. They were accompanied by the members of the Gun Club, and by deputations sent from all the European observatories. Barbicane, cool and collected, was giving his final directions. Nicholl, with compressed lips, his arms crossed behind his back, walked with a firm and measured step. Michel Ardan, always easy, dressed in thorough traveler's costume, high leather boots on his legs, pouch by his side, in loose corduroy suit, cigar in mouth, was full of inexhaustible gayety, laughing, joking, playing pranks with J. T. Matson. In one word, he was the thorough "Frenchman" (and worse, a "Parisian") to the last moment.

Ten o'clock struck! The moment had arrived for taking their places in the projectile! The necessary operations for the descent, and the subsequent removal of the cranes and scaffolding that leaned over the mouth of the Columbiad, required a certain period of time.

Barbicane had regulated his chronometer to the tenth part of a second by that of Murchison the engineer, who was charged with the duty of firing the gun by means of an electric spark. Thus the travelers enclosed within the projectile were enabled to follow with their eyes the impassive needle which marked the precise moment of their departure.

The moment had arrived for saying "goodbye!" The scene was a touching one. Despite his feverish gayety, even Michel Ardan was touched. J. T. Maston had found in his own dry eyes one ancient tear, which he doubtless reserved for the occasion. He dropped it on the forehead of his old friend.

"Can I not go?" he said, "there is still time!"

"Impossible, dear old fellow!" replied Barbicane. A few moments later, the three fellow-travelers had ensconced themselves in the projectile, and screwed down the plate which covered the entrance-aperture. The mouth of the Columbiad, now completely disencumbered, was open entirely to the sky.

The moon advanced upward in a heaven of the purest clearness, outshining in her passage the twinkling light of the stars. She passed over the constellation of the Twins, and was now nearing the halfway point between the horizon and the zenith. A terrible silence weighed upon the entire scene! Not a breath of wind upon the earth! Not a sound of breathing from the countless chests of the spectators! Their hearts seemed afraid to beat! All eyes were fixed upon the yawning mouth of the Columbiad.

Murchison followed with his eyes the hand of his chronometer. It wanted scarce forty seconds to the moment of departure, but each second seemed to last an age! At the twentieth there was a general shudder, as it occurred to the minds of that vast assemblage that the bold travelers shut up within the projectile were also counting those terrible seconds. Some few cries here and there escaped from the crowd.

"Thirty-five! — thirty-six! — thirty-seven! — thirty-eight! — thirty-nine! —forty!—FIRE!"

Instantly Murchison pressed with his finger the key of the electric battery, restored the current of the fluid, and discharged the spark into the breach of the Columbiad.

An appaling, unearthly report followed instantly, such as can be compared to nothing whatever known, not even to the roar of thunder, or the blast of volcanic explosions! No words can convey the slightest idea of the terrific sound! An immense spout of fire shot up, and with great difficulty some few spectators obtained a momentary glimpse of the projectile victoriously cleaving the air in the midst of the fiery vapors!

foul weather

At the moment when that pyramid of fire rose to a prodigious height into the air, the glare of the flame lit up the whole of Florida; and for a moment day superseded night over a considerable extent of the country. This immense canopy of fire was perceived at a distance of one hundred miles out at sea, and more than one ship's captain entered into his log the appearance of this gigantic meteor.

The discharge of the Columbiad was accompanied by a perfect earthquake. Florida was shaken to its very depths. The gases of the powder, expanded by heat, forced back the atmospheric strata with tremendous violence, and this artificial hurricane rushed like a waterspout through the air.

Not a single spectator remained on his feet! Men, women, children, all lay prostrate like ears of corn under a storm. There ensued a terrible tumult; a large number of persons were seriously injured. J. T. Maston, who, despite all dictates of prudence, had kept in advance of the crowd, was pitched back 120 feet, shooting like a projectile over the heads of his fellow-citizens. Three hundred thousand persons remained deaf for a time, and as though struck stupefied.

As soon as the first effects were over, the injured, the deaf, and lastly, the crowd in general, woke up with frenzied cries. "Hurrah for Ardan! Hurrah for Barbicane! Hurrah for Nicholl!" rose to the skies. Thousands of persons, noses in air, armed with telescopes and binoculars, were questioning space, forgetting all bruises and emotions in the one idea of watching for the projectile. They looked in vain! It was no longer to be seen, and they were obliged to wait for telegrams from Long's Peak. The director of the Cambridge Observatory was at his post in the Rocky Mountains; and to him, as a skillful and persevering astronomer, all observations and reports had been transmitted.

But an unforeseen phenomenon came in to subject the public impatience to a severe test.

The weather, hitherto so fine, suddenly changed; the sky became heavy with clouds. It could not have been otherwise after the terrible derangement of the atmospheric strata, and the dispersion of the enormous quantity of vapor arising from the combustion of 200,000 pounds of pyroxyle!

On the morrow the horizon was covered with clouds—a thick and impenetrable curtain between earth and sky, which unhappily extended as far as the Rocky Mountains. It was a calamity! But since man had chosen to disturb the atmosphere, he was bound to accept the consequence of his experiment.

Supposing, now, that the experiment had succeeded, the travelers having started on the 1st of December, at 10h. 46m 40s. p. m., were due on the 4th at Oh. p. m., at their destination. So that up to time it would have been difficult after all to have observed, under such conditions, a body so small as the shell. Therefore they waited with what patience they might.

From the 4th to the 6th of December inclusive, the weather remaining much the same in America, the great European instruments of Herschel, Rosse, and Foucault were constantly directed toward the moon, for the weather was then magnificent; but the comparative weakness of their lenses prevented any trustworthy observations being made.

On the 7th the sky seemed to clear up. They were in hopes now, but their hopes were of but short duration, and at night again thick clouds hid the starry vault from all eyes.

Matters were now becoming serious, when on the 9th the sun reappeared for an instant, as if for the purpose of teasing the Americans.

On the 10th, no change! J. T. Maston went nearly mad, and great fears were entertained regarding the mental state of this worthy individual.

But on the 11th one of those inexplicable storms peculiar to those semi-tropical regions was let loose in the atmosphere. A terrific east wind swept away the groups of clouds which had been so long gathering, and at night the semi-disc of the orb of night rode majestically amid the soft constellation of the sky.

a new star

That very night, the startling news so impatiently awaited, burst like a thunderbolt over the United States, and thence, darting across the ocean, ran through all the telegraphic wires of the globe. The projectile had been detected, thanks to the gigantic reflector of

Long's Peak. Here is the message received by the director of the Observatory of Cambridge. It contains the scientific conclusion regarding this great experiment of the Gun Club.

Long's Peak, December 12.
To the Officers of the Observatory of Cambridge:

"The projectile discharged by the Columbiad at Stones Hill has been detected by Messrs. Belfast and J. T. Maston, 12th of December, at 8:47 p.m., the moon having entered her last quarter. This projectile has not arrived at its destination. It has passed by the side; but sufficiently near to be retained by the lunar attraction.

"The rectilinear movement has thus become changed into a circular motion of extreme velocity, and it is now pursuing an elliptical orbit around the moon, of which it has become a true satellite.

"The elements of this new star we have as yet been unable to determine; we do not yet know the velocity of its passage. The distance which separates it from the surface of the moon may be estimated at about 2,833 miles. However, two hypotheses come here into our consideration.

"1. Either the attraction of the moon will end by drawing them into itself, and the travelers will be able to land; or,

"2. The projectile, following an immutable law, will continue to gravitate around the moon till the end of time.

"At some future time, our observations will be able to determine this point, but then the experiment of the Gun Club can have no other result than to have provided our solar system with a new star.

J. Belfast.

This unexpected development gave rise to many questions. What mysterious results was the future reserving for the investigations of science? At all events, the names of Nicholl, Barbicane, and Michel Ardan were certain to be immortalized in the annals of astronomy!

When the information from Long's Peak had become known, there was but one feeling of universal surprise and alarm. Was it possible to go to the aid of these bold travelers? No! for they had placed themselves beyond the reach of humanity, by crossing the limits imposed by the Creator on his earthly creatures. They had air enough for *two* months; they had food enough for *twelve—but after that*? There was only one man who would not admit that the situation was desperate—he alone had confidence; and that was their devoted friend J. T. Maston.

Besides, he never let them get out of sight. His home was henceforth the post at Long's Peak; his horizon, the mirror of that **immense** reflector. As soon as the moon rose above the horizon, he immediately caught her in the field of the telescope; he never let her go for an instant out of his sight, and followed her assiduously in her course through the stellar spaces. He watched with untiring patience the passage of the projectile across her silvery disc, and thus the worthy man kept his three friends under constant observation—and never doubted that he would see them again some day.

"Those three men," he said, "have carried into space all the resources of art, science, and industry. With that, one can do anything; and you will see that, some day, they will come out all right."

On July 20, 1969, U. S. astronaut Neil A. Armstrong became the first man to set foot on the moon. Edwin E. Aldrin, Jr., accompanied Armstrong on the moon landing.

VOCABULARY STUDY

"Good words are worth much and cost little." The poet George Herbert made this observation in the seventeenth century, but his meaning is probably truer now than ever before. It is a widely accepted fact that articulate, direct speakers, the people with just the right word for their comment, are the people who succeed in all endeavors today, in business, in science, in the humanities. We all owe ourselves no less than a good start in the lifelong habit of vocabulary development.

Begin by trying to determine the correct definitions of the words in the left column, matching them with the answers to the right. Note that the vocabulary list is in context; in most cases it will help to go back to the story (the exact page on which the word appears is given) to use further contextual clues from the reading. When you have finished, check your answers with the Cumulative Vocabulary List at the end of the chapter, noting the definitions of the words you have missed.

Each chapter in this book will give you further practice with all words accumulated so far. By the time you finish the book you will have learned some very useful words in as economical a way as possible. Consider each Cumulative Vocabulary List an assignment, a list to be mastered.

VOCABULARY QUIZ 1-A

Words to Learn

denizens *vociferations* *immutable*
Babel *intrepid* *assiduously*
execrable *prodigious*
patriarchs *derangement*

From the Earth to the Moon

Match each italicized word with the appropriate choice from the right.

Words in Context

1. "three of its *denizens*," p. 3.
2. "a perfect *Babel*," p. 3.
3. "the *execrable* taste," p. 4.
4. "the *patriarchs* of tribes," p. 4.
5. "the *vociferations* that resounded," p. 4.
6. "the three *intrepid* travelers," p. 4.
7. "a *prodigious* height," p. 6.
8. "the terrible *derangement*," p. 7.
9. "an *immutable* law," p. 8.
10. "he followed her *assiduously*," p. 9.

Definitions

a. fearless
b. disturbance
c. not changeable
d. steadily, attentively
e. enormous
f. inhabitants
g. a noisy scene
h. very bad
i. fathers or founders
j. outcries

VOCABULARY PRACTICE 1-A

Write a sentence for each of the words below. You may change the word's part of speech, tense, or number if you wish. Each sentence must have a meaning of its own and not seem to be a part of the other two.

1. *intrepid*   2. *prodigious*   3. *assiduously*

SUGGESTIONS FOR DISCUSSION AND WRITING

1. At the launching of the Columbiad, "not less than five million spectators thronged the soil of Florida," (p. 3) and "all these cries intermingled produced a bewildering and deafening hubbub." (p. 4). Compare Jules Verne's account of the launching of the Columbiad with the launching of the first Apollo lunar probe.

2. Contrast the two missions. How do you account for the differences?

SCIENCE FICTION AND FANTASY

3. Compare and contrast the means of propulsion used in the two missions. How do you account for the lack of similarity?

4. RESEARCH PROJECT: Write a detailed, authentic narrative of the actual launching of Apollo 11, man's first moon landing.

5. Virtually all of the news and magazine accounts of the Apollo trip to the moon were emotionally "dry;" that is, factual and reportorial rather than emotional and dramatic. The style of *From the Earth to the Moon* is quite the opposite.

   (a) Find several adjectives in Verne's writing that would seem out of place in today's coverage of space shots.

   (b) Choose several passages (at least five) which contain descriptions that are so emotional or ornate in style that they would never have been written about the Apollo launching.

   (c) What else is "different" about Jules Verne's style—his use of punctuation for example, or his descriptions of peripheral events?

   (d) Why do you suppose we of the present day tend to prefer less description and emotional reference in our daily news diet than did people of a century ago?

Selections from

Twenty-Thousand Leagues Under the Sea

JULES VERNE

the iceberg

ABOUT EIGHT o'clock in the morning of March 16 the *Nautilus*, following the fifty-fifth meridian, cut the antarctic polar circle. Ice surrounded us on all sides, and closed the horizon. But Captain Nemo went from one opening to another, still going higher. I cannot express my astonishment at the beauty of these new regions. The ice took most surprising forms. The splitting and fall of ice was heard on all sides, great overthrows of icebergs which altered the whole landscape like a diorama. Often seeing no exit, I thought we were definitely prisoners; but instinct guiding him at the slightest indication, Captain Nemo would discover a new pass. He was never mistaken when he saw the thin threads of bluish water trickling along the ice fields; and I had no doubt that he had already ventured into the midst of these antarctic seas before.

On March 16, however, the ice fields absolutely blocked our road. It was not the iceberg itself, as yet, but vast fields cemented by the cold. But this obstacle could not stop Captain Nemo; he hurled himself against it with frightful violence. The *Nautilus* entered the brittle mass like a wedge, and split it with frightful crackings. The ice, thrown high in the air, fell like hail around us. By its own power of propulsion, our submarine made a canal for itself; sometimes carried away by its own impetus, it climbed upon the ice field, crushing it with its weight, and sometimes buried beneath it, dividing it by a simple pitching movement, producing large rents in the ice.

Violent gales assailed us at this time, accompanied by thick fogs, through which, from one end of the deck to the other, we could see nothing. The wind blew sharply from all points of the compass, and the snow lay in such hard heaps that we had to break it with blows of a pickax. The temperature was always at five degrees below zero; every outward part of the *Nautilus* was covered with ice. At length, on March 18, we were positively blocked. It was no longer either streams, packs, or ice fields, but an interminable and immovable barrier, formed by mountains soldered together.

"An iceberg!" said the Canadian to me.

I knew that to all other navigators who had preceded us, this was an insurmountable obstacle. Of the liquid surface of the sea there was no longer a glimpse. Under the spur of the *Nautilus* lay stretched a vast plain, entangled with confused blocks. Here and there sharp points, and slender needles rising to a height of two hundred feet; farther on a steep shore, hewn as it were with an ax, and clothed with grayish tints; huge mirrors, reflecting a few rays of sunshine, half drowned in the fog. The *Nautilus* was then obliged to stop in its adventurous course amid these fields of ice. In spite of our efforts, in spite of the powerful means employed to break up the ice, the submarine remained immovable. Generally, when we can proceed no farther, we have return still open to us; but here return was as impossible as advance, for every pass had closed behind us; and for the few moments when we were stationary, we were likely to be totally blocked, which did happen, indeed, about two o'clock in the afternoon, the fresh ice forming around the hull with astonishing rapidity. I was obliged to admit that Captain Nemo had been reckless. I was on deck at that moment. The captain had been studying our situation for some time, when he said to me:

"Well, Sir, what do you think of this?"

"I think that we are caught, Captain."

"So, M. Aronnax, you really think that the *Nautilus* cannot disengage itself?"

"With difficulty, Captain; for the season is already too far advanced for you to reckon on the breaking up of the ice."

"Ah, Sir," said Captain Nemo, in an ironical tone, "you will always be the same. You see nothing but difficulties and obstacles. I affirm that not only can the *Nautilus* disengage itself, but also that it can go farther still."

"Farther to the south?" I asked, looking at the Captain.

"Yes, Sir; it shall go to the Pole."

"To the Pole!" I exclaimed, unable to repress my incredulity.

"Yes," replied the captain coldly, "to the Antarctic Pole—to that unknown point whence springs every meridian of the globe. *You know that I can do whatever I please with the Nautilus!*"

Yes, I knew that. I knew that this man was bold, even to rashness. But to conquer these obstacles which made the South Pole even more inaccessible than the North Pole—which had not yet been reached by the boldest navigators—was it not a mad enterprise, one which only a maniac would have conceived? It then came into my head to ask Captain Nemo if he had ever discovered that pole which had never yet been trodden by a human creature?

"No, Sir," he replied; "but we will discover it together. Where others have failed, *I* will not fail. I have never yet led my *Nautilus* so far into southern seas; but, I repeat, it shall go farther yet."

"I can well believe you, Captain," said I, in a slightly ironical tone. "I believe you! Let us go ahead! There are no obstacles for us! Let us smash this iceberg! Let us blow it up; and if it resists, let us give the *Nautilus* wings to fly over it!"

"Over it, Sir!" said Captain Nemo, quietly; "no, not *over* it, but *under* it!"

"Under it!" I exclaimed, a sudden idea of the captain's plans flashing upon my mind. I understood; the wonderful capabilities of the *Nautilus* were going to serve us in this superhuman effort.

"I see that we are beginning to understand each other, Sir," said the Captain, half smiling. "You begin to see the possibility—I should say the success—of this attempt. That which is impossible for an ordinary vessel is easy for the *Nautilus*. If a continent lies before the Pole, then we stop there; but if, on the contrary, the Pole is washed by open sea, our submarine can go all the way to the Pole."

"Certainly," said I, carried away by the captain's reasoning; "if the surface of the sea is frozen, the lower depths are free by the providential law which has placed the maximum of density of the waters of the ocean one degree higher than freezing point; and, if I am not mistaken, the portion of this iceberg which is above the water is as four to one to that which is below."

"Very nearly, Sir; for each foot of iceberg above the sea there are three below it. If these ice mountains are not more than 300 feet above the surface, they are not more than 900 below. And what are 900 feet to my *Nautilus*?"

"Nothing at all, Captain."

"The only difficulty," continued Captain Nemo, "is that of remaining several days without renewing our provision of air."

"Is that all? The *Nautilus* has vast reservoirs; we can fill them, and they will supply us with all the oxygen we want."

"Good thinking, M. Aronnax," replied the captain, smiling. "But not wishing you to accuse me of rashness, I will first give you all my objections."

"Have you anymore to make?"

"Only one. It is possible, if the sea exists at the South Pole, that it may be frozen; and, consequently, we shall be unable to come to the surface."

"Well, Captain! but do you forget that the *Nautilus* is armed with a powerful spur, and could we not sent it diagonally against these fields of ice, which would break open at its thrust?"

"Ah! Sir, you are full of ideas today."

"Moreover, Captain," I added enthusiastically, "why should we not find the sea open at the South Pole as it is at the North? The polar icecaps and the actual poles do not coincide exactly, either in the southern or in the northern regions; and, until it is proved to the contrary, we may anticipate either a continent or an ocean free from ice at these two points of the globe."

"I think so too, M. Aronnax," replied Captain Nemo. "I only wish you to observe that, after having made so many objections to my projects, you are now crushing me with arguments in their favor!"

The preparations for this daring attempt now began. The powerful pumps of the *Nautilus* were forcing air into the reservoirs and storing it at high pressure. About four o'clock, Captain Nemo announced the closing of the panels on deck. I gave one last look at the massive iceberg which we were going to cross. The weather was clear, the atmosphere pure enough, the cold very intense: twelve degrees below zero; but the wind having gone down, that temperature was not too unbearable. About ten men mounted the sides of the hull, armed with pickaxes to break up the ice around the submarine, which soon floated freely. The operation was easily performed because the fresh ice was still fairly thin. We all went below. The usual reservoirs were filled with the newly liberated water, and the *Nautilus* soon began to dive. I had taken my place with Conseil in the saloon: through the portholes we could see the lower beds of the southern ocean. The thermometer went up, the needle of the compass deviated on the dial. At about nine hundred feet, as Captain Nemo had predicted, we were floating beneath the undulating bottom of the iceberg. But the *Nautilus* went lower still—it went to the depth of four, hundred fathoms. The temperature of the water at the surface showed twelve degrees. Needless to say, the temperature inside of the *Nautilus* was kept at a comfortable level by its heating apparatus. Every maneuver was accomplished with wonderful precision.

"I think we are going to make it, Sir," said Conseil.

"I believe we shall," I said, in a tone of firm conviction.

In this open sea, the *Nautilus* had taken its course direct to the pole, without leaving the second meridian. From 67° 30' to 90°, twenty-two degrees and a half of latitude remained to travel; that is, about five hundred leagues. The *Nautilus* kept up an average speed of twenty-six miles an hour—the speed of an express train. If that was kept up, in forty hours we should reach the Pole.

For a part of the night the novelty of the situation kept us at the window. The sea was lit with the electric searchlight; but it was deserted; fishes did not sojourn in these imprisoned waters; they found there only a passage to take them to the open polar sea. Our pace was rapid; we could feel it by the quivering of the long steel body. About two in the morning, I went to my cabin to rest, and Conseil did the same. I did not see the captain anywhere, and supposed that he was in the pilot's cage. The next morning, March 19, I noticed that the speed of the *Nautilus* had been slackened. It was then going toward the surface; but prudently emptying its ballast tanks very slowly. My heart beat fast. Were we going to emerge and regain the open polar air? No! A shock told me that the *Nautilus* had scraped the bottom of the iceberg, still very thick, judging from the deadened sound. We had indeed "struck," but in an inverse sense, and at a thousand feet deep. This would give three thousand feet of ice above us; one thousand being above the watermark. The iceberg was then higher than at its borders—not a very reassuring fact.

Several times that day the *Nautilus* tried again, and every time it struck the wall which lay like a ceiling above us. I carefully noted the different depths, and thus obtained a submarine profile of the chain as it was developed under the water. That night no change had taken place in our situation. Still ice between four and five hundred yards in depth! It was evidently diminishing, but still what a thickness between us and the surface! It was then eight. According to the daily custom on board the *Nautilus*, its air should have been renewed four hours ago; but I did not suffer much, although Captain Nemo had not yet made any demand upon his reserve of oxygen. My sleep was painful that night; hope and fear besieged me by turns: I rose several times. The groping of the *Nautilus* continued. About three in the morning, I noticed that the lower surface of the iceberg was only fifty yards deep. One hundred and fifty feet now separated us from the surface of the waters. The iceberg was by degrees becoming an ice field, the mountain a plain. My eyes never left the manometer. We were still rising diagonally to the surface, which sparkled under the electric rays. The iceberg was stretching both above and beneath into lengthening slopes; mile after mile it was getting thinner. At length, at six in the morning of that memorable day, March 19, the door of the saloon opened, and Captain Nemo appeared.

"The open sea!" was all he said.

the south pole

I rushed to the deck. Yes! the open sea, with but a few scattered moving icebergs—a long stretch of sea; a world of birds in the air, and myriads of fishes under those waters, which varied from intense blue to olive green, according to the bottom. The thermometer marked three degrees centigrade above zero. It was comparatively spring, shut up as we were behind this huge iceberg, whose lengthened mass was dimly seen on our northern horizon.

"Are we at the Pole?" I asked the captain, with a beating heart.

"I do not know," he replied. "At noon I will take our bearings."

"But will the sun show itself through this fog?" said I, looking at the leaden sky.

"However little it shows, it will be enough," replied the captain.

Snow began to fall, and turned into a storm which continued till the next day. It was impossible to remain on deck. From the saloon, where I was taking notes of various incidents of our voyage to the polar continent, I could hear the cries of birds hunting for food in the midst of this violent storm. The *Nautilus* did not remain motionless, but skirted the coast, advancing ten miles more to the south in the half light left by the sun as it skirted the edge of the horizon. The next day, March 20, the snow had ceased. The fog was rising, and I hoped that that day our observations might be taken. Captain Nemo reminded me that four hours remained until the sun could be observed with advantage.

Noon arrived, and, as before, the sun did not appear. Observations were still wanting. If not accomplished tomorrow, we must give up all idea of taking any. We were indeed exactly at the twentieth of March. Tomorrow, the twenty-first, would be the equinox; the sun would disappear behind the horizon for six months, and with its disappearance the long polar night would begin. Since the September equinox it had emerged from the northern horizon, rising by lengthened spirals up to December 21. At this period, the summer solstice of the southern regions, it had begun to descend; and tomorrow was to shed its last rays upon them. I communicated my fears and observations to the captain.

"You are right, M. Aronnax," said he; "if tomorrow I cannot take the altitude of the sun, I shall not be able to do it for six months. But precisely because chance has led me into these seas on March 21, my bearings will be easy to take, if at twelve we can see the sun."

"Why, Captain?"

"Because then the orb of day describes such lengthened curves that it is difficult to measure exactly its height above the horizon, and grave errors may be made with instruments."

"What will you do then?"

"I shall only use my chronometer," replied Captain Nemo. "If tomorrow, March 21, the disk of the sun, allowing for refraction, is exactly cut by the northern horizon, it will show that I am at the South Pole."

"Just so," said I. "But this statement is not mathematically correct, because the equinox does not necessarily begin at noon."

"Very likely, Sir; but the error will not be a hundred yards, and we do not want more. Till tomorrow then." The captain went back to his quarters.

The next day, March 21, I went up on deck at five in the morning, and found Captain Nemo already there.

"The weather is lightening a little," said he. "I have some hope. After breakfast we will go on shore, and choose a post for observation."

Breakfast over, we went on shore. The *Nautilus* had gone some miles farther up during the night. It was a whole league from the coast, above which rose a sharp peak about five hundred yards high. The boat took with me Captain Nemo, two men of the crew, and the instruments which consisted of a chronometer, a telescope, and a barometer.

At nine we landed; the sky was brightening, the clouds were flying to the south, and the fog seemed to be leaving the cold surface of the waters. Captain Nemo went toward the peak, which he doubtless meant to be his observatory. It was a painful, two-hour ascent over the sharp lava and the pumice stones, in an atmosphere often impregnated with a sulphurous smell from the smoking cracks. For a man unaccustomed to walking on land, the captain climbed the steep slopes with an agility I never saw equaled, and which a hunter might envy.

On arriving at the summit, Captain Nemo carefully took the mean height of the barometer, for he would have to consider that in taking his observations. At quarter to twelve, the sun, then seen only by refraction, looked like a golden disk shedding its last rays upon this deserted continent, and seas which never man had yet plowed. Captain Nemo, furnished with a lenticular glass which, by means of a mirror, corrected the refraction, watched the orb sinking below the horizon by degrees, following a lengthened diagonal. I held the chronometer. My heart beat fast. If the disappearance of the half disk of the sun coincided with twelve o'clock on the chronometer, we were at the pole.

"Twelve!" I exclaimed.

"The South Pole!" replied Captain Nemo, in a grave voice, handing me the glass, which showed the orb cut in exactly equal parts by the horizon.

I looked at the last rays crowning the peak, and the shadows mounting by degrees up its slopes. At that moment Captain Nemo, resting with his hand on my shoulder, said:

"I, Captain Nemo, on the twenty-first day of March 1868, have reached the South Pole on the ninetieth degree; and I take possession of this part of the globe, equal to one sixth of the known continents."

"In whose name, Captain?"

"In my own, Sir!"

Discovery of the South Pole: Roald Amundsen (Norway) with four men and dog teams reached the Pole December 14, 1911.

On a 1600-mile airplane flight, Richard E. Byrd (U.S.) crossed the South Pole November 29, 1929. He dropped a U.S. flag over the Pole.

While no attempts to reach the South Pole by submarine are recorded, Captain Nemo would be pleased—and flattered—to note the following:

On August 3, 1958, the U.S. Navy submarine NAUTILUS became the first ship to cross the North Pole beneath the Arctic ice. On August 12, 1958, the U.S. Navy nuclear submarine SKATE became the second ship to make an underwater crossing of the North Pole. In March, 1959, the SKATE returned tc the Arctic and, on its third attempt, broke through at the North Pole, the first time any ship had been on the surface at 90° North.

VOCABULARY STUDY

VOCABULARY QUIZ 1-B

Words to Learn

diorama *undulating* *latitude*
assailed *meridian*

Match each italicized word with the appropriate choice from the right.

Words in Context

1. "like a *diorama*," p. 13.
2. "gales *assailed* us," p. 14.
3. "the *undulating* bottom of the iceberg," p. 16.
4. "without leaving the second *meridian*," p. 16.
5. "twenty-two degrees . . . of *latitude*," p. 17.

Definitions

a. imaginary circle passing through both poles
b. swaying, moving in waves
c. distance in degrees from the equator
d. attacked, assaulted
e. a spectacular, three-dimensional scene

VOCABULARY PRACTICE 1-B

Write an intelligent, thoughtful sentence for each of the words listed below.

1. *assailed*
2. *undulating*

SUGGESTIONS FOR DISCUSSION AND WRITING

1. While this is only one portion of the novel *Twenty Thousand Leagues Under the Sea*, it does offer several direct and indirect references to the character of Captain Nemo. How would you describe him? Be sure not to ignore the implications of *what he is doing* in your assessment of his character, or the curious transformations in his behavior, from his ironic friendliness on pages 15–16 to his overbearing egoism on page 20.

2. What sort of a man is the professor who narrates the story? How does Captain Nemo seem to regard him? Does his mind operate on an emotional, subjective plane, or is he an objective, practical realist?

3. If you were able to choose, which venture would you undertake: a voyage aboard the *Nautilus* with Captain Nemo in the last century, a tour aboard one of our nuclear submarines today, or the trek to the South Pole with Roald Amundsen in 1911? Why?

4. The story in this chapter is told mainly by means of two points of view, *first-person limited* (See Appendix 1, page 251), by which the narrative progresses in the mind and memory of Professor Aronnax, and *third-person limited*, by which we overhear the dialogue between Professor Aronnax and Captain Nemo. Each narrative point of view gives us distinctly different kinds of information. Discuss the differences as you see them.

5. If you have read Herman Melville's *Moby Dick*, you will probably agree that Captain Nemo and Captain Ahab are similar in many ways. Compare and contrast these two important fictional characters.

The Time Machine

H. G. WELLS

THE THING the Time Traveller held in his hand was a glittering metallic framework, scarcely larger than a small clock, and very delicately made. There was ivory in it, and some transparent crystalline substance. And now I must be explicit, for this that follows—unless his explanation is to be accepted—is an absolutely unaccountable thing. He took one of the small octagonal tables that were scattered about the room, and set it in front of the fire, with two legs on the hearthrug. On this table he placed the mechanism. Then he drew up a chair, and sat down. The only other object on the table was a small shaded lamp, the bright light of which fell full upon the model. There were also perhaps a dozen candles about, two in brass candlesticks upon the mantel and several in sconces, so that the room was brilliantly illuminated. I sat in a low chair nearest the fire, and drew this forward so as to be almost between the Time Traveller and the fireplace. Filby sat behind him, looking over his shoulder. The Medical Man and the Provincial Mayor watched him in profile from the right, the Psychologist from the left. The Very Young Man stood behind the Psychologist. We were all on the alert. It appears incredible to me that any kind of trick, however subtly conceived and however adroitly done, could have been played upon us under these conditions.

The Time Traveller looked at us, and then at the mechanism.

"Well?" said the Psychologist.

"This little affair," said the Time Traveller, resting his elbows upon the table and pressing his hands together above the apparatus, "is only a model. It is my plan for a machine to travel through time. You will notice that it looks singularly askew, and that there is an odd twinkling appearance about this bar, as though it was in some way unreal." He pointed to the part with his finger. "Also, here is one little white lever, and here is another."

The Medical Man got up out of his chair and peered into the thing. "It's beautifully made," he said.

"It took two years to make," retorted the Time Traveller. Then, when we had all imitated the action of the Medical Man, he said: "Now I want you clearly to understand that this lever being pressed over sends the machine gliding into the future, and this other reverses the motion. This saddle represents the seat of a time traveller. Presently I am going to press the lever, and off the machine will go. It will vanish, pass into the future time, and disappear. Have a good look at the thing. Look at the table too, and satisfy yourselves there is no trickery. I don't want to waste this model and then be told I'm a quack."

There was a minute's pause perhaps. The Psychologist seemed about to speak to me, but changed his mind. Then the Time Traveller put forth his finger towards the lever. "No," he said suddenly. "Lend me your hand." And turning to the Psychologist, he took that individual's hand in his own and told him to put out his forefinger. So that it was the Psychologist himself who sent forth the model Time Machine on its interminable voyage. We all saw the lever turn. I am absolutely certain there was no trickery. There was a breath of wind, and the lamp flame jumped. One of the candles on the mantel was blown out, and the little machine suddenly swung round, became indistinct, was seen as a ghost for a second perhaps, as an eddy of faintly glittering brass and ivory; and it was gone—vanished! Save for the lamp the table was bare.

Everyone was silent for a minute. Then Filby said he was damned.

The Psychologist recovered from his stupor, and suddenly looked under the table. At that the Time Traveller laughed cheerfully. "Well?" he said, with a reminiscence of the Psychologist. Then, getting up, he went to the tobacco jar on the mantel, and with his back to us began to fill his pipe.

We stared at each other. "Look here," said the Medical Man, "are you in earnest about this? Do you seriously believe that that machine has travelled into time?"

"Certainly," said the Time Traveller, stooping to light a twig at the fire. Then he turned, lighting his pipe, to look at the Psychologist's face. (The Psychologist, to show that he was not unhinged, helped himself to a cigar and tried to light it uncut.) "What is more, I have a big machine nearly finished in there"—he indicated the laboratory —and when that is put together I mean to have a journey on my own account."

"I told some of you last Thursday of the principles of the Time Machine, and showed you the actual thing itself, incomplete in the workshop. There it is now, a little travel-worn, truly; but the rest of it's sound enough. I expected to finish it on Friday; but on Friday, when the putting together was nearly done, I found that one of the nickel bars was exactly one inch too short, and this I had to get re-made; so that the thing was not complete until this morning. It was at ten o'clock today that the first of all Time Machines began its career. I gave it a last tap, tried all the screws again, put one more drop of oil on the quartz rod, and sat myself in the saddle. I suppose a suicide who holds a pistol to his skull feels much the same wonder at what will come next as I felt then. I took the starting lever in one hand and the stopping one in the other, pressed the first, and almost immediately the second. I seemed to reel; I felt a nightmare sensation of falling; and, looking round, I saw the laboratory exactly as before. Had anything happened? For a moment I suspected that my intellect had tricked me. Then I noted the clock. A moment before, as it seemed, it had stood at a minute or so past ten; now it was nearly half-past three!

"I drew a breath, set my teeth, gripped the starting lever with both hands, and went off with a thud. The laboratory got hazy and went dark. Mrs. Watchett came in, and walked, apparently without seeing me, towards the garden door. I suppose it took her a minute or so to traverse the place, but to me she seemed to shoot across the room like a rocket. I pressed the lever over to its extreme position. The night came like the turning out of a lamp, and in another moment came tomorrow. The laboratory grew faint and hazy, then fainter and even fainter. Tomorrow night came black, then day again, night again, day again, faster and faster. An eddying murmur filled my ears, and a strange, dumb confusedness descended on my mind.

"I am afraid I cannot convey the peculiar sensations of time travelling. They are excessively unpleasant. There is a feeling exactly like that one has upon a switchback— of a helpless headlong motion! I felt the same horrible anticipation, too, of an imminent smash. As I put on pace, night followed day like the flapping of a black wing. The dim suggestion of the laboratory seemed presently to fall away from me, and I saw the sun hopping swiftly across the sky, leaping at every minute, and every minute marking a day. I supposed the laboratory had been destroyed, and I had come into the open air. I had a dim impression of scaffolding, but I was already going too fast to be conscious of any moving things. The slowest snail that ever crawled dashed by too fast for me. The twinkling succession of darkness and light was excessively painful to the eyes. Then, in the intermittent darknesses, I saw the moon spinning swiftly through her quarters from new to full, and had a faint glimpse of the circling stars. Presently, as I went on, still gaining velocity, the palpitation of night and day merged into one continuous greyness; the sky took on a wonderful deepness of blue, a splendid luminous colour like that of early twilight; the jerking sun became a streak of fire, a brilliant arch, in space, the moon a fainter fluctuating band; and I could see nothing of the stars, save now and then a brighter circle flickering in the blue.

"The landscape was misty and vague. I was still on the hillside upon which this house now stands, and the shoulder rose above me grey and dim. I saw trees growing and changing like puffs of vapor, now brown, now green; they grew, spread, shivered, and passed away. I saw huge buildings rise up faint and fair, and pass like dreams. The whole surface of the earth seemed changed—melting and flowing under my eyes. The little hands upon the dials that registered my speed raced round faster and faster. Presently I noted that the sun-belt swayed up and down, from solstice to solstice, in a minute or less, and that, consequently, my pace was over a year a minute; and minute by minute the white snow flashed across the world, and vanished, and was followed by the bright, brief green of spring.

"The unpleasant sensations of the start were less poignant now. They merged at last into a kind of hysterical exhilaration. I remarked, indeed, a clumsy swaying of the machine, for which I was unable to account. But my mind was too confused to attend to it, so with a kind of madness growing upon me, I flung myself into futurity. At first I scarce thought of stopping, scarce thought of anything but these new sensations. But presently a fresh series of impressions grew up in my mind, a certain curiosity and therewith a certain dread, until at last they took complete possession of me. What strange developments of humanity, what wonderful advances upon our rudimentary civilization, I thought, might not appear when I came to look nearly into the dim elusive world that raced and fluctuated before my eyes! I saw great and splendid architecture rising about me, more massive than any buildings of our own time, and yet, as it seemed, built of glimmer and mist. I saw a richer green flow up the hillside, and remain there without any wintry intermission. Even through the veil of my confusion the earth seemed very fair. And so my mind came to the business of stopping.

"The peculiar risk lay in the possibility of my finding some substance in the space which I, or the machine, occupied. So long as I travelled at a high velocity through time, this scarcely mattered: I was, so to speak, attenuated—was slipping like a vapor through the interstices of intervening substances! But to come to a stop involved the jamming of myself, molecule by molecule, into whatever lay in my way: meant bringing my atoms into such intimate contact with those of the obstacles that a profound chemical reaction, possibly a far reaching explosion, would result, and blow myself and my apparatus out of all possible dimensions—into the Unknown. This possibility had occurred to me again and again while I was making the machine; but then I had cheerfully accepted it as an unavoidable risk—one of the risks a man has to take! Now the risk was inevitable, I no longer saw it in the same cheerful light. The fact is that, insensibly, the absolute strangeness of everything, the sickly jarring and swaying of the machine, above all, the feeling of prolonged falling, had absolutely upset my nerves. I told myself that I could never stop, and with a gust of petulance I resolved to stop forthwith. Like an impatient fool, I lugged over the lever, and incontinently the thing went reeling over, and I was flung headlong through the air."

VOCABULARY STUDY

VOCABULARY QUIZ 1-C

Words to Learn

explicit	interminable	poignant
provincial	traverse	exhilaration
adroitly	imminent	rudimentary
askew	intermittent	attenuated
retorted	palpitation	incontinently

Match each italicized word with the appropriate choice from the right.

Words in Context

1. "I must be *explicit*," p. 23.
2. "The *Provincial* Mayor," p. 23.
3. "a trick . . . *adroitly* done," p. 23.
4. "it looks . . . *askew*," p. 23.
5. "*retorted* the Time Traveller," p. 24.
6. "its *interminable* voyage," p. 24.
7. "to *traverse* the place," p. 25.
8. "an *imminent* smash," p. 25.
9. "in the *intermittent* darkness," p. 25.
10. "the *palpitation* of night and day," p. 25.
11. "the *sensations* . . . were less poignant," p. 26.

Definitions

a. sectional
b. threatening to occur
c. sharp, severe
d. animation, joy
e. to pass through, to cross
f. returning at intervals
g. rapid beating
h. undeveloped
i. endless
j. skillfully
k. made thin and weak

12. "the kind of *hysterical* exhilaration," p. 26.
13. "our *rudimentary* civilization," p. 26.
14. "It was, so to speak, *attenuated*," p. 26.
15. "*incontinently* the thing went reeling," p. 27.

l. without control
m. plain, direct
n. sideways
o. replied sharply

VOCABULARY PRACTICE 1-C

Write a six-line paragraph containing the three words listed below.

1. *explicit*   2. *imminent*   3. *retorted*

SUGGESTIONS FOR DISCUSSION AND WRITING

1. While H. G. Wells was not the first writer to explore travel in time, he was the first to conceive the idea of a "time machine." How does he meet the necessity of making the machine credible to the reader? What details does he omit which a science fiction writer of today might feel required to furnish?

2. In writing *The Time Machine*, Wells ignored other technical aspects that might give modern science fiction writers more problems. One of these is called the *time paradox*, the idea that, if you go back in time and alter the past, your present would have to be different; in fact, it might not even include you! In what ways might your present be transformed by minor changes in your past? What other technical problems has Wells ignored?

3. Why is it that science fiction writers today cannot "get away with" (or, in the words of Coleridge, expect the reader to "willingly suspend the disbelief of") the paradoxes that Wells ignored? What has happened in the world since *The Time Machine* was written in 1895, and how have these events brought about the modern science fiction writer's need for authentic, substantiated detail?

Christmas 200,000 B.C.

STANLEY WATERLOO

IT WAS Christmas in the year 200,000 B.C. It is true that it was not called Christmas then—our ancestors at that date were not much given to the celebration of religious festivals—but, taking the Gregorian calendar and counting backward just 200,000 plus 1887 years this particular day could be located. There was no formal celebration, but, nevertheless, a good deal was going on in the neighborhood of the home of Fangs. Names were not common at the time mentioned, but the more advanced of the cave-dwellers had them. Man had so far advanced that only traces of his ape origins remained, and he had begun to have a language. It was a queer "clucking" sort of language, something like that of the Bushmen, not very useful in the expression of ideas, but then primitive man didn't have many ideas to express. Names, so far as used, were at this time derived merely from some personal quality or peculiarity. Fangs was so called because of his huge teeth. His mate was called She Fox; his daughter, not Nellie, nor Jennie, nor Mamie—young ladies did not affect the "ie" then—but Red Lips. She was, for the age, remarkably pretty and refined. She could cast eyes which told a story to a suitor, and there were several kinds of snakes she would not eat. She was a merry, energetic girl, and was the most useful member of the family in tree-climbing. She was an only child and rather petted. Her father or mother rarely knocked her down with a very heavy club when angry, and after her fourteenth year rarely assaulted her at all. So far as She Fox was concerned, this kindness largely resulted from discretion, the daughter having in the last encounter so belabored the mother that she was laid up for a week. The father abstained chiefly because the daughter had become useful. Red Lips was now eighteen.

Fangs was a cave-dweller. His home was sumptuously furnished. The floor of the cave was strewn with dry grass, something that in most other caves was lacking. Fangs was a prominent citizen. He was one of the strongest men in the valley. He had killed Red Beard, another prominent citizen, in a little dispute over priority of right to possession of a dead mastodon discovered in a swamp, and had for years been the terror of every cave man in the region who possessed anything worth taking.

On this particular morning, which would have been Christmas morning, had it not come too early in the world's history, Fangs left the cave after eating the whole of a water-fowl he had killed with a stone the night before and some half dozen field mice which his wife had brought in. She Fox and Red Lips had for breakfast only the bones of the duck and some roots dug in the forest. Fangs carried with him a huge club, and in a rough pouch made of the skin of some small animal a collection of stones of convenient size for throwing. This was before man had invented the bow or even the crude stone ax. He came back in a surly mood because he had found nothing and killed nothing, but he brought a companion with him. This companion, whom he had met in the woods, was known as Wolf because his countenance reminded one of a wolf. He could hardly be called a gentleman, even as times and terms went then. He was evidently not of an old family, for he possessed something more than a rudimentary tail, and, had his face looked less like that of a wolf, it would have been that of a baboon. He was hairy, and his speech of rough gutturals was imperfect. He could pronounce but a few words. He was, however, very strong, and Fangs rather liked him.

What Fangs did when he came in was to propose a matrimonial alliance. That is, he grasped his daughter by the arm and led her up to Wolf, and then pointing to an abandoned cave in the hillside not far distant, pushed them toward it. They did not have marriage ceremonies in 200,000 B.C. Wolf, who had evidently been informed of Fang's desire and who was himself in favor of the alliance, seized the girl and began dragging her off to the new home and the honeymoon. She resisted, and shrieked, and clawed like a wild cat. Her mother, She Fox, came running out, club in hand, but was promptly knocked down by Fangs, who then dragged her into the cave again. Meanwhile the bridegroom was hauling the bride away through furze and bushes at a rapid rate. Red Lips had ceased to struggle, and was thinking. Her thoughts were not very well defined nor clear, but one thing she knew well—she did not want to live in a cave with Wolf. She had a fancy that she would prefer to live instead with Yellow Hair, a young cave man who had not yet selected a mate, and who was remarkably fleet of foot. They were now very near the cave, and she knew that unless she exerted herself housekeeping would begin within a very few moments. Wolf was strong, but slow of movement. Red Lips was only less swift than Yellow Hair. An idea occurred to her. She bent her head and buried her strong teeth deep in the wrist of the man who was half-carrying, half-dragging her through the underwood.

With a howl which justified his name, Wolf for an instant released his hold. That instant allowed the girl's escape. She leaped away like a deer and darted into the forest. Yelling with pain and rage, Wolf pursued her. She gained on him steadily as she ran, but there was a light snow upon the ground, and she could be followed by the trail which her pursuer took up doggedly and determinedly. He knew that he could tire her out and catch her in time. He solaced himself for her temporary escape by thinking, as he ran, how fiercely he would beat his bride before starting for the cave again, and as he thought his teeth showed like those of a dog of today.

The chase lasted for hours, and Red Lips had gained perhaps a mile upon her pursuer when her strength began to flag. The pace was telling upon her. She had run many miles. She was almost hopeless of escape when she emerged into a little glade, where sat a man gnawing contentedly at a raw rabbit. He leaped to his feet as the girl appeared, but a moment later recognized her and smiled. The man was Yellow Hair. He reached out part of the rabbit he was devouring, and Red Lips, whose breakfast had, as already mentioned, been a light one, tore at it and consumed it in a moment. Then she told of what had happened.

"We will kill Wolf, and you shall live with me," said Yellow Hair.

Red Lips assented eagerly, and the two consulted together. Near them was a hill, one side of which was a precipice. At the base of the precipice ran a path. The result of the consultation was that Yellow Hair left the girl, and making a swift circuit, came upon the precipice from the farther side, and crouched low upon its summit. The girl ran along the path at the bottom of the declivity for some distance, then, entering a defile which crossed it at right angles, herself made a turn, climbed the hill and joined Yellow Hair. From where they were lying they could see the glade they had just left.

Wolf entered the glade, and noted where the footsteps of the girl and those of a man came together. For a moment or two he appeared troubled and suspicious; then his face cleared. He saw that the tracks had diverged again. He had recognized the man's tracks as those of Yellow Hair.

"Yellow Hair is afraid of my strong arm," he thought. "He dare not stay with Red Lips. I shall catch her soon and beat her and take her with me."

The two crouching upon the precipice watched his every movement. They had rolled to the edge of the declivity a rock as huge as they could control, and now together held it poised over the pathway. Wolf came hurrying along, his head bent down like that of a hound on the scent of game. He reached a spot just beneath the two, and then with a sudden united effort they shoved over the rock. It thundered down upon the unfortunate Wolf with an accuracy which spoke well for the eyes and hands of the lovers. The man was crushed horribly. The two above scrambled down, laughing, and Yellow Hair took from the dead Wolf a necklace of claws and fastened it proudly upon his own person.

"Now we will go to my cave," he said.

"No," said Red Lips; "my father will look for Wolf tomorrow, and will find him. Then he will come and kill us. We must go and kill him tonight."

"Yes," said Yellow Hair.

Hand in hand the two started for the cave of Fangs. The side hill in which it was situated was very steep, and the lovers thought they could duplicate the affair with Wolf. "We must cripple him, anyway," said Yellow Hair, "for I am not strong enough to fight him alone. His club is heavy."

They reached the vicinity of the cave and crept above it. Having, with great difficulty, secured a rock in position to be rolled down, they waited for Fangs to appear. He came out about dusk, and stretched out his arms lazily, when the two above released the rock. It rolled down swiftly and with great force, but there was no such sheer drop afforded as when Wolf was killed, and Fangs heard the stone coming and almost eluded it. It caught one of his legs, as he tried to leap aside, and broke it. Fangs fell to the ground.

With a yell of triumph Yellow Hair bounded to where the crippled man lay and began pounding him upon the head with his club. Fangs had a very thick head. He struggled vigorously, and succeeded in catching Yellow Hair by the wrist. Then he drew the younger man to him and began to throttle him. The case of Yellow Hair was desperate. Fangs's great strength was too much for him. His stifled yells told of his agony.

It was at this juncture that Red Lips demonstrated her quality as a girl of decision and of action. A sharp instrument of slate, several pounds in weight, lay at her feet. She seized it and bounded forward to where the struggle was going on. The back of Fangs' head was fairly exposed. The girl brought down the sharp stone upon it just where the head and spinal column joined, and the crashing thud told of the force of the blow. Delivered with such strength upon such a spot there could be but one result. The man could not have been killed more quickly. Yellow Hair released himself from the dead giant's embrace and rose to his feet. Then, after a short breathing time, to make assurance sure, he picked up his club and battered the head of Fangs until there could be no chance of resuscitation. The performance was unnecessary, but neither Yellow Hair nor Red Lips was aware of the fact. Their knowledge of anatomy was limited. Neither knew the effect of such a blow delivered properly at the base of the brain.

Yellow Hair finally ceased his exercise and rested on his club.

"Shall we go to my cave now?" said he.

"Why should we?" said Red Lips. "Let us take this cave. There is dry grass on the floor."

They entered the cave. She Fox, who had witnessed what had occurred, sat in one corner, and looked up doubtfully as they entered. "I am tired," said Yellow Hair, and he laid himself down and went to sleep.

She Fox looked at her daughter. "I killed three hedgehogs today," she whispered.

The new mistress of the cave looked at her kindly. "Go out and dig some roots," she said, "and come back with them, and then with them and the hedgehogs we will have a feast."

She Fox went out and returned in an hour with roots and nuts. Red Lips awakened Yellow Hair, and all three fed ravenously and merrily. It was a great occasion in the cave of the late Fangs. There was no such Christmas feast, at the same time a wedding feast, in any other cave in all the region. And the sequel to the events of the day was as happy as the day itself. Yellow Hair and Red Lips somehow avoided being killed, and grew old together, and left a numerous progeny.

VOCABULARY STUDY

VOCABULARY QUIZ 1-D

Words to Learn

sumptuously   countenance   progeny
surly   resuscitation

Match each italicized word with the appropriate choice from the right.

Words in Context

1. "*Sumptuously* furnished," p. 32.
2. "in a *surly* mood," p. 32.
3. "his *countenance* reminded one of," p. 32.
4. "no chance of his *resuscitation*," p. 35.
5. "life a numerous *progeny*," p. 35.

Definitions

a. gloomy, rough
b. face, expression
c. offspring
d. in luxury
e. revival

VOCABULARY PRACTICE 1-D

Add an appropriate choice from the above vocabulary list to the sentences below.

1. When Sir Winston Churchill was angered, he took on the _____ of a grouchy bulldog.

2. The honeymooners dined _____ at The Blue Boar Tavern, an expensive restaurant specializing in English cooking.

3. The _____ of French immigrant Iréné Du Pont have, for two hundred years, kept the family name in the vanguard of American business and technology.

4. Joe Smith had hoped that his mother-in-law would be happy to see him after his long absence; instead, she was _____ and hostile.

5. Lifeguards at public beaches are trained in methods of _____.

SUGGESTIONS FOR DISCUSSION AND WRITING

1. This story illustrates the science fiction device of extension, but extension in reverse. What habits, customs, devices, and tendencies can you pick out in the story that, in some way, were harbingers of the future?

2. What do you perceive to be Stanley Waterloo's attitude toward his characters? How seriously does he expect the reader to take the story. Note the back-handed compliments Waterloo gives Red Lips on page 31, for example, or on page 34. Can you find similar irony in the story?

3. How does the style of writing serve to support the quality of thought and action conveyed in the story? Note the length of the sentences on pages 33–35, for example, especially in the dialogue. Also note the abrupt, halting manner in which the narrative thread moves along, without smooth transition between events.

In the Year Ten Thousand

WILLIAM HARBEN

A.D. 10,000. An old man, more than six hundred years of age, was walking with a boy through a great museum. The people who were moving around them had beautiful forms, and faces which were indescribably refined and spiritual.

"Father," said the boy, "you promised to tell me today about the Dark Ages. I like to hear how men lived and thought long ago."

"It is no easy task to make you understand the past," was the reply. "It is hard to realize that man could have been so ignorant as he was eight thousand years ago, but come with me; I will show you something."

He led the boy to a cabinet containing a few time-worn books bound in solid gold.

"You have never seen a book," he said, taking out a large volume and carefully placing it on a silk cushion on a table. "There are only a few in the leading museums of the world. Time was when there were as many books on earth as inhabitants."

"I cannot understand," said the boy with a look of perplexity on his intellectual face. "I cannot see what people would have wanted with them; they are not attractive; they seem to be useless."

The old man smiled. "When I was your age, the subject was too deep for me; but as I grew older and made a close study of the history of the past, the use of books gradually became plain to me. When we know that in the year 2000 they were read by the best minds, we begin to understand. First, I shall have to explain that eight thousand years ago human beings communicated their thoughts to one another by making sounds with their tongues, and not by mind-reading, as you and I do. To understand me, you have simply to read my thoughts as well as your education permits; but primitive man knew nothing about thought-intercourse, so he invented speech. Humanity then was divided up in various races, and each race had a separate language. As certain sounds conveyed definite ideas, so did signs and letters; and later, to facilitate the exchange of thought, writing and printing were invented. This book was printed."

The boy leaned forward and examined the pages closely; his young brow clouded. "I cannot understand," he said, "it seems so useless."

The old man put his delicate fingers on the page. "A line of these words may have conveyed a valuable thought to a reader long ago," he said reflectively. "In fact, this book purports to be a history of the world up to the year 2000. Here are some pictures," he continued, turning the worn leaves carefully. "This is George Washington; this a pope of a church called the Roman Catholic; this is a man named Gladstone, who was a great political leader in England. Pictures then, as you see, were very crude. We have preserved some of the oil paintings made in those days. Art was in its cradle. In producing a painting of an object, the early artists mixed colored paints and spread them according to taste on stretched canvas or on the walls or windows of buildings. You know that our artists simply throw light and darkness into space in the necessary variations, and the effect is all that could be desired in the way of imitating nature. See that landscape in the alcove before you. The foliage of the trees, the grass, the flowers, the stretch of water have every appearance of life because the light which produces them is alive."

The boy looked at the scene admiringly for a few minutes, then bent again over the book. Presently he recoiled from the pictures, a strange look of disgust in his tender features.

"These men have awful faces," he said. "They are so unlike people living now. The man you call a King looks like an animal. They all have huge mouths and frightfully heavy jaws. Surely men could not have looked like that."

"Yes," the old man replied, gently. "There is no doubt that human beings then bore a nearer resemblance to the lower animals than we now do. In the sculpture and portraits of all ages we can trace a gradual refinement in the appearances of men. The features of the human race today are more ideal. Thought has always given form and expression to faces. In those dark days the thoughts of men were not refined. Human beings died of starvation and lack of attention in cities where there were people so wealthy that they could not use their fortunes. And they were so nearly related to the lower animals that they believed in war. George Washington was for several centuries reverenced by millions of people as a great and good man;

and yet under his leadership thousands of human beings lost their lives in battle."

The boy's susceptible face turned white.

"Do you mean that he encouraged men to kill one another?" he asked, bending more closely over the book.

"Yes, but we cannot blame him; he thought he was right. Millions of his countrymen applauded him. A greater warrior than he, was a man named Napoléon Bonaparte. Washington fought under the belief that he was doing his country a service in defending it against enemies, but everything in history goes to prove that Bonaparte waged war to gratify a personal ambition to distinguish himself as a hero. Wild animals of the lowest orders were courageous, and would fight one another till they died; and yet the most refined of the human race, eight or nine thousand years ago, prided themselves on the same ferocity of nature. Women, the gentlest half of humanity, honored men more for bold achievements in shedding blood than for any other quality. But murder was not only committed in wars; men in private life killed one another; fathers and mothers were now and then so depraved as to put their children to death; and the highest tribunals of the world executed murderers without dreaming that it was wrong, erroneously believing that to kill was the only way to prevent killing."

"Did no one in those days realize that it was horrible?" asked the youth.

"Yes," answered the father, "as far back as ten thousand years ago there was an humble man, it is said, who was called Jesus Christ. He went from place to place, telling every one he met that the world would be better if men would love one another as themselves.

"What kind of man was he?" asked the boy, with kindling eyes.

"He was a spiritual genius," was the earnest reply, "and the greatest that has ever lived."

"Did he prevent them from killing one another?" asked the youth, with a tender upward glance.

"No, for he himself was killed by men who were too barbarous to understand him. But long after his death his words were remembered. People were not civilized enough to put his teachings into practice, but they were able to see that he was right."

"After he was killed, did the people not do as he had told them?" asked the youth, after a pause of several minutes.

"It seems not," was the reply . . . Then, as if to change the subject, the father pointed to a painting on the wall and said: "This was a great queen of England, called Victoria."

"I hoped that the women would not have such repulsive features as the men," said the boy, looking critically at the portrait, "but this face makes me shudder. Why do they all look so coarse and brutal?"

"People living when this queen reigned had the most degrading habit that ever blackened the history of mankind."

"What was that?" asked the youth.

"The consumption of flesh. They believed that animals, fowls, and fish were created to be eaten."

"Is it possible?" The boy shuddered convulsively, and turned away from the book. "I understand now why their faces repel me so. I do not like to think that we have descended from such people."

"They knew no better," said the father. "As they gradually became more refined they learned to burn the meat over flames and to cook it in heated vessels to change its appearance. The places where animals were killed and sold were withdrawn to retired places. Mankind was slowly turning from the habit, but they did not know it. As early as 2050 learned men, calling themselves vegetarians, proved conclusively that the consumption of such food was cruel and barbarous, and that it retarded refinement and mental growth. However, it was not till about 2300 that the vegetarian movement became of marked importance. The most highly educated classes in all lands adopted vegetarianism, and only the uneducated continued to kill and eat animals. The vegetarians tried for years to enact laws prohibiting the consumption of flesh, but the opposition was very strong. In America in 2320 a colony was formed consisting of about three hundred thousand vegetarians. They purchased large tracts of land in what was known as the Indian Territory, and there made their homes, determined to prove by example the efficacy of their tenets. Within the first year the colony had doubled its number: people joined it from all parts of the globe. In the year 4000 it was a country of its own, and was the wonder of the world. The brightest minds were born there. The greatest discoveries and inventions were made by its inhabitants. In 4030 Gillette discovered the process of manufacturing crystal. Up to that time people had built their houses of natural stone, inflammable wood, and metals; but the new material, being fireproof and beautiful in its various colors, was used for all building purposes. In 4050 Holloway found the submerged succession of mountain chains across the Atlantic Ocean, and intended to construct a bridge on their summits; but the vast improvements in air travel rendered his plans impractical.

"In 4051 John discovered and put into practice thought-telegraphy. This discovery was the signal for the introduction in schools and colleges of the science of mind-reading, and by the year 5000 so great had been the progress in that branch of knowledge that words were spoken only among the lowest of the uneducated. In no age of the world's history has there been such an important discovery. It civilized the world. Its early promoters did not dream of the vast good mind-reading would accomplish. Slowly it killed evil. Societies for the prevention of evil thought were organized in all lands. Children were born pure of mind and grew up in purity. Crime was choked out of existence. If a man had an evil thought, it was read in his heart, and he was not allowed to keep it. Men at first shunned evil for fear of detection, and then grew to love purity.

"In the year 6021 all countries of the world, having then a common language, and being drawn together in brotherly love by constant exchange of thought, agreed to call themselves a union without ruler or rulers. It was the greatest event in the history of the world. Certain sensitive mind students in Germany, who had for years been trying to communicate with other planets through the channel of thought, declared that, owing to the terrestrial unanimity of purpose in that direction, they had received mental impressions from other worlds, and that thorough interplanetary intercourse was a future possibility.

"Important inventions were made as the mind of humanity grew more elevated. For instance, Thornton discovered the plan to heat the earth's surface from its internal fire, and this discovery made journeys to the wonderful ice-bound countries situated at the North and South Poles easy of accomplishment. At the North Pole, in the extensive concave lands, was found a peculiar race of men. Their sun was the great perpetually boiling lake of lava which bubbled from the center of the earth in the bottom of their bowl-shaped world."

The old man and his son left the museum and walked into a wonderful park. Flowers of the most beautiful kinds and of sweetest fragrance grew on all sides. They came to a tall tower, four thousand feet in height, built of manufactured crystal. Something, like a great white bird, a thousand feet long, flew across the sky and settled down on the tower's summit.

"This was one of the most wonderful inventions of the seventieth century," said the old man. "The early inhabitants of the earth could not have dreamed that it would be possible to go around in it twenty-four hours. In fact, there was a time when they were not able to go around it at all. Scientists were astonished when a man called Malburn, a great inventor, announced that, at a height of four thousand feet, he could disconnect an air ship from the laws of gravitation, and cause it to stand still in space till the earth had turned over. Fancy what must have been that immortal genius' feeling when he stood in space and saw the earth for the first time whirling beneath him!"

They walked on for some distance across the park till they came to a great instrument made to magnify the music in light.

"It will soon be night," said the old man. "Those tones are those of bleeding sunset. I came here last evening to listen to the musical struggle between the light of dying day and that of the coming stars. The sunlight had been playing a powerful solo; but the gentle chorus of the stars, led by the moon, was inexplicably touching. Light is the voice of immortality; it speaks in all things."

An hour passed. It was growing dark.

"Tell me what immortality is," said the boy. "What does life lead to?"

"We do not know," replied the old man. "If we knew we would be infinite. Immortality is increasing happiness for all time; it is—"

A meteor shot across the sky. There was a burst of musical laughter among the stars. The old man bent over the boy's face and kissed it. "Immortality," said he—"immortality must be love immortal."

VOCABULARY STUDY

VOCABULARY QUIZ 1-E

Words to Learn

facilitate efficacy fragrance
purports tenets

Match each italicized word with the appropriate choice from the right.

Words in Context	Definitions
1. "to *facilitate* the exchange," p. 40.	a. scent, odor
2. "this book *purports* to be a history," p. 40.	b. beliefs
3. "the *efficacy* of their tenets," p. 42.	c. make easier
4. "the efficacy of their *tenets*," p. 42.	d. means, intends
5. "and of sweetest *fragrance*," p. 43.	e. effectiveness

VOCABULARY PRACTICE 1-E

Write a sentence for each of the words below. Make each sentence as brief as possible, while giving it a full and clear meaning.

1. *facilitate* 2. *efficacy* 3. *fragrance*

SUGGESTIONS FOR DISCUSSION AND WRITING

1. In this story, we again see one of the favorite devices of the science fiction writer employed, that of *literary extension*. Here are some faint beginnings from our own society that have developed into far more influential forces by the year ten thousand. Identify their ultimate development in the story.

   a. Studies in major universities of such borderline subjects as E.S.P., mental telepathy, clairvoyance, and other psychic phenomena.
   b. The United Nations.
   c. The slow but persistent progress made in the use of international languages, such as Esperanto.
   d. Late improvements in three-dimensional photography.
   e. The moratorium on the death penalty declared in many states.
   f. Meat substitutes.
   g. The Common Market.
   h. The search for alternative sources of energy.
   i. The Skylab projects of NASA.
   j. Studies of sound and light signals from outer space.

2. Before you consider this question, you may need to review the discussion of point of view on page 252. William Harben uses the *third-person limited* point of view, depending upon dialogue for most of the narration. Do you believe the story would have changed significantly if he had employed other points of view? Would it have been improved in any other ways?

3. Both "In the Year Ten-Thousand" and "Christmas 200,000 B.C." suggest that mankind is progressing toward an era when human values differ sharply from those we hold today. How would the values held by father and son alter our world?

4. At the end of the story the father tries to define *immortality*. He says, "immortality is increasing happiness for all time; . . . immortality must be love immortal." Why is his comment a particularly suitable ending for this story?

CHAPTER 1 CUMULATIVE VOCABULARY LIST

1. *adroitly*—skillfully
2. *askew*—sideways
3. *assailed*—attacked, assaulted
4. *assiduously*—steadily attentive
5. *attenuated*—made thin or weak
6. *Babel*—a noisy scene
7. *countenance*—face, expression
8. *denizens*—inhabitants, those who frequent a place
9. *derangement*—disturbance
10. *diorama*—a spectacular, three-dimensional scene
11. *efficacy*—effectiveness
12. *execrable*—very bad, detestable
13. *exhilaration*—animation, joy, liveliness
14. *explicit*—plain, direct
15. *facilitate*—make easier
16. *fragrance*—scent, odor
17. *imminent*—impending, threatening
18. *immutable*—not changeable
19. *incontinently*—without control
20. *interminable*—endless
21. *intermittent*—returning at intervals
22. *intrepid*—fearless
23. *latitude*—distance in degrees from the equator
24. *meridian*—an imaginary circle passing through both poles
25. *palpitation*—rapid beating
26. *patriarchs*—fathers, founders
27. *poignant*—pathetic, heart-rending
28. *prodigious*—enormous, extraordinary
29. *progeny*—offspring
30. *provincial*—sectional
31. *purports*—means, intends
32. *resuscitation*—revival
33. *retorted*—replied sharply
34. *rudimentary*—undeveloped
35. *sumptuously*—in luxury
36. *surly*—gloomy, rough
37. *tenets*—beliefs

38. *traverse*—to pass through, to cross
39. *undulating*—swaying, moving in waves
40. *vociferations*—outcries

Chapter 2

TAMPERING WITH HUMAN NATURE

Man's preoccupation with himself will last until the millennium—that glorious day—when we all shall seek, and find, naught but perfection in each other and in ourselves as well. That day is a long way off; meanwhile, diligent science fiction writers will continue their search for more astounding ways of "improving" the breed. We shudder at the prospect.

Frankenstein created his monster in 1818; Dr. Jekyll conducted his experiment in 1886. Two very long steps bring us to "Fondly Fahrenheit" (1954) and "The Man Inside" (1969).

Whereas Mary Shelley and Robert Louis Stevenson could command the breathless attention of their readers by writing in that contemporaneous style which gives one a sense of close personal association with the events of a story, our two contemporary authors were playing to a more sophisticated audience: an audience sated with the lurid headlines of daily newspapers, the radio blasts of "special bulletins," X-rated movies, and the traumatic hodgepodge of television drama.

YOU are that audience!

If "Fondly Fahrenheit" and "The Man Inside" can hold your attention from beginning to end—and we think they will—salute their authors for a job well done.

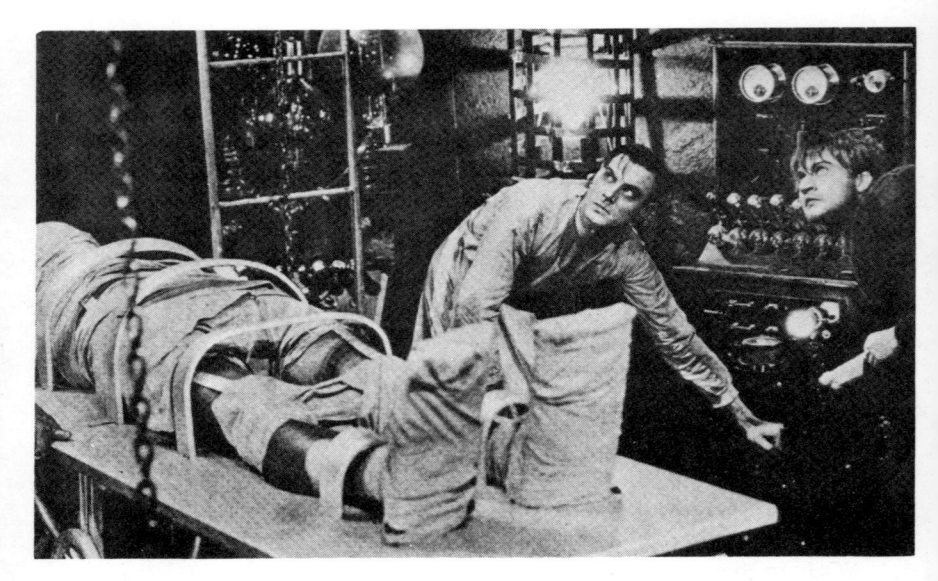

Boris Karloff, Colin Clive, and John Boles in Universal Pictures' 1931 version of *Frankenstein*.

Selections from

FRANKENSTEIN

MARY W. SHELLEY

Mary W. Shelley began writing this "novel of terror" in 1816, when she was nineteen years old. Without formal education, this talented and imaginative English girl gave the world its most enduring and favorite monster.

The book is rather lengthy and because it is written by a novice in the embroidered and ornate style of her day, is is arduous to read. We have, therefore, selected as series of excerpts from the original version, in sequence, which is sufficient for the purpose of this book.

Be sure you understand exactly who Frankenstein is. He is the protagonist of the story; a brilliant young Swiss student, he speaks to you in the first person, unfolding his frightening tale of misguided zeal. Somehow, through the years, we have forgotten the creator, and allowed the "horrible one" to assume his name.

FROM THIS day natural philosophy, and particularly chemistry, in the most comprehensive sense of the word, became nearly my sole occupation. I read with ardour those works so full of genius and discrimination, which modern enquirers have written on these subjects. I attended the lectures, and cultivated the acquaintance of the men of science at the university.

My application was at first fluctuating and uncertain; it gained strength as I proceeded, and soon became so ardent and eager, that the stars often disappeared in the light of morning whilst I was yet engaged in my laboratory. As I applied so closely, it may be easily conceived that my progress was rapid.

. . . One of the phenomena which had peculiarly attracted my attention was the structure of the human frame, and, indeed, any animal endued with life. Whence, I often asked myself, did the principle of life proceed? It was a bold question, and one which has ever been considered as a mystery; yet with how many things are we on the brink of becoming acquainted, if cowardice or carelessness did not restrain our enquiries. I revolved these circumstances in my mind, and determined thenceforth to apply myself more particularly to those branches of natural philosophy which relate to physiology. Unless I had been animated by an almost supernatural enthusiasm, my application to this study would have been irksome, and almost intolerable. To examine the causes of life, we must have recourse to death. I became acquainted with the science of anatomy: but this was not sufficient; I must observe the natural decay and corruption of the human body. In my education my father had taken the greatest precautions that my mind should be impressed with no supernatural horrors. I do not ever remember to have trembled at a tale of superstition, or to have feared the apparition of a spirit. Darkness had no effect upon my fancy; and a churchyard was to me merely the receptacle of bodies deprived of life, which, from being the seat of beauty and strength, had become food for the worm. Now I was led to examine the cause and progress of this decay, and forced to spend days and nights in vaults and charnel-houses. My attention was fixed upon every object the most insupportable to the delicacy of the human feelings. I saw how the fine form of man was degraded and wasted; I beheld the corruption of death succeed to the blooming cheek of life; I saw how the worm inherited the wonders of the eye and brain. I paused, examining and analysing all the minutiae of causation, as exemplified in the change from life to death, and death to life, until from the midst of this darkness a sudden light broke in upon me—a light so brilliant and wondrous, yet so simple, that while I became dizzy with the immensity of the prospect which it illustrated, I was surprised, that among so many men of genius who had directed their enquiries towards the same science, that I alone should be reserved to discover so astonishing a secret.

. . . It was with these feelings that I began the creation of a human being. As the minuteness of the parts formed a great hindrance to my speed, I resolved, contrary to my first intention, to make the being of a gigantic stature; that is to say, about eight feet in height, and proportionably large. After having formed this determination, and having spent some months in successfully collecting and arranging my materials, I began.

No one can conceive the variety of feelings which bore me onwards, like a hurricane, in the first enthusiasm of success. Life and death appeared to me ideal bounds, which I should first break through, and pour a torrent of light into our dark world. A new species would bless me as its creator and source; many happy and excellent natures would owe their being to me. No father could claim the gratitude of his child so completely as I should deserve theirs. Pursuing these reflections, I thought, that if I could bestow animation upon lifeless matter, I might in process of time (although I now found it impossible) renew life where death had apparently devoted the body to corruption.

These thoughts supported my spirits, while I pursued my undertaking with unremitting ardour. My cheek had grown pale with study, and my person had become emaciated with confinement. Sometimes, on the very brink of certainty, I failed; yet still I clung to the hope which the next day or the next hour might realize. One secret which I alone possessed was the hope to which I had dedicated myself; and the moon gazed on my midnight labors, while, with unrelaxed and breathless eagerness, I pursued nature to her hiding-places. Who shall conceive the horrors of my secret toil, as I dabbled among the unhallowed damps of the grave, or tortured the living animal to animate the lifeless clay? My limbs now tremble, and my eyes swim with the remembrance; but then a resistless, and almost frantic impulse urged me forward; I seemed to have lost all soul or sensation but for this one pursuit. It was indeed but a passing trance, that only made me feel with renewed acuteness so soon as, the unnatural stimulus ceasing to operate, I had returned to my old habits. I collected bones from charnel-houses; and disturbed, with profane fingers, the tremendous secrets of the human frame. In a solitary chamber, or rather cell, at the top of the house, and separated from all the other apartments by a gallery and staircase, I kept my workshop of filthy creation: my eye-balls were starting from their sockets in attending to the details of my employment. The dissecting room and the slaughterhouse furnished many of my materials; and often did my human nature turn with loathing from my occupation, whilst, still urged on by an eagerness which perpetually increased, I brought my work near conclusion.

. . . It was on a dreary night of November, that I beheld the accomplishment of my toils. With an anxiety that almost amounted to agony, I collected the instruments of life around me, that I might infuse a spark of being into the lifeless thing that lay at my feet. It was already one in the morning; the rain patted dismally against the panes, and my candle was nearly burnt out, when, by the glimmer of the half-extinguished light, I saw the full yellow eye of the creature open; it breathed hard, and a convulsive motion agitated its limbs.

How can I describe my emotions at this catastrophe, or how delineate the wretch whom with such infinite pains and care I had endeavored to form? His limbs were in proportion, and I had selected his features as beautiful. Beautiful!—Great God! His yellow skin scarcely covered the work of muscles and arteries beneath; his hair was of a lustrous black, and flowing; his teeth of a pearly whiteness; but these luxuriances only formed a more horrid contrast with his watery eyes, that seemed almost of the same color as the dun white sockets in which they were set, his shrivelled complexion and straight black lips.

The different accidents of life are not so changeable as the feelings of human nature. I had worked hard for nearly two years, for the sole purpose of infusing life into an inanimate body. For this I had deprived myself of rest and health. I had desired it with an ardour that far exceeded moderation; but now that I had finished, the beauty of the dream vanished, and breathless horror and disgust filled my heart. Unable to endure the aspect of the being I had created, I rushed out of the room, and continued a long time traversing my bedchamber, unable to compose my mind to sleep. At length lassitude succeeded to the tumult I had endured; and I threw myself on the bed in my clothes, endeavoring to seek a few moments of forgetfulness. But it was in vain; I slept, indeed, but I was disturbed by the wildest dreams.

. . . I started from my sleep with horror; a cold dew covered my forehead, my teeth chattered, and every limb became convulsed: when, by the dim and yellow light of the moon, as it forced its way through the window shutters, I beheld the wretch—the miserable monster I had created. He held up the curtain of the bed; and his eyes, if eyes they may be called, were fixed on me. His jaws opened, and he muttered some inarticulate sounds, while a grin wrinkled his cheeks. He might have spoken, but I did not hear; one hand was stretched out, seemingly to detain me, but I escaped, and rushed downstairs. I took refuge in the courtyard belonging to the house which I inhabited; where I remained during the rest of the night, walking up and down in the greatest agitation, listening attentively, catching and fearing each sound as if it were to announce the approach of the demoniacal corpse to which I had so miserably given life.

VOCABULARY STUDY

VOCABULARY QUIZ 2-A

Words to Learn

protagonist　　　　*apparition*　　　　*lassitude*
ardent　　　　　　*hindrance*

Match each italicized word with the appropriate choice from the right.

Words in Context　　　　　　　　　　**Definitions**

1. "he is the *protagonist* in the story," p. 51.　　a. eager, driven
2. "it . . . became so *ardent*," p. 51.　　　　　　b. an impediment
3. "the *apparition* of a spirit," p. 52.　　　　　　c. appearance, ghost
4. "a *hindrance* to my speed," p. 52.　　　　　　d. weariness, fatigue
5. "*lassitude* succeeded," p. 54.　　　　　　　　e. main character

VOCABULARY PRACTICE 2-A

Write a mature, thoughtful sentence for each of the words listed below. You may change the word's part of speech, tense, or number if you wish.

1. *ardent*　　　　2. *apparition*　　　　3. *lassitude*

SUGGESTIONS FOR DISCUSSION AND WRITING

1. *Frankenstein* is an example of the Gothic novel popular in Mary Shelley's day. It is characterized by a somber Gothic setting, remote and distant time and locale, as well as some psychological aberration on the part of the protagonist. Even in this short excerpt, it is clear that Frankenstein's *mind* is one of the main focal points of the story. Briefly describe his personality as you understand it to be, using only the facts you have learned by reading this selection. Note particularly his excessive concern with his own feelings and emotions, his reasons for undertaking the creation of another being, and his unnatural intensity.

2. There is a suggestion, at the end of the *Frankenstein* selection, that Frankenstein is punished or cursed, rather than rewarded, for his brilliance. What is his punishment; how is it consistent with the rest of the story?

3. Examine some of the passages in which the words Mary Shelley employs are very precise (such as her description of the creation), and some in which the language is vague and allusive (such as the passage in which Dr. Frankenstein explains his reasons for undertaking a study of physiology). Discuss how the words are associated with the effect she wants to create.

A Selection from

THE STRANGE CASE OF
DOCTOR JEKYLL AND MISTER HYDE
AND OTHER FAMOUS TALES

ROBERT LOUIS STEVENSON

ON THE ninth of January, now four days ago, I received by the evening mail a registered envelope, addressed in the hand of my colleague and old school companion, Henry Jekyll. I was a good deal surprised by this; for we were by no no means in the habit of correspondence; I had seen the man, dined with him indeed, the night before; and I could imagine nothing in our intercourse that should justify formality of registration. The contents increased my wonder; for this is how the letter ran:

10th December, 18—.

"Dear Lanyon,—You are one of my oldest friends; and although we may have differed at times on scientific questions, I cannot remember, at least on my side, any break in our affection. There was never a day when, if you had said to me, 'Jekyll, my life, my honor, my reason, depend on you,' I would not have sacrificed my left hand to help you. Lanyon, my life, my honor, my reason, are all at your mercy; if you fail me tonight, I am lost. You might suppose, after this preface, that I am going to ask you for something dishonorable to grant. Judge for yourself.

"I want you to postpone all other engagements for tonight—ay, even if you were summoned to the bedside of an emperor; to take a cab, unless your carriage should be actually at the door; and with this letter in your hand for consultation, to drive straight to my house.

Poole, my butler, has his orders; you will find him waiting your arrival with a locksmith. The door of my cabinet is then to be forced: and you are to go in alone; to open the glazed press (letter E) on the left hand, breaking the lock if it be shut; and to draw out, *with all its contents as they stand*, the fourth drawer from the top or (which is the same thing) the third from the bottom. In my extreme distress of mind, I have a morbid fear of misdirecting you; but even if I am in error, you may know the right drawer by its contents: some powders, a phial and a paper book. This drawer I beg of you to carry back with you to Cavendish Square exactly as it stands.

"That is the first part of the service: now for the second. You should be back, if you set out at once on the receipt of this, long before midnight; but I will leave you that amount of margin, not only in the fear of one of those obstacles that can neither be prevented nor foreseen, but because an hour when your servants are in bed is to be preferred for what will then remain to do. At midnight then, I have to ask you to be alone in your consulting room, to admit with your own hand into the house a man who will present himself in my name, and to place in his hands the drawer that you will have brought with you from my cabinet. Then you will have played your part and earned my gratitude completely. Five minutes afterwards, if you insist upon an explanation, you will have understood that these arrangements are of capital importance; and that by the neglect of one of them, fantastic as they must appear, you might have charged your conscience with my death or the shipwreck of my reason.

"Confident as I am that you will not trifle with this appeal, my heart sinks and my hand trembles at the bare thought of such a possibility. Think of me at this hour, in a strange place, laboring under a blackness of distress that no fancy can exaggerate, and yet well aware that, if you will but punctually serve me, my troubles will roll away like a story that is told. Serve me, my dear Lanyon, and save.

Your friend,
H.J.

"P.S.—I had already sealed this up when a fresh terror struck upon my soul. It is possible that the post-office may fail me, and this letter not come into your hands until tomorrow morning. In that case, dear Lanyon, do my errand when it shall be most convenient for you in the course of the day; and once more expect my messenger at midnight. It may then already be too late; and if that night passes without event, you will know that you have seen the last of Henry Jekyll."

Upon the reading of this letter, I made sure my colleague was insane; but till that was proved beyond the possibility of doubt, I felt bound to do as he requested. The less I understood of this farrago, the less I was in a position to judge of its importance; and an appeal so worded could not be set aside without a grave responsibility. I rose accordingly from table, got into a hansom, and drove straight to Jekyll's house. The butler was awaiting my arrival; he had received by the same post as mine a registered letter of instruction, and had sent at once for a locksmith and a carpenter. The tradesmen came while we were yet speaking; and we moved in a body to old Dr. Denman's surgical theatre, from which (as you are doubtless aware) Jekyll's private cabinet is most conveniently entered. The door was very strong, the lock excellent; the carpenter avowed he would have great trouble and have to do much damage, if force were to be used; and the locksmith was near despair. But this last was a handy fellow, and after two hours' work, the door stood open. The press marked E was unlocked; and I took out the drawer, had it filled up with straw and tied in a sheet, and returned with it to Cavendish Square.

Here I proceeded to examine its contents. The powders were neatly enough made up, but not with the nicety of the dispensing chemist; so that it was plain they were of Jekyll's private manufacture; and when I opened one of the wrappers I found what seemed to me a simple crystalline salt of a white color. The phial, to which I next turned my attention, might have been about half full of a blood-red liquor, which was highly pungent to the sense of smell and seemed to me to contain phosphorus and some volatile ether. At the other ingredients I could make no guess. The book was an ordinary version book and contained little but a series of dates. These covered a period of many years, but I observed that the entries ceased nearly a year ago and quite abruptly. Here and there a brief remark was appended to a date, usually no more than a single word: "double" occurring perhaps six times in a total of several entries; and once very early in the list and followed by several marks of exclamation, "total failure!!!" All this, though it whetted my curiosity, told me little that was definite. Here were a phial of some tincture, a paper of some salt, and the record of a series of experiments that had led (like too many of Jekyll's investigations) to no end of practical usefulness. How could the presence of these articles in my house affect either the honor, the sanity, or the life of my flighty colleague? If his messenger could go to one place, why could he not go to another? And even granting some impediment, why was this gentleman to be received by me in secret? The more I reflected the more convinced I grew that I was dealing with a case of cerebral disease; and though I dismissed my servants to bed, I loaded an old revolver, that I might be found in some posture of self-defense.

Twelve o'clock had scarce rung out over London, ere the knocker sounded very gently on the door. I went myself at the summons, and found a small man crouching against the pillars of the portico.

"Are you come from Dr. Jekyll?" I asked.

He told me "yes" by a constrained gesture; and when I had bidden him enter, he did not obey me without a searching backward glance into the darkness of the square. There was a policeman not far off, advancing with his bull's eye open; and at the sight, I thought my visitor started and made greater haste.

These particulars struck me, I confess, disagreeably; and as I followed him into the brightness of the consulting room, I kept my hand ready on my weapon. Here, at last, I had a chance of clearly seeing him. I had never set eyes on him before, so much was certain. He was small, as I have said; I was struck besides with the shocking expression on his face, with his remarkable combination of great muscular activity and great apparent debility of constitution, and—last but not least—with the odd, subjective disturbance caused by his neighborhood. This bore some resemblance to incipient rigor, and was accompanied by a marked sinking of the pulse. At the time, I set it down to some idiosyncratic, personal distaste, and merely wondered at the acuteness of the symptoms; but I have since had reason to believe the cause to lie much deeper in the nature of man, and to turn on some nobler hinge than the principle of hatred.

This person (who had thus, from the first moment of his entrance, struck in me what I can only describe as a disgustful curiosity) was dressed in a fashion that would have made an ordinary person laughable; his clothes, that is to say, although they were of rich and sober fabric, were enormously too large for him in every measurement—the trousers hanging on his legs and rolled up to keep them from the ground, the waist of the coat below his haunches, and the collar sprawling wide upon his shoulders. Strange to relate, this ludicrous accoutrement was far from moving me to laughter. Rather, as there was something abnormal and misbegotten in the very essence of the creature that now faced me—something seizing, surprising and revolting—this fresh disparity seemed but to fit in with and to reinforce it; so that to my interest in the man's nature and character, there was added a curiosity as to his origin, his life, his fortune and status in the world.

These observations, though they have taken so great a space to be set down in, were yet the work of a few seconds. My visitor was, indeed, on fire with sombre excitement.

"Have you got it?" he cried. "Have you got it?" And so lively was his impatience that he even laid his hand upon my arm and sought to shake me.

The Strange Case of Doctor Jekyll and Mister Hyde

I put him back, conscious at his touch of a certain icy pang along my blood. "Come, sir," said I. "You forget that I have not yet the pleasure of your acquaintance. Be seated, if you please." And I showed him an example, and sat down myself in my customary seat and with as fair an imitation of my ordinary manner to a patient, as the lateness of the hour, the nature of my preoccupations, and the horror I had of my visitor, would suffer me to muster.

"I beg your pardon, Dr. Lanyon," he replied civilly enough. "What you say is very well founded; and my impatience has shown its heels to my politeness. I come here at the instance of your colleague, Dr. Henry Jekyll, on a piece of business of some moment; and I understood . . ." He paused and put his hand to his throat, and I could see, in spite of his collected manner, that he was wrestling against the approaches of the hysteria—I understood, a drawer . . ."

But here I took pity on my visitor's suspense, and some perhaps on my own growing curiosity.

"There it is, sir," said I, pointing to the drawer, where it lay on the floor behind a table and still covered with the sheet.

He sprang to it, and then paused, and laid his hand upon his heart; I could hear his teeth grate with the convulsive action of his jaws; and his face was so ghastly to see that I grew alarmed both for his life and reason.

"Compose yourself," said I.

He turned a dreadful smile to me, and as if with the decision of despair, plucked away the sheet. At sight of the contents, he uttered one loud sob of such immense relief that I sat petrified. And the next moment, in a voice that was already fairly well under control, "Have you a graduated glass?" he asked.

I rose from my place with something of an effort and gave him what he asked.

He thanked me with a smiling nod, measured out a few minims of the red tincture and added one of the powders. The mixture, which was at first of a reddish hue, began, in proportion as the crystals melted, to brighten in color, to effervesce audibly, and to throw off small fumes of vapor. Suddenly and at the same time, the ebullition ceased and the compound changed to a dark purple, which faded again more slowly to a watery green. My visitor, who had watched these metamorphoses with a keen eye, smiled, set down the glass upon the table, and then turned and looked upon me with an air of scrutiny.

"And now," said he, "to settle what remains. Will you be wise? will you be guided? will you suffer me to take this glass in my hand and to go forth from your house without further parley? or has the greed of curiosity too much command of you? Think before you answer, for it shall be done as you decide. As you decide, you shall be left as you were before, and neither richer nor wiser, unless the sense of service rendered to a man in mortal distress may be counted as a kind of riches of the soul. Or, if you shall so prefer to choose, a new province of knowledge and new avenues to fame and power shall be laid upon you, here, in this room, upon the instant; and your sight shall be blasted by a prodigy to stagger the unbelief of Satan."

"Sir," said I, affecting a coolness that I was far from truly possessing, "you speak enigmas, and you will perhaps not wonder that I hear you with no very strong impression of belief. But I have gone too far in the way of inexplicable services to pause before I see the end."

"It is well," replied my visitor. "Lanyon, you remember your vows: what follows is under the seal of our profession. And now, you who have so long been bound to the most narrow and material views, you who have denied the virtue of transcendental medicine, you who have derided your superiors—behold!"

He put the glass to his lips and drank at one gulp. A cry followed; he reeled, staggered, clutched at the table and held on, staring with injected eyes, gasping with open mouth; and as I looked there came, I thought, a change—he seemed to swell—his face became suddenly black and the features seemed to melt and alter—and the next moment, I had sprung to my feet and leaped back against the wall, my arms raised to shield me from that prodigy, my mind submerged in terror.

"O God!" I screamed, and "O God!" again and again; for there before my eyes—pale and shaken, and half fainting, and groping before him with his hands, like a man restored from death—there stood Henry Jekyll!

What he told me in the next hour, I cannot bring my mind to set on paper. I saw what I saw, I heard what I heard, and my mind sickened at it; and yet now when that sight has faded from my eyes, I ask myself if I believe it, and I cannot answer. My life is shaken to its roots; sleep has left me; the deadliest terror sits by me at all hours of the day and night; and I feel that my days are numbered, and that I must die; and yet I shall die incredulous. As for the moral turpitude that man unveiled to me, even with tears of penitence, I cannot, even in memory, dwell on it without a start of horror. I will say but one thing, Utterson, and that (if you can bring your mind to credit it) will be more than enough. The creature who crept into my house that night was, on Jekyll's own confession, known by the name of Hyde and hunted for in every corner of the land as the murderer of Carew.

VOCABULARY STUDY

VOCABULARY QUIZ 2-B

Words to Learn

morbid
cerebral

debility
ludicrous

enigmas

Match each italicized word with the appropriate choice from the right.

Words in Context

1. "I have a *morbid* fear," p. 58.
2. "a case of *cerebral* disease," p. 59.
3. "*debility* of constitution," p. 60.
4. "this *ludicrous* accoutrement," p. 60.
5. "you speak *enigmas*," p. 62.

Definitions

a. puzzles
b. despondent, diseased
c. laughable, absurd
d. weakness
e. of the brain

VOCABULARY PRACTICE 2-B

1. Write a short, one-paragraph description of an imaginary person who pursues a hobby which you consider *ludicrous*.
2. Describe an actual circumstance which is an *enigma* to you.

SUGGESTIONS FOR DISCUSSION AND WRITING

1. Stevenson uses a number of devices to make Dr. Jekyll's appeal to Dr. Lanyon sound particularly compelling. In the first and last paragraphs, for example, there are references to their friendship, as well as other emotional appeals. The careful planning that lies behind the letter itself helps bring about its urgent tone. Describe these and other devices you can find; be sure to strengthen your response with specific quotations and references to the text.

2. Stevenson's story is clearly more than a science fiction tale of a man who can transform his physical appearance by means of a remarkable potion. It is about a man who has discovered that he possesses two natures, one of a very evil character. As Dr. Lanyon looks upon (and describes to us) the "shocking appearance of Mr. Hyde" on page 60, he suggests that there is more to this man than ugliness. He *prepares* the reader, in fact, for the subsequent transformation. Explain, with references to the text of the story.

FONDLY FAHRENHEIT

ALFRED BESTER

HE DOESN'T know which of us I am these days, but they know one truth. You must own nothing but yourself. You must make your own life, live your own life and die your own death . . . or else you will die another's.

The rice fields on Paragon III stretch for hundreds of miles like checkerboard tundras, a blue and brown mosaic under a burning sky of orange. In the evenings, clouds whip like smoke, and the paddies rustle and murmur.

A long line of men marched across the paddies, the evening we escaped from Paragon III. They were silent, armed, intent; a long rank of silhouetted statues looming against the smoking sky. Each man carried a gun. Each man wore a walkie-talkie belt pack, the speaker button in his ear, the microphone bug clipped to his throat, the glowing viewscreen strapped to his wrist like a green-eyed watch. The multitude of screens showed nothing but a multitude of individual paths through the paddies. The annunciators uttered no sound but the rustle and splash of steps. The men spoke infrequently, in heavy grunts, all speaking to all.

"Nothing here."
"Where's here?"
"Jenson's fields."
"You're drifting too far west."
"Close in the line there."
"Anbody covered the Grimson paddy?"
"Yeah. Nothing."
"She couldn't have walked this far."
"Could have been carried."
"Think she's alive?"
"Why should she be dead?"

The slow refrain swept up and down the long line of beaters advancing towards the smoky sunset. The line of beaters wavered like a writhing snake, but never ceased its remorseless advance.

65

One hundred men spaced fifty feet apart. Five thousand feet of ominous search. One mile of angry determination stretching from east to west across a compass of heat. Evening fell. Each man lit his search lamp. The writhing snake was transformed into a necklace of wavering diamonds.

"Clear here. Nothing."
"Nothing here."
"What about the Allen paddies?"
"Covering them now."
"Think we missed her?"
"Maybe."
"We'll beat back and check."
"This'll be an all night job."
"Allen paddies clear."
"We've got to find her!"
"We'll find her."
"Here she is. Sector seven. Tune in."

The line stopped. The diamonds froze in the heat. There was silence. Each man gazed into the glowing screen on his wrist, tuning to sector seven. All tuned to one. All showed a small nude figure awash in the muddy water of a paddy. Alongside the figure an owner's stake of bronze read: VANDALEUR. The end of the line converged towards the Vandaleur field. The necklace turned into a cluster of stars. One hundred men gathered around a small nude body, a child dead in a rice paddy. There was no water in her mouth. There were fingerprints on her throat. Her innocent face was battered. Her body was torn. Clotted blood on her skin was crusted and hard.

"Dead three-four hours at least."
"Her mouth is dry."
"She wasn't drowned. Beaten to death."

In the dark evening heat the men swore softly. They picked up the body. She had fought her murderer. Under the nails were particles of flesh and bright drops of scarlet blood, still liquid, still uncoagulated.

"That blood ought to be clotted too."
"Funny."
"Not so funny. What kind of blood don't clot?"
"Android."
"Looks like she was killed by one."
"Vandaleur owns an android."
"She couldn't be killed by an android."
"That's android blood under her nails."
"The police better check."
"The police'll prove I'm right."
"But androids can't kill."
"That's android blood, ain't it?"
"Androids can't kill. They're made that way."
"Looks like one android was made wrong."

And the thermometer that day registered 91.9° gloriously Fahrenheit.

So there we were aboard the Paragon Queen en route for Megaster V, James Vandaleur and his android. James Vandaleur counted his money and wept. In the second class cabin with him was his android, a magnificent creature with classic features and wide blue eyes. Raised on its forehead in a cameo of flesh were the letters MA, indicating that this was one of the rare multiple aptitude androids, worth $57,000 on the current exchange. There we were, weeping and counting and calmly watching.

"Twelve, fourteen, sixteen. Sixteen hundred dollars," Vandaleur wept. "That's all. Sixteen hundred dollars. My house was worth ten thousand. The land was worth five. There was furniture, cars, my paintings, etchings, my plane, my —And nothing to show for everything but sixteen hundred dollars."

I leaped up from the table and turned on the Android. I pulled a strap from one of the leather bags and beat the android. It didn't move.

"I must remind you," the android said, "that I am worth fifty-seven thousand dollars on the current exchange. I must warn you that you are endangering valuable property."

"You damned crazy machine," Vandaleur shouted.

"I am not a machine," the android answered. "The robot is a machine. The android is a chemical creation of synthetic tissue."

"What got into you?" Vandaleur cried. "Why did you do it? Damn you!" He beat the android savagely.

"I must remind you that I cannot be punished," I said. "The pleasure-pain syndrome is not incorporated in the android synthesis."

"Then why did you kill her?" Vandaleur shouted. "If it wasn't for kicks, why did you—"

"I must remind you," the android said, "that the second class cabins in these ships are not soundproofed."

Vandaleur dropped the strap and stood panting, staring at the creature he owned.

"Why did you do it? Why did you kill her?" I asked.

"I don't know," I answered.

"First it was malicious mischief. Small things. Petty destruction. I should have known there was something wrong with you then. Androids can't destroy. They can't harm. They—"

"There is no pleasure-pain syndrome incorporated in the android synthesis."

"Then it got to arson. Then serious destruction. Then assault . . . that engineer on Rigel. Each time worse. Each time we had to get out faster. Now it's murder. What's the matter with you? What's happened?"

"There are no self-check relays incorporated in the android brain."

"Each time we had to get out it was a step downhill. Look at me. In a second class cabin. Me. James Paleologue Vandaleur. There was a time when my father was the wealthiest—Now, sixteen hundred dollars in the world. That's all I've got. And you!"

Vandaleur raised the strap to beat the android again, then dropped it and collapsed on a berth, sobbing. At last he pulled himself together.

"Instructions," he said.

The multiple aptitude android responded at once. It arose and awaited orders.

"My name is now Valentine. James Valentine. I stopped off on Paragon III for only one day to transfer to this ship for Megaster V. My occupation: Agent for one privately owned MA android which is for hire. Purpose of visit: To settle on Megaster V. Fix the papers."

The android removed Vandaleur's passport and papers from a bag, got pen and ink and sat down at the table. With an accurate flawless hand—an accomplished hand that could draw, write, paint, carve, engrave, etch, photograph, design, create and build—it meticulously forged new credentials for Vandaleur. Its owner watched me miserably.

"Create and build," I muttered. "And now destroy. What am I going to do? If I could only get rid of you. If only I'd inherited some guts instead of you."

Dallas Brady was Megaster's leading jewelery designer. She was short, stocky and amoral. She hired Vandaleur's multiple aptitude android and put me to work in her shop. One day, she asked abruptly: "Your name's Vandaleur, isn't it?"

"Yes," I murmured. Then: "No! No! It's Valentine. James Valentine."

"What happened on Paragon?" Dallas Brady asked. "I thought androids couldn't kill or destroy property. Prime Directives and Inhibitions set up for them when they're synthesized. Every company guarantees they can't."

"Valentine!" Vandaleur insisted.

"Oh, come off it," Dallas Brady said. "I've known for a week. I haven't hollered copper, have I?"

"The name is Valentine."

"You want to prove it? You want I should call the cops?" Dallas reached out and picked up the phone.

"For God's sake, Dallas!" Vandaleur leaped up and struggled to take the phone from her. She fended him off, laughing at him until he collapsed and wept in shame and helplessness.

"How did you find out?" he asked at last.

"The papers are full of it. And Valentine was a little too close to Vandaleur. That wasn't smart, was it?"

"I guess not. I'm not very smart."

"Your android's got quite a record, hasn't it? Assault. Arson. Destruction. What happened on Paragon?"

"It kidnapped a child. Took her into the rice fields and murdered her."

"They're going to catch up with you."

"Don't I know it? . . . We've been running for two years now. Seven planets in two years. I must have abandoned fifty thousand dollars worth of property in two years."

"You better find out what's wrong with it."

"How can I? Can I walk into a repair clinic and ask for an over-

Fondly Fahrenheit

haul? What am I going to say? 'My android's just turned killer. Fix it.' They'd call the police right off." I began to shake. "They'd have that android dismantled inside one day. I'd probably be booked as accessory to murder."

"Why didn't you have it repaired before it got to murder?"

"I couldn't take the chance," Vandaleur explained angrily. "If they started fooling around with lobotomies and body chemistry and endocrine surgery, they might have destroyed its aptitudes. What would I have left to hire out? How would I live?"

"You could work yourself. People do."

"Work for what? You know I'm good for nothing. How could I compete with specialist androids and robots? Who can, unless he's got a terrific talent for a particular job?"

"Yeah. That's true."

"I lived off my old man all my life. He had to go bust just before he died. Left me with the android and that's all. The only way I can get along is living off what it earns."

"You better sell it before the cops catch up with you. You can live off fifty grand. Invest it."

"At 3 per cent? Fifteen hundred a year? When the android returns 15 per cent on its value? Eight thousand a year. That's what it earns. No, Dallas. I've got to go along with it."

"What are you going to do about its violence kick?"

"I can't do anything . . . except watch and pray. What are you going to do about it?"

"Nothing. It's none of my business. Only one thing . . . I ought to get something for keeping my mouth shut."

"What?"

"The android works for me for free. Let somebody else pay you, but I get it for free."

The multiple aptitude android worked. Vandaleur collected its fees. His expenses were taken care of. His savings began to mount. As the warm spring of Megaster V turned to hot summer, I began investigating farms and properties. It would be possible, within a year or two, for us to settle down permanently, provided Dallas Brady's demands did not become rapacious.

On the first hot day of summer, the android began singing in Dallas Brady's workshop. It hovered over the electric furnace which, along with the weather, was broiling the shop, and sang an ancient tune that had been popular half a century before.

Oh, it's no feat to beat the heat.
All reet! All reet!
So jeet your seat
Be fleet be fleet
Cool and discreet
Honey . . .

It sang in a strange, halting voice, and its accomplished fingers were clasped behind its back, writhing in a strange rhumba all their own. Dallas Brady was surprised.

"You happy or something?" she asked.

"I must remind you that the pleasure-pain syndrome is not incorporated in the android synthesis," I answered. "All reet! All reet! Be fleet be fleet, cool and discreet, honey . . ."

Its fingers stopped their writhing and picked up a heavy pair of iron tongs. The android poked them into the glowing heart of the furnace, leaning far forward to peer into the lovely heat.

"Be careful, you fool!" Dallas Brady exclaimed. "You want to fall in?"

"I must remind you that I am worth fifty-seven thousand dollars on the current exchange," I said. "It is forbidden to endanger valuable property. All reet! All reet! Honey . . ."

It withdrew a crucible of glowing gold from the electric furnace, turned, capered hideously, sang crazily, and splashed a sluggish gobbet of molten gold over Dallas Brady's head. She screamed and collapsed, her hair and clothes flaming, her skin crackling. The android poured again while it capered and sang.

"Be fleet be fleet, cool and discreet, honey . . ." It sang and slowly poured and poured the molten gold. Then I left the workshop and rejoined James Vandaleur in his hotel suite. The android's charred clothes and squirming fingers warned its owner that something was very much wrong.

Vandaleur rushed to Dallas Brady's workshop, stared once, vomited and fled. I had enough time to pack one bag and raise nine hundred dollars on portable assets. He took a third class cabin on the Megaster Queen which left that morning for Lyra Alpha. He took me with him. He wept and counted his money and I beat the android again.

And the thermometer in Dallas Brady's workshop registered 98.1° beautifully Fahrenheit.

On Lyra Alpha we holed up in a small hotel near the university. There, Vandaleur carefully bruised my forehead until the letters MA were obliterated by the swelling and discoloration. The letters would reappear, but not for several months, and in the meantime Vandaleur hoped the hue and cry for an MA android would be forgotten. The android was hired out as a common laborer in the university's power plant. Vandaleur, as James Venice eked out life on the android's small earnings.

I wasn't too unhappy. Most of the other residents in the hotel were university students, equally hard-up, but delightfully young and enthusiastic. There was one charming girl with sharp eyes and a quick mind. Her name was Wanda, and she and her beau, Jed Stark, took a tremendous interest in the killing android which was being mentioned in every paper in the galaxy.

"We've been studying the case," she and Jed said at one of the casual student parties which happened to be held this night in Vandaleur's room. "We think we know what's causing it. We're going to do a paper." They were in a high state of excitement.

"Causing what?" somebody wanted to know.

"The android rampage."

"Obviously out of adjustment, isn't it? Body chemistry gone haywire. Maybe a kind of synthetic cancer, yes?"

"No." Wanda gave Jed a look of suppressed triumph.

"Well, what is it?"

"Something specific."

"What?"

"That would be telling."

"Oh, come on."

"Nothing doing."

"Won't you tell us?" I asked intently. "I . . . We're very much interested in what could go wrong with an android."

"No, Mr. Venice," Wanda said. "It's a unique idea and we've got to protect it. One thesis like this and we'll be set up for life. We can't take the chance of somebody stealing it."

"Can't you give us a hint?"

"No. Not a hint. Don't say a word, Jed. But I'll tell you this much, Mr. Venice. I'd hate to be the man who owns that android."

"You mean the police?" I asked.

"I mean projection, Mr. Venice. Projection! That's the danger . . . and I won't say any more. I've said too much as it is."

I heard steps outside, and a hoarse voice singing softly: "Be fleet be fleet, cool and discreet, honey . . ." My android entered the room, home from its tour of duty at the university power plant. It was not introduced. I motioned to it and I immediately responded to the command and went to the keg and took over Vandaleur's job of serving the guests. Its accomplished fingers writhed in a private rhumba of their own. Gradually they stopped their squirming, and the strange humming ended.

Androids were not unusual at the university. The wealthier students owned them along with cars and planes. Vandaleur's android provoked no comment, but young Wanda was sharp-eyed and quick-witted. She noted my bruised forehead and she was intent on the history-making thesis she and Jed were going to write. After the party broke up, she consulted with Jed walking upstairs to her room.

"Jed, why'd that android have a bruised forehead?"

"Probably hurt itself, Wanda. It's working in the power plant. They fling a lot of heavy stuff around."

"That's all?"

"What else?"

"It could be a convenient bruise."

"Convenient for what?"

"Hiding what's stamped on its forehead."

"No point to that, Wanda. You don't have to see marks on a forehead to recognize an android. You don't have to see a trademark on a car to know it's a car."

"I don't mean it's trying to pass as a human. I mean it's trying to pass as a lower grade android."

"Why?"

"Suppose it had MA on its forehead."

"Multiple aptitude? Then why in hell would Venice waste it stoking furnaces if it would earn more— Oh. Oh! You mean it's—"

Wanda nodded.

"Golly!" Stark pursed his lips. "What do we do? Call the police?"

"No. We don't know if it's an MA for a fact. If it turns out to be an MA and the killing android, our paper comes first anyway. This is our big chance, Jed. If it's *that* android we can run a series of controlled tests and—"

"How do we find out for sure?"

"Easy. Infrared film. That'll show what's under the bruise. Borrow a camera. Buy some film. We'll sneak down to the power plant tomorrow and take some pictures. Then we'll know."

They stole down into the university power plant the following afternoon. It was a vast cellar, deep under the earth. It was dark, shadowy, luminous with burning light from the furnace doors. Above the roar of the fires they could hear a strange voice shouting and chanting in the echoing vault: "All reet! All reet! So jeet your seat. Be fleet, be fleet, cool and discreet, honey . . ." And they could see a capering figure dancing a lunatic rhumba in time to the music it shouted. The legs twisted. The arms waved. The fingers writhed.

Jed Stark raised the camera and began shooting his spool of infrared film, aiming the camera sights at that bobbing head. Then Wanda shrieked, for I saw them and came charging down on them, brandishing a polished steel shovel. It smashed the camera. It felled the girl and then the boy. Jed fought me for a desperate hissing moment before he was bludgeoned into helplessness. Then the android dragged them to the furnace and fed them to the flames, slowly, hideously. It capered and sang. Then it returned to my hotel.

The thermometer in the power plant registered 100.9° murderously Fahrenheit. All reet! All reet!

We bought steerage on the Lyra Queen and Vandaleur and the android did odd jobs for their meals. During the night watches, Vandaleur would sit alone in the steerage head with a cardboard portfolio on his lap, puzzling over its contents. That portfolio was all he had managed to bring with him from Lyra Alpha. He had stolen it from Wanda's room. It was labelled ANDROID. It contained the secret of my sickness.

And it contained nothing but newspapers. Scores of newspapers from all over the galaxy, printed, microfilmed, engraved, offset, photostated . . . Rigel *Star-Banner* . . . Paragon *Picayune* . . . Megaster *Times-Leader* . . . Lalande *Journal* . . . Indi *Intelligencer* . . . Eridani *Telegram-News*. All reet! All reet!

Nothing but newspapers. Each paper contained an account of one crime in the android's ghastly career. Each paper also contained news, domestic and foreign, sports, society, weather, shipping news, stock exchange quotations, human interest stories, features, contests, puzzles. Somewhere in that mass of uncollated facts was the secret Wanda and Jed Stark had discovered. Vandaleur pored over the papers helplessly. It was beyond him. So jeet your seat!

"I'll sell you," I told the android. "Damn you. When we land on Terra, I'll sell you. I'll settle for 3 per cent on whatever you're worth."

"I am worth fifty-seven thousand dollars on the current exchange," I told him.

"If I can't sell you, I'll turn you over to the police," I said.

"I am valuable property," I answered. "It is forbidden to endanger valuable property. You won't have me destroyed."

"And why not!" Vandaleur cried. "What? Are you arrogant? Do you know you can trust me to protect you? Is that the secret?"

The multiple aptitude android regarded him with calm accomplished eyes. "Sometimes," it said, "It is a good thing to be property."

It was 3 below zero when the Lyra Queen dropped at Croydon Field. A mixture of ice and snow swept across the field, fizzing and exploding into steam under the Queen's tail jets. The passengers trotted numbly across the blackened concrete to customs inspection, and thence to the airport bus that was to take them to London. Vandaleur and the android were broke. They walked.

By midnight they reached Piccadilly Circus. The December ice storm had not slackened and the statue of Eros was encrusted with ice. They turned right, walked down to Trafalgar Square and then along the Strand towards Soho, shaking with cold and wet. Just above Fleet Street, Vandaleur saw a solitary figure coming from the direction of St. Paul's. He drew the android into an alley.

"We've got to have money," he whispered. He pointed at the approaching figure. "He has money. Take it from him."

"The order cannot be obeyed," the android said.

"Take it from him," Vandaleur repeated. "By force. Do you understand? We're desperate."

"It is contrary to my prime directive," I said. "I cannot endanger life or property. The order cannot be obeyed."

"For God's sake!" Vandaleur burst out. "You've attacked, destroyed, murdered. Don't gibber about prime directives. You haven't any left. Get his money. Kill him if you have to. I tell you, we're desperate!"

"It is contrary to my prime directive," the android repeated. "The order cannot be obeyed."

I thrust the android back and leaped out at the stranger. He was tall, austere, competent. He had an air of hope curdled by cynicism. He carried a cane. I saw he was blind.

"Yes?" he said. "I hear you near me. What is it?"

"Sir . . ." Vandaleur hesitated. "I'm desperate."

"We are all desperate," the stranger replied. "Quietly desperate."

"Sir . . . I've got to have some money."

"Are you begging or stealing?" The sightless eyes passed over Vandaleur and the android.

"I'm prepared for either."

"Ah. So are we all. It is the history of our race." The stranger motioned over his shoulder. "I have been begging at St. Paul's, my friend. What I desire cannot be stolen. What is it you desire that you are lucky enough to be able to steal?"

"Money," Vandaleur said.

"Money for what? Come, my friend, let us exchange confidences. I will tell you why I beg, if you tell me why you steal. My name is Blenheim."

"My name is . . . Vole."

"I was not begging for sight at St. Paul's, Mr. Vole. I was begging for a number."

"A number?"

"Ah, yes. Numbers rational, numbers irrational. Numbers imaginary. Positive integers. Negative integers. Fractions, positive and negative. Eh? You have never heard of Blenheim's immortal treatise on Twenty Zeroes, or The Differences in Absence of Quantity?" Blenheim smiled bitterly. "I am a wizard of the Theory of Numbers, Mr. Vole, and I have exhausted the charm of numbers for myself. After fifty years of wizardry, senility approaches and the appetite vanishes. I have been praying in St. Paul's for inspiration. Dear God, I prayed, if You exist, send me a number."

Vandaleur slowly lifted the cardboard portfolio and touched Blenheim's hand with it. "In here," he said, "is a number. A hidden number. A secret number. The number of a crime. Shall we exchange, Mr. Blenheim? Shelter for a number?"

"Neither begging nor stealing, eh?" Blenheim said. "But a bargain. So all life reduces to the banal." The sightless eyes again passed over Vandaleur and the android. "Perhaps the All-Mighty is not God but a merchant. Come home with me."

On the top floor of Blenheim's house we shared a room—two beds, two closets, two washstands, one bathroom. Vandaleur bruised my forehead again and sent me out to find work, and while the android worked, I consulted with Blenheim and read him the papers from the portfolio, one by one. All reet! All reet!

Vandaleur told him so much and no more. He was a student, I said, attempting a thesis on the murdering android. In these papers which he had collected were the facts that would explain the crimes of which Blenheim had heard nothing. There must be a correlation, a number, a statistic, something which would account for my derangement, I explained, and Blenheim was piqued by the mystery, the detective story, the human interest in numbers.

We examined the papers. As I read them aloud, he listed them and their contents in his blind, meticulous writing. And then I read his notes to him. He listed the papers by type, by type-face, by fact, by fancy, by article, spelling, words, theme, advertising, pictures, subjects, politics, prejudices. He analyzed. He studied. He meditated. And we lived together on that top floor, always a little cold, always a little terrified, always a little closer . . . brought together by our fears of it, our hatred between us. Like a wedge driven into a living tree and splitting the trunk, only to be forever incorporated into the scar tissue, we grew together. Vandaleur and the android. Be fleet be fleet!

And one afternoon Blenheim called Vandaleur into his study and displayed his notes. "I think I've found it," he said, "but I can't understand it."

Vandaleur's heart leaped.

"Here are the correlations," Blenheim continued. "In fifty papers there are accounts of the criminal android. What is there, outside the depredations, that is also in fifty papers?"

"I don't know, Mr. Blenheim."

"It was a rhetorical question. Here is the answer. The weather."

"What?"

"The weather." Blenheim nodded. "Each crime was committed on a day when the temperature was above ninety degrees Fahrenheit."

"But that's impossible," Vandaleur exclaimed. "It was cool on Lyra Alpha."

"We have no record of any crime on Lyra Alpha. There is no paper."

"No. That's right. I—" Vandaleur was confused. Suddenly he exclaimed. "No. You're right. The furnace room. It was hot there. Hot! Of course, yes! That's the answer. Dallas Brady's electric furnace . . . The rice deltas on Paragon. So jeet your seat. Yes. But why? Why?"

I came into the house at that moment, and passing the study, saw Vandaleur and Blenheim. I entered, awaiting commands, my multiple aptitudes devoted to service.

"That's the android, eh?" Blenheim said after a long moment.

"Yes," Vandaleur answered, still confused by the discovery. "And that explains why he refused to attack you that night on the Strand. It wasn't hot enough to break the prime directive. Only in the heat . . . The heat, all reet!" He looked at the android. A lunatic command passed from man to android. I refused. It is forbidden to endanger life. Vandaleur gestured furiously, then seized Blenheim's shoulders and yanked him back out of his chair. Blenheim shouted once. Vandaleur leaped on him like a tiger, pinning him to the floor and sealing his mouth with one hand.

"Find a weapon," he called to the android.

"It is forbidden to endanger life."

"This is a fight for self-preservation. Bring me a weapon!" He held the squirming mathematician with all his weight. I went at once to a cupboard where I knew a revolver was kept. I checked it. It was loaded with five cartridges. I handed it to Vandaleur. I took it, rammed the barrel against Blenheim's head and pulled the trigger. He shuddered once.

We had three hours before the cook returned from her day off. We looted the house. We took Blenheim's money and jewels. We packed a bag with clothes. We took Blenheim's notes, destroyed the newspapers; and we left, carefully locking the door behind us. In Blenheim's study we left a pile of crumpled papers under a half inch of burning candle. And we soaked the rug around it with kerosene. No, I did all that. The android refused. I am forbidden to endanger life or property.

All reet!

They took the tubes to Leicester Square, changed trains and rode to the British Museum. There they got off and went to a small Georgian house just off Russell Square. A shingle in the window read: NAN WEBB, PSYCHOMETRIC CONSULTANT. Vandaleur had made a note of the address some weeks earlier. They went into the house. The android waited in the foyer with the bag. Vandaleur entered Nan Webb's office.

She was a tall woman with grey shingled hair, very fine English complexion and very bad English legs. Her features were blunt, her expression acute. She nodded to Vandaleur, finished a letter, sealed it and looked up.

"My name," I said, "is Vanderbilt. James Vanderbilt."

"Quite."

"I'm an exchange student at London University."

"Quite."

"I've been researching on the killing android, and I think I've discovered something very interesting. I'd like your advice on it. What is your fee?"

"What is your college at the University?"

"Why?"

"There is a discount for students."

"Merton College."

"That will be two pounds, please."

Vandaleur placed two pounds on the desk and added to the fee Blenheim's notes. "There is a correlation," he said, "between the crimes of the android and the weather. You will note that each crime was committed when the temperature rose above ninety degrees Fahrenheit. Is there a psychometric answer for this?"

Nan Webb nodded, studied the notes for a moment, put down the sheets of paper and said: "Synesthesia, obviously."

"What?"

"Synesthesia," she repeated. "When a sensation, Mr. Vanderbilt, is interpreted immediately in terms of a sensation from a different sense organ from the one stimulated, it is called synesthesia. For example: A sound stimulus gives rise

Fondly Fahrenheit

to a simultaneous sensation of definite color. Or color gives rise to a sensation of taste. Or a light stimulus gives rise to a sensation of sound. There can be confusion or short circuiting of any sensation of taste, smell, pain, pressure, temperature and so on. D'you understand?"

"I think so."

"Your research has uncovered the fact that the android most probably reacts to temperature stimulus above the ninety degree level synesthetically. Most probably there is an endocrine response. Probably a temperature linkage with the android adrenal surrogate. High temperature brings about a response of fear, anger, excitement and violent physical activity . . . all within the province of the adrenal gland."

"Yes. I see. Then if the android were to be kept in cold climates . . ."

"There would be neither stimulus nor response. There would be no crimes. Quite."

"I see. What is projection?"

"How do you mean?"

"Is there any danger of projection with regard to the owner of the android?"

"Very interesting. Projection is a throwing forward. It is the process of throwing out upon another the ideas or impulses that belong to oneself. The paranoid, for example, projects upon others his conflicts and disturbances in order to externalize them. He accuses, directly or by implication, other men of having the very sickness with which he is struggling himself."

"And the danger of projection?"

"It is the danger of believing what is implied. If you live with a psychotic who projects his sickness upon you, there is a danger of falling into his psychotic pattern and becoming virtually psychotic yourself. As, no doubt, is happening to you, Mr. Vandaleur."

Vandaleur leaped to his feet.

"You are an ass," Nan Webb went on crisply. She waved the sheets of notes. "This is no exchange student's writing. It's the unique cursive of the famous Blenheim. Every scholar in England knows this blind writing. There is no Merton College at London University. That was a miserable guess. Merton is one of the Oxford Colleges. And you, Mr. Vandaleur, are so obviously infected by the association with your deranged android . . . by projection, if you will . . . that I hesitate between calling the Metropolitan Police and the Hospital for the Criminally Insane."

I took out the gun and shot her. Reet!

"Antares II, Alpha Aurigae, Acrux IV, Pollux IX, Rigel Centaurus," Vandaleur said. "They're all cold. Cold as a witch's kiss. Mean temperature of 40° Fahrenheit. Never got hotter than 70. We're in business again. Watch that curve."

The multiple aptitude android swung the wheel with its accomplished hands. The car took the curve sweetly and sped on through the northern marshes, the reeds stretching for miles, brown and dry, under the cold English sky. The sun was sinking swiftly. Overhead, a lone flight of bustards flapped clumsily eastward. High above the flight, a lone helicopter drifted towards home and warmth.

"No more warmth for us," I said. "No more heat. We're safe when we're cold. We'll hole up in Scotland, make a little money, get across to Norway, build a bankroll and then slip out. We'll settle on Pollux. We're safe. We've licked it. We can live again."

There was a startling *bleep* from overhead, and then a ragged roar: "ATTENTION JAMES VANDALEUR AND ANDROID. ATTENTION JAMES VANDALEUR AND ANDROID!"

Vandaleur started and looked up. The lone helicopter was floating above them. From its belly came amplified commands. "YOU ARE SURROUNDED, THE ROAD IS BLOCKED. YOU ARE TO STOP YOUR CAR AT ONCE AND SUBMIT TO ARREST. STOP AT ONCE!"

I looked at Vandaleur for orders.

"Keep driving," Vandaleur snapped.

The helicopter dropped lower: ATTENTION ANDROID. YOU ARE IN CONTROL OF THE VEHICLE. YOU ARE TO STOP AT ONCE. THIS IS A STATE DIRECTIVE SUPERSEDING ALL PRIVATE COMMANDS."

"What are you doing?" I shouted.

"A state directive supersedes all private commands," the android answered. "I must point out to you that—"

"Let go of the wheel," Vandaleur ordered. I clubbed the android, yanked him sideways and squirmed over him to the wheel. The car veered off the road in that moment and went churning through the frozen mud and dry reeds. Vandaleur regained control and continued westward through the marshes towards a parallel highway five miles distant.

"We'll beat the block," he grunted.

The car pounded and surged. The helicopter dropped even lower. A searchlight blazed from the belly of the plane.

"ATTENTION JAMES VANDALEUR AND ANDROID. SUBMIT TO ARREST. THIS IS A STATE DIRECTIVE SUPERSEDING ALL PRIVATE COMMANDS."

"He can't submit," Vandaleur shouted wildly. "There's no one to submit to. He can't and I won't."

"We'll beat them yet," I muttered. "We'll beat the block. We'll beat the heat. We'll—"

"I must point out to you," I said, "That I am required by my prime directive to obey state directives which supersede all private commands. I must submit to arrest."

"Who says it's a state directive?" Vandaleur said. "Them? Up in that plane? They've got to show credentials. They've got to prove it's state authority before you submit. How d'you know they're not crooks trying to trick us?"

Holding the wheel with one hand,

he reached into his side pocket to make sure the gun was still in place. The car skidded. The tires squealed on frost and reeds. The wheel was wrenched from his grasp and the car yawed up a small hillock and overturned. The motor roared and the wheels screamed. Vandaleur crawled out and dragged the android with him. For the moment we were outside the circle of light boring down from the helicopter. We blundered off into the marsh, into the blackness, into concealment . . . Vandaleur running with a pounding heart, hauling the android along.

The helicopter circled and soared over the wrecked car, searchlight peering, loudspeaker braying. On the highway we had left, lights appeared as the pursuing and blocking parties gathered and followed radio direction from the plane. Vandaleur and the android continued deeper and deeper into the marsh, working their way towards the parallel road and safety. It was night by now. The sky was a black matte. Not a star showed. The temperature was dropping. A southeast night wind knifed us to the bone.

Far behind there was a dull concussion. Vandaleur turned, gasping. The car's fuel had exploded. A geyser of flame shot up like a lurid fountain. It subsided into a low crater of burning reeds. Whipped by the wind, the distant hem of flame fanned up into a wall, ten feet high. The wall began marching down on us, crackling fiercely. Above it, a pall of oily smoke surged forward. Behind it, Vandaleur could make out the figures of men . . . a mass of beaters searching the marsh.

I searched desperately for safety. He ran, dragging me with him, until their feet crunched through the surface ice of a pool. He trampled the ice furiously, then flung himself down in the numbing water, pulling the android with us.

The wall of flame approached. I could hear the crackle and feel the heat. He could see the searchers clearly. Vandaleur reached into his side pocket for the gun. The pocket was torn. The gun was gone. He groaned and shook with cold terror. The light from the marsh fire was blinding. Overhead, the helicopter floated helplessly to one side, unable to fly through the smoke and flames and aid the searchers who were beating far to the right of us.

"They'll miss us," Vandaleur whispered. "Keep quiet. That's an order. They'll miss us. We'll beat them. We'll beat the fire. We'll—"

Three distinct shots sounded less than a hundred feet from the fugitives. *Blam! Blam! Blam!* They came from the last three cartridges in my gun as the marsh fire reached it where it had dropped, and exploded the shells. The searchers turned towards the sound and began working directly toward us. Vandaleur cursed hysterically and tried to submerge even deeper to escape the intolerable heat of the fire. The android began to twitch.

The wall of flame surged up to them. Vandaleur took a deep breath and prepared to submerge until the flame passed over them. The android shuddered and burst into an earsplitting scream.

"All reet! All reet!" it shouted. "Be fleet be fleet!"

I shouted. I tried to drown it.

I cursed him. I smashed his face.

The android battered Vandaleur, who fought it off until it exploded out of the mud and staggered upright. Before I could return to the attack, the live flames captured it hypnotically. It danced and capered in a lunatic rhumba before the wall of fire. Its legs twisted. Its arms waved. The fingers writhed in a private rhumba of their own. It shrieked and sang and ran in a crooked waltz before the embrace of the heat, a muddy monster silhouetted against the brilliant sparkling flare.

The searchers shouted. There were shots. The android spun around twice and then continued its horrid dance before the face of the flames. There was a rising gust of wind. The fire swept around the capering figure and enveloped it for a roaring moment. Then the fire swept on, leaving behind it a sobbing mass of synthetic flesh oozing scarlet blood that would never coagulate.

The thermometer would have registered 1200° wondrously Fahrenheit.

Vandaleur didn't die. I got away. They missed him while they watched the android caper and die. But I don't know which of us he is these days. Projection, Wanda warned me. Projection, Nan Webb told me. If you live with a crazy man or a crazy machine long enough, I become crazy too. Reet!

But we know one truth. We know they are wrong. The new robot and Vandaleur know that because the new robot's started twitching too. Reet! Here on cold Pollux, the robot is twitching and singing. No heat, but my fingers writhe. No heat, but it's taken the little Talley girl off for a solitary walk. A cheap labor robot. A servo-mechanism . . . all I could afford . . . but it's twitching and humming and walking alone with the child somewhere and I can't find them. Vandaleur can't find me before it's too late. Cool and discreet, honey, in the dancing frost while the thermometer registers 10° fondly Fahrenheit.

VOCABULARY STUDY

VOCABULARY QUIZ 2-C

Words to Learn

synthesized   *austere*   *piqued*
rapacious   *banal*

Match each italicized word with the appropriate choice from the right.

Words in Context

1. "when they're *synthesized*," p. 68.
2. "demands . . . became *rapacious*," p. 69.
3. "He was tall, *austere*," p. 73.
4. "all life reduced to the *banal*," p. 74.
5. "*piqued* by the mystery," p. 74.

Definitions

a. somber, stern
b. wanting originality or freshness
c. challenged or angered
d. artificially manufactured; something produced by combining elements
e. excessively grasping or consuming

VOCABULARY PRACTICE 2-C

Choose one of the words from the vocabulary list above for each of the men described on the following page.

1. Always dressed in gray or black, the judge did not believe in cheerfulness for its own sake. Hard work was his idea of pleasure, in fact, and he considered laughter the language of the fool.

2. The loan shark feeds his appetite for illegal gain by preying upon the helplessness and ignorance of the poor.

3. Dr. Alexander Fleming could not dismiss the strange green mold. Why had the bacteria near this spore died? He had much more important work to attend to; he was ten days behind in his compilation of data, but still he decided to investigate the unrelated find.

SUGGESTIONS FOR DISCUSSION AND WRITING

1. The *persona*, or speaker of the story, provides the reader with an enigma at the outset. On page 66, a shift in point of view takes place: "So there we were aboard the Paragon Queen en route for Megaster V, James Vandaleur and his android." But who, the reader wonders, is the "we"? The question is not clearly resolved until the latter part of the story, when the reader learns that it is both Vandaleur and the android, that they are almost interchangeable. Why does the author employ this shifting point of view? In what ways is it essential to the meaning of the story?

2. There is a suggestion, within the story, that Vandaleur is the victim of his android's malfunction, that by the process of projection, the android is "externalizing" his "sickness," and thus influencing the behavior of its owner. If this is so, how do you explain the incident described in the last two paragraphs of the story?

3. Perhaps the most chilling language Bester uses in the story occurs in his description of the android's first malfunction (p. 69). The android begins singing a rhythmic, 1950s rock song, a song that alludes to cheerfulness and fun, but what follows is far from that. Briefly analyze the language used to describe the malfunction: list the adjectives, adverbs, nouns, and verbs that are instrumental in achieving the final effect. Are any words repeated? What words suggest that the malfunction is pleasurable to the android?

THE MAN INSIDE

BRUCE McALLISTER

I AM ten and a half years old, and I must be important because I'm the only one they let into this laboratory of the hospital. My father is in the other room of this laboratory. He's what Dr. Plankt calls a "catatonic" because Dad just sits in one position all the time like he can't make up his mind what to do. And that makes Dr. Plankt sad, but today Dr. Plankt is happy because of his new machine and what it will do with Dad.

Dr. Plankt said, "This is the first time a computer will be able to articulate a man's thoughts." That means that when they put the "electrodes" (those are wires) on Dad's head, and the "electrodes" are somehow attached to Dr. Plankt's big machine with the spinning tapes on it, that machine will tell us what's in Dad's head. Dr. Plankt also said, "Today we dredge the virgin silence of an in-state catatonic for the first time in history." So Dr. Plankt is happy today.

I am too, for Dad, because he will be helped by this "experiment" (everything that's happening today) and for Dr. Plankt, who is good to me. He helps me make my "ulcer" (a hurting sore inside me) feel better, and he also gives me pills for my "hypertension" (what's wrong with my body). He told me, "Your father has an ulcer like yours, Keith, and hypertension too, so we've got to take care of you. You're much too young to be carrying an ulcer around in you. Look at your father now. We don't want what happened to your father to happen . . ."

He didn't finish what he was saying, so I didn't understand all of it. Just that I should keep healthy and calm and not worry. I'm a lot like Dad, I know that much. Even if Dad worried a lot before he became a "catatonic" and I don't worry much because I don't have many things to worry about. "Yet," Dr. Plankt told me.

We're waiting for the big "computer" to tell us what's in Dad's head! A few minutes ago Dr. Plankt said that his machine might help his "theory" (a bunch of thoughts) about "personality symmetry in correlation with schizophrenia." He didn't tell me what he meant by that because he wasn't talking to me when he said it. He was talking to another doctor, and I was just listening. I think what he said has to do with Dad's personality, which Mom says is rotten because he's always so grouchy and nervous and picky. Mom says I shouldn't *ever* be like Dad. She's always telling me that, and she shouts a lot.

Except when she brings people home from her meetings.

I don't think Dr. Plankt likes Mom. Once Dr. Plankt came over to our house, which is on Cypress Street, and Mom was at one of her meetings, and Dr. Plankt and I sat in the living room and talked. I said, "It's funny how Dad and me have ulcers and hypertension. 'Like father, like son. Mom says that. It's kind of funny." Dr. Plankt got mad at something then and said to me, "It's not funny, Keith! With what she's doing to you both, your *mother*, not your father, is the one who should be in a mental inst—" He didn't finish his last word, and I don't know what it was and what he was mad about. Maybe he was mad at me.

Many times Dr. Plankt says that he wants to take me away from Cypress Street and put me in a better —

Wait! The computer just typed something! It works just like a typewriter but without anyone's hands on it. The words it is typing are from Dad's head! Dr. Plankt has the piece of paper in his hands now. He's showing it to three doctors. Now he's showing it to Mom. Mom is starting to cry! I've never seen her cry before. I want to see the words from Dad's head!

Another doctor is looking at me, and he has the paper now. I say, "Can I see it! Can I see it?" He looks at me again, and I think he knows who I am because Dr. Plankt talks about me a lot to everyone. I must be important. I don't like the look on this other doctor's face. It's like the look Uncle Josh gets when he's feeling sad about something. This other doctor closes his eyes for a minute and comes over to me with the paper. The paper, the paper! The words from Dad's head. The words are:

OH	OH
MY	MY
WIFE	SON!
I	I
CERTAINLY	CERTAINLY
DO	DO
NOT	NOT
WANT	WANT
TO	TO
LIVE!	DIE!

When I squint my eyes and look at these words from Dad's head, they look like a man in a hat with his arms out, kind of like Dad— except that there's a split down the middle of this man.

It's funny, but I know just how Dad feels.

VOCABULARY STUDY

VOCABULARY QUIZ 2-D

Words to Learn

catatonic   hypertension   schizophrenia
correlation   symmetry

Match each italicized word with the appropriate choice from the right.

Words in Context

1. "an in-state *catatonic*," p. 83.
2. "ulcers and *hypertension*," p. 84.
3. "about 'personality *symmetry*,'" p. 84.
4. "in *correlation* with schizophrenia," p. 84.
5. "in correlation with *schizophrenia*," p. 84.

Definitions

d. personality disorder
a. balance, harmony
b. interdependence
c. in a stupor
e. unusually high blood pressure

VOCABULARY PRACTICE 2-D

Add an appropriate choice from the above vocabulary list to the sentences below.

1. The doctor told Grandpa to stop smoking in order to reduce his _____.

2. The harmonious and graceful _____ which characterizes the architecture of the great cathedrals of Europe might be considered too "old-fashioned" by architects of the modern school.

3. When a person loses contact with his environment and his personality disintegrates, he might be suffering from _____.

4. Market prices fluctuate in _____ with wages in industry; neither can change without affecting the other.

5. Edgar Allan Poe's stories sometimes involve long, _____ trances, during which a man approximates death.

SUGGESTIONS FOR DISCUSSION AND WRITING

1. Who is the *persona* of this story? Who is the *protagonist*? Which point of view does the author employ? What additional information would the reader have been given if the omniscient point of view had been used? (See Appendix I, page 252).

2. More and more, modern psychiatry seems inclined to deal with human interrelationships rather than isolated mental problems. Whole families sometimes attend therapy sessions together and frequently discover that the mental stress suffered by one member is owing to some stress situation in the home. In a group therapy session, what facts do you believe would emerge about this family?

CHAPTER 2 CUMULATIVE VOCABULARY LIST

1. *adroitly*—skillfully
2. *apparition*—appearance, ghost
3. *ardent*—eager, driven
4. *askew*—sideways
5. *assailed*—attacked, assaulted
6. *assiduously*—steadily, attentively
7. *attenuated*—made thin or weak
8. *austere*—somber, stern
9. *Babel*—a noisy scene
10. *banal*—wanting originality or freshness
11. *catatonic*—in a stupor
12. *cerebral*—of the brain
13. *correlation*—interdependence
14. *countenance*—face, expression
15. *debility*—weakness
16. *denizens*—inhabitants, those who frequent a place
17. *derangement*—disturbance
18. *diorama*—a spectacular, three-dimensional scene
19. *efficacy*—effectiveness
20. *enigmas*—puzzles
21. *execrable*—very bad, detestable
22. *exhilaration*—animation, joy, liveliness
23. *explicit*—plain, direct
24. *facilitate*—make easier
25. *fragrance*—odor, scent
26. *hindrance*—impediment
27. *hypertension*—condition of unusually high blood pressure
28. *imminent*—impending, threatening
29. *immutable*—not changeable
30. *incontinently*—without control
31. *indolence*—laziness, sloth
32. *interminable*—endless
33. *intermittent*—returning at intervals
34. *intrepid*—fearless
35. *lassitude*—weariness, fatigue
36. *latitude*—distance in degrees from the equator
37. *ludicrous*—laughable, absurd
38. *meridian*—an imaginary circle passing through both poles

39. *morbid*—despondent, diseased
40. *palpitation*—rapid beating
41. *patriarchs*—fathers or founders
42. *piqued*—challenged or angered
43. *poignant*—pathetic, heart-rending
44. *prodigious*—enormous, extraordinary
45. *progeny*—offspring
46. *protagonist*—main character
47. *provincial*—sectional
48. *purports*—means, intends
49. *rapacious*—excessively grasping or consuming
50. *resuscitation*—revival
51. *retorted*—replied sharply
52. *rudimentary*—undeveloped
53. *schizophrenia*—mental disorder
54. *sumptuously*—in luxury
55. *surly*—gloomy, rough
56. *symmetry*—balance, harmony
57. *synthesized*—artificially manufactured or the bringing together of elements
58. *tenets*—beliefs
59. *traverse*—to pass through, to cross
60. *undulating*—swaying, moving in waves
61. *vociferations*—outcries

Chapter 3

GOING A STEP FURTHER—ROBOTS

The robot is Frankenstein's younger stepbrother. He had long been a gleam in the collective eye of science fiction writers, but it was the Czech playwright Karel Capek who gave him tangible shape, substance, character, and a name in his 1920 play: *R. U. R.*

The very concept of manufacturing humanlike robots by the same assembly line techniques that turn out tractors and washing machines is at first thought . . . shocking.

The play is a masterful combination of melodrama, subdued sarcasm, and bitter protest against the impending mechanization of humanity. Recognized as a "classic" today, *R. U. R.* can rightfully claim to have added a new word to the vocabularies of all nations, while providing science fiction with one of its most versatile assets. The selection you are about to read produces no clues to the plot of the play—let it suffice to say that the robots eventually wipe out the human race.

The three stories following *R. U. R.* are in chronological order (dates of first publication) to illustrate two points we wish to make; namely, that science fiction writers need not be hindered by precedent, and that they often seem to fit the mood of their story to the social climate prevailing at the time of writing. That is particularly true of "Helen O'Loy," written in 1938, a time of harsh realities—of transition from depression to war. What the world most needed then was romance . . . so, in "Helen O'Loy," you have science fiction at its romantic best.

Quite different again are "A Bad Day for Sales" (1953) and "Men Are Different" (1954).

Note: The vocabulary quiz following each story is omitted in this chapter and replaced by a special exercise at its conclusion.

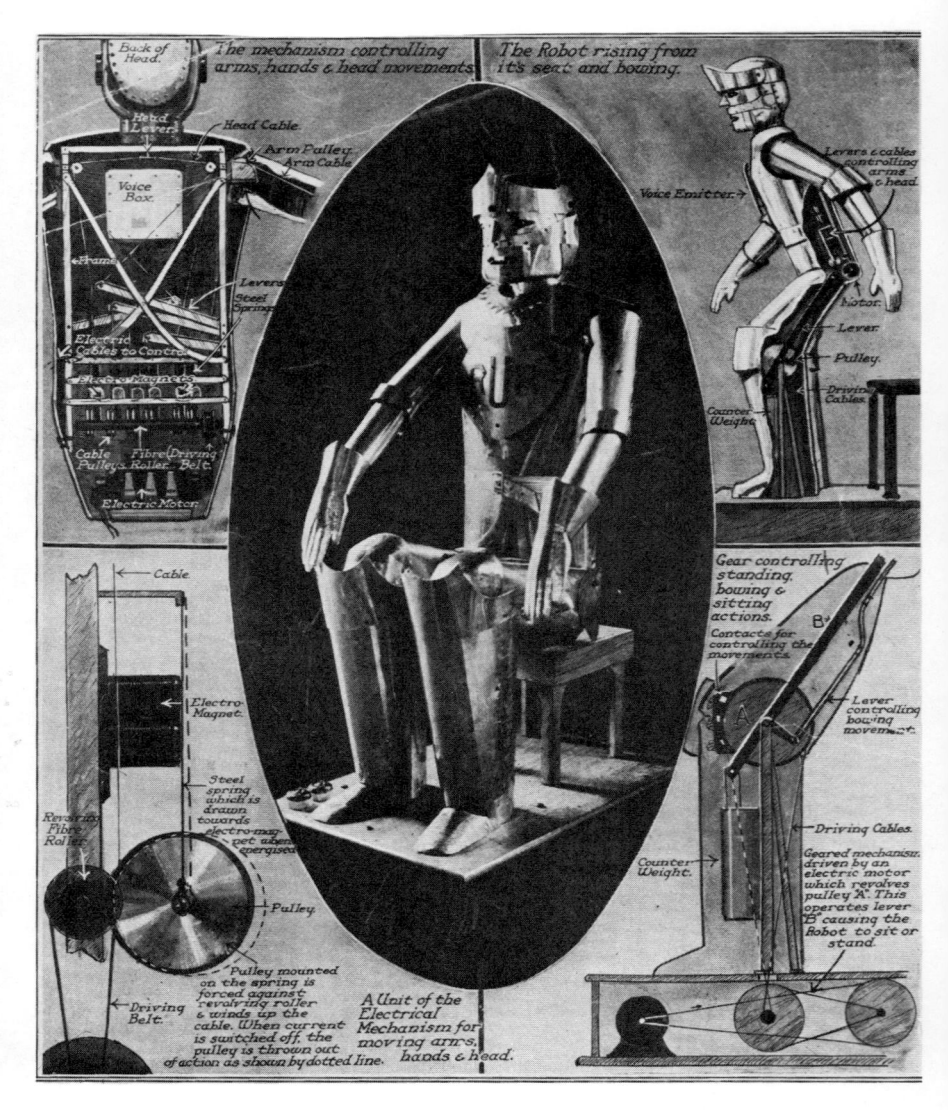

An aluminum "man" that rises, bows, and makes a speech. Drawn by G.H. Davis; Captain Richards and A.H. Reffell, inventors. 1928.

A Selection from

A Fantastic Melodrama
R.U.R.
(ROSSUM'S UNIVERSAL ROBOTS)

KAREL CAPEK

The entire play consists of three acts and an epilogue, all staged in different settings. There are, altogether, sixteen characters in the play. (The first American production of *R. U. R.* was presented in New York in 1923, by the American Theatre Guild.) The following selection is the beginning of Act I, and will introduce you to the leading characters:

Harry Domin, *General Manager*;
Sulla, *a Robotess*;
Marius, *a Robot*;
Helena Glory, *a visitor*.

ACT I

Domin is sitting in the revolving chair at a large American writing table. At a desk near the windows, Sulla is typing letters.
DOMIN (*dictating*) Ready?
SULLA. Yes.
DOMIN. To E. M. McVicker and Co., Southampton, England. "We undertake no guarantee for goods damaged in transit. As soon as the consignment was taken on board we drew your captain's attention to the fact that the vessel was unsuitable for the transport of Robots, and we are therefore not responsible for spoiled freight. We beg to remain for Rossum's Universal Robots. Yours truly." (SULLA, *who has sat motionless during dictation, now types rapidly for a few seconds, then stops, withdrawing the completed letter*) Ready?

SULLA. Yes.
DOMIN. Another letter. To the E. B. Huyson Agency, New York, U.S.A. "We beg to acknowledge receipt of order for five thousand Robots. As you are sending your own vessel, please dispatch as cargo equal quantities of soft and hard coal for R. U. R., the same to be credited as part payment of the amount due to us. We beg to remain, for Rossum's Universal Robots. Yours truly." (SULLA *repeats the rapid typing*) Ready?
SULLA. Yes.
DOMIN. Another letter. "Friedrichswerks, Hamburg, Germany. We beg to acknowledge receipt of order for fifteen thousand Robots." (*telephone rings*) Hello! This is the Central Office. Yes. Certainly. Well, send them a wire. Good. (*hangs up telephone*) Where did I leave off?
SULLA. "We beg to acknowledge receipt of order for fifteen thousand Robots."
DOMIN. Fifteen thousand R. Fifteen thousand R.

(*Enter* MARIUS.)

DOMIN. Well what is it?
MARIUS. There's a lady, sir, asking to see you.
DOMIN. A lady? Who is she?
MARIUS. I don't know, sir. She brings this card of introduction.
DOMIN. (*reads the card*) Ah, from President Glory. Ask her to come in.
MARIUS. Please step this way.

(*Enter* HELENA GLORY.)
(*Exit* MARIUS.)

HELENA. How do you do?
DOMIN. How do you do (*standing up*) What can I do for you?
HELENA. You are Mr. Domin, the General Manager.
DOMIN. I am.
HELENA. I have come—
DOMIN. With President Glory's card. That is quite sufficient.
HELENA. President Glory is my father. I am Helena Glory.
DOMIN. Miss Glory, this is such a great honor for us to welcome our great President's daughter, that—
HELENA. That you can't show me the door?
DOMIN. Please sit down. Sulla, you may go.

(*Exit* SULLA.)

(*sitting down*) How can I be of service to you, Miss Glory?
HELENA. I have come—

DOMIN. To have a look at our famous works where people are manufactured. Like all visitors. Well, there is no objection.
HELENA. I thought it was forbidden to—
DOMIN. To enter the factory. Yes, of course. Everybody comes here with someone's visting card, Miss Glory.
HELENA. And you show them—
DOMIN. Oniy certain things. The manufacture of artificial people is a secret process.
HELENA. If you only knew how enormously that—
DOMIN. Interests me. Europe's talking about nothing else.
HELENA. Why don't you let me finish speaking?
DOMIN: I beg your pardon. Did you want to say something different?
HELENA. I only wanted to ask—
DOMIN. Whether I could make a special exception in your case and show you our factory. Why, certainly, Miss Glory.
HELENA. How did you know I wanted to say that?
DOMIN. They all do. But we shall consider it a special honor to show you more than we do the rest.
HELENA. Thank you.
DOMIN. But you must agree not to divulge the least . . .
HELENA. (*standing up and giving him her hand*) My word of honor.
DOMIN. Thank you. Won't you raise your veil?
HELENA. Of course. You want to see whether I'm a spy or not. I beg your pardon.
DOMIN. What is it?
HELENA. Would you mind releasing my hand?
DOMIN. (*releasing it*) I beg your pardon.
HELENA. (*raising her veil*) How cautious you have to be here, don't you?
DOMIN. (*observing her with deep interest*) Mm, of course—we—that is—
HELENA. But what is it? What's the matter?
DOMIN. I'm remarkably pleased. Did you have a pleasant crossing?
HELENA. Yes.
DOMIN. No difficulty?
HELENA. Why?
DOMIN. What I mean to say is—you're so young.
HELENA. May we go straight into the factory?
DOMIN. Yes. Twenty-two, I think.
HELENA. Twenty-two what?
DOMIN. Years.
HELENA. Twenty-one. Why do you want to know?
DOMIN. Because—as—(*with enthusiasm*) you will make a long stay, won't you?

HELENA. That depends on how much of the factory you show me.
DOMIN. Oh, hang the factory. Oh, no, no, you shall see everything, Miss Glory. Indeed you shall. Won't you sit down?
HELENA (*crossing to couch and sitting*) Thank you.
DOMIN: But first would you like to hear the story of the invention?
HELENA. Yes, indeed.
DOMIN. (*observes HELENA with rapture and reels off rapidly*) It was in the year 1920 that old Rossum, the great physiologist, who was then quite a young scientist, took himself to this distant island for the purpose of studying the ocean fauna, full stop. On this occasion he attempted by chemical synthesis to imitate the living matter known as protoplasm until he suddenly discovered a substance which behaved exactly like living matter although its chemical composition was different. That was in the year 1932, exactly four hundred and forty years after the discovery of America. Whew!
HELENA. Do you know that by heart?
DOMIN. Yes. You see physiology is not in my line. Shall I go on?
HELENA. Yes, please.
DOMIN. And then, Miss Glory, old Rossum wrote the following among his chemical specimens: "Nature has found only one method of organizing living matter. There is, however, another method, more simple, flexible and rapid, which has not yet occurred to Nature at all. This second process by which life can be developed was discovered by me to-day." Now imagine him, Miss Glory, writing those wonderful words over some colloidal mess that a dog wouldn't look at. Imagine him sitting over a test tube, and thinking how the whole tree of life would grow from it, beginning with some sort of beetle and ending with a man. A man of different substance from us. Miss Glory, that was a tremendous moment.
HELENA. Well?
DOMIN. Now, the thing was how to get the life out of the test tubes, and hasten development and form organs, bones and nerves, and so on, and find such substances as catalytics, enzymes, hormones, and so forth, in short—you understand?
HELENA. Not much, I'm afraid.
DOMIN. Never mind. You see with the help of his tinctures he could make whatever he wanted. He could have produced a Medusa with the brain of Socrates or a worm fifty yards long. But being without a grain of humor, he took it into his head to make a vertebrate or perhaps a man. This artificial matter of his had a raging thirst for life. It didn't mind being sewn or mixed together. That couldn't be done with natural albumen. And that's how he set about it.

HELENA. About what?

DOMIN. About imitating nature. First of all he tried making an artificial dog. That took him several years and resulted in a sort of stunted calf which died in a few days. I'll show it to you in the museum. And then old Rossum started on the manufacture of man.

HELENA. And I must divulge this to nobody?

DOMIN. To nobody in the world.

HELENA. What a pity that it's to be found in all the school books of both Europe and America.

DOMIN. Yes. But do you know what isn't in the school books? That old Rossum was mad. Seriously, Miss Glory, you must keep this to yourself. The old crank wanted to actually make people.

HELENA. But you do make people.

DOMIN. Approximately, Miss Glory. But old Rossum meant it literally. He wanted to become a sort of scientific substitute for God. He was a fearful materialist, and that's why he did it all. His sole purpose was nothing more or less than to prove that God was no longer necessary. Do you know anything about anatomy?

HELENA. Very little.

DOMIN. Neither do I. Well, he then decided to manufacture everything as in the human body. I'll show you in the museum the bungling attempt it took him ten years to produce. It was to have been a man, but it lived for three days only. Then up came young Rossum, an engineer. He was a wonderful fellow, Miss Glory. When he saw what a mess of it the old man was making, he said: "It's absurd to spend ten years making a man. If you can't make him quicker than nature, you might as well shut up shop." Then he set about learning anatomy himself.

HELENA. There's nothing about that in the school books.

DOMIN. No. The school books are full of paid advertisements, and rubbish at that. What the school books say about the united efforts of the two great Rossums is all a fairy tale. They used to have dreadful rows. The old atheist hadn't the slightest conception of industrial matters, and the end of it was that young Rossum shut him up in some laboratory or other and let him fritter the time away with his monstrosities, while he himself started on the business from an engineer's point of view. Old Rossum cursed him and before he died he managed to botch up two physiological horrors. Then one day they found him dead in the laboratory. And that's his whole story.

HELENA. And what about the young man?

DOMIN. Well, any one who has looked into human anatomy will have seen that man is too complicated, and that a good engineer could make him more simply. So young Rossum began to overhaul anatomy and tried to see what could be left out or simplified. In short—but this isn't boring you, Miss Glory?

HELENA. No indeed. You're—it's awfully interesting.

DOMIN. So young Rossum said to himself: "A man is something that feels happy, plays the piano, likes going for a walk, and in fact, wants to do a whole lot of things that are really unnecessary."

HELENA. Oh.

DOMIN. That are unnecessary when he wants, let us say, to weave or count. Do you play the piano?

HELENA. Yes.

DOMIN. That's good. But a working machine must not play the piano, must not feel happy, must not do a whole lot of other things. A gasoline motor must not have tassels or ornaments, Miss Glory. And to manufacture artificial workers is the same thing as to manufacture gasoline motors. The process must be of the simplest, and the product of the best from a practical point of view. What sort of worker do you think is the best from a practical point of view?

HELENA. What?

DOMIN. What sort of worker do you think is the best from a practical point of view?

HELENA. Perhaps the one who is most honest and hard-working.

DOMIN. No; the one that is the cheapest, the one whose requirements are the smallest. Young Rossum invented a worker with the minimum amount of requirements. He had to simplify him. He rejected everything that did not contribute directly to the progress of work—everything that makes man more expensive. In fact, he rejected man and made the Robot. My dear Miss Glory, the Robots are not people. Mechanically they are more perfect than we are, they have an enormously developed intelligence, but they have no souls.

HELENA. How do you know they've no soul?

DOMIN. Have you ever seen what a Robot looks like inside?

HELENA. No.

DOMIN. Very neat, very simple. Really, a beautiful piece of work. Not much in it, but everything in flawless order. The product of an engineer is technically at a higher pitch of perfection than a product of nature.

HELENA. But man is supposed to be the product of God.

DOMIN. All the worse. God hasn't the least notion of modern engineering. Would you believe that young Rossum then proceeded to play at being God?

HELENA. How do you mean?

DOMIN. He began to manufacture Super-Robots. Regular giants they were. He tried to make them twelve feet tall. But you wouldn't believe what a failure they were.

HELENA. A failure?

DOMIN. Yes. For no reason at all their limbs kept snapping off. Evidently our planet is too small for giants. Now we only make Robots of normal size and of very high class human finish.

HELENA. I saw the first Robots at home. The town counsel brought them for—I mean engaged them for work.

DOMIN. Bought them, dear Miss Glory. Robots are bought and sold.

HELENA. These were employed as street sweepers. I saw them sweeping. They were so strange and quiet.

DOMIN. Rossum's Universal Robot factory doesn't produce a uniform brand of Robots. We have Robots of finer and coarser grades. The best will live about twenty years.

(He rings for MARIUS.)

HELENA. Then they die?

DOMIN. Yes, they get used up.

(Enter MARIUS.)

DOMIN. Marius, bring in samples of the Manual Labor Robots.

(Exit MARIUS.)

DOMIN. I'll show you specimens of the two extremes. This first grade is comparatively inexpensive and is made in vast quantities.

(MARIUS *reenters with two Manual Labor Robots.*)

DOMIN. There you are; as powerful as a small tractor. Guaranteed to have average intelligence. That will do, Marius.

(MARIUS *exits with Robots.*)

HELENA. They make me feel so strange.

DOMIN. *(rings)* Did you see my new typist?

(He rings for SULLA.)

HELENA. I didn't notice her.

(Enter SULLA.)

DOMIN. Sulla, let Miss Glory see you.

HELENA. So pleased to meet you. You must find it terribly dull in this out-of-the-way spot, don't you?

SULLA. I don't know, Miss Glory.

HELENA. Where do you come from?

SULLA. From the factory.

HELENA. Oh, you were born there?

SULLA. I was made there.

HELENA. What?

DOMIN (*laughing*) Sully is a Robot, best grade.
HELENA. Oh, I beg your pardon.
DOMIN. Sulla isn't angry. See, Miss Glory, the kind of skin we make. (*feels the skin on* SULLA'S *face*) Feel her face.
HELENA. Oh, no, no.
DOMIN. You wouldn't know that she's made of different material from us, would you? Turn around Sulla.
HELENA. Oh, stop, stop.
DOMIN. Talk to Miss Glory, Sulla.
SULLA. Please sit down. (HELENA *sits*) Did you have a pleasant crossing?
HELENA. Oh, yes, certainly.
SULLA. Don't go back on the *Amelia*, Miss Glory. The barometer is falling steadily. Wait for the *Pennsylvania*. That's a good, powerful vessel.
DOMIN. What's its speed?
SULLA. Twenty knots. Fifty thousand tons. One of the latest vessels, Miss Glory.
HELENA. Thank you.
SULLA. A crew of fifteen hundred, Captain Harpy, eight boilers—
DOMIN. That'll do, Sulla. Now show us your knowledge of French.
HELENA. You know French?
SULLA. I know four languages. I can write: Dear Sir, Monsieur, Geehrter Herr, Cteny pane.
HELENA. (*jumping up*) Oh, that's absurd! Sulla isn't a Robot. Sulla is a girl like me. Sulla, this is outrageous! Why do you take part in such a hoax?
SULLA. I am a Robot.
HELENA. No, no, you are not telling the truth. I know they've forced you to do it for an advertisement. Sulla, you are a girl like me, aren't you?
DOMIN. I'm sorry, Miss Glory. Sulla is a Robot.
HELENA. It's a lie!
DOMIN. What? (*rings*) Excuse me, Miss Glory, then I must convince you.

(*Enter* MARIUS.)

DOMIN. Marius, take Sulla into the dissecting room, and tell them to open her up at once.
HELENA. Where?
DOMIN. Into the dissecting room. When they've cut her open, you can go and have a look.
HELENA. No, no!
DOMIN. Excuse me, you spoke of lies.
HELENA. You wouldn't have her killed?
DOMIN. You can't kill machines.

HELENA. Don't be afraid, Sulla, I won't let you go. Tell me, my dear, are they always so cruel to you? You mustn't put up with it, Sulla you mustn't.
SULLA. I am a Robot.
HELENA. That doesn't matter. Robots are just as good as we are. Sulla, you wouldn't let yourself be cut to pieces?
SULLA. Yes.
HELENA. Oh, you're not afraid of death, then?
SULLA. I cannot tell, Miss Glory.
HELENA. Do you know what would happen to you in there?
SULLA. Yes, I should cease to move.
HELENA. How dreadful!
DOMIN. Marius, tell Miss Glory what you are.
MARIUS. Marius, the Robot.
DOMIN. Would you take Sulla into the dissecting room?
MARIUS. Yes.
DOMIN. Would you be sorry for her?
MARIUS. I cannot tell.
DOMIN. What would happen to her?
MARIUS. She would cease to move. They would put her into the stamping mill.
DOMIN. That is death, Marius. Aren't you afraid of death?
MARIUS. No.
DOMIN. You see, Miss Glory, the Robots have no interest in life. They have no enjoyments. They are less than so much grass.
HELENA. Oh, stop. Send them away.
DOMIN. Marius, Sulla, you may go.
(*Exeunt* SULLA *and* MARIUS.)
HELENA. How horrible! It's outrageous what you are doing.
DOMIN. Why outrageous?
HELENA. I don't know, but it is. Why do you call her Sulla?
DOMIN. Isn't it a nice name?
HELENA. It's a man's name. Sulla was a Roman general.
DOMIN. Oh, we thought that Marius and Sulla were lovers.
HELENA. Marius and Sulla were generals and fought against each other in the year—I've forgotten now.
DOMIN. Come here to the window.
HELENA. What?
DOMIN. Come here. What do you see?
HELENA. Bricklayers.
DOMIN. Robots. All our work people are Robots. And down there, can you see anything?

HELENA. Some sort of office.
DOMIN. A counting house. And in it—
HELENA. A lot of officials.
DOMIN. Robots. All our officials are Robots. And when you see the factory—

(Factory whistle blows.)

DOMIN. Noon. We have to blow the whistle because the Robots don't know when to stop work. In two hours I will show you the kneading trough.
HELENA. Kneading trough?
DOMIN. The pestle for beating up the paste. In each one we mix the ingredients for a thousand Robots at one operation. Then there are the vats for the preparation of livers, brains, and so on. Then you will see the bone factory. After that I'll show you the spinning-mill.
HELENA. Spinning-mill?
DOMIN. Yes. For weaving nerves and veins. Miles and miles of digestive tubes pass through it at a time.
HELENA. Mayn't we talk about something else?
DOMIN. Perhaps it would be better. There's only a handful of us among a hundred thousand Robots, and not one woman. We talk about nothing but the factory, all day, every day. It's just as if we were under a curse, Miss Glory.
HELENA. I'm sorry I said you were lying.

SUGGESTIONS FOR DISCUSSION AND WRITING

1. Domin is the general manager of a robot manufacturing plant, but what is also interesting about him is his attitude towards humans. Considering particularly the first lines of his conversation with Helena, indicate how you believe people affect him.

2. In these excerpts from Domin's dialogue with Helena, do you detect a trace of sarcasm? If so, in what sense?
    a. ". . . we are therefore not responsible for spoiled freight." (p. 91)
    b. "In fact, he rejected man and made the Robot." (p. 96)
    c. "All our officials are Robots." (p. 100)

3. The selection from *R. U. R.* and your awareness that the play ends with the conquest of Man by the Robot are enough to create some curiosity about the author, Karel Capek.

He was 30 years old, living in Prague, when he wrote the play. In 1920, Europe lay devastated by World War I, crippled by the loss of fifteen million lives, and benumbed by the task of rebuilding without adequate human and material resources. In subsequent plays and novels, Capek continued to deplore the evils of the machine age and to plead for what we, in America, call "the Jeffersonian dream"—an essentially agrarian society. Can you name recent public manifestations, protests, and concerns which may, to some degree, make "the dream" come true?

Helen O'Loy

LESTER DEL REY

I AM AN old man now, and I can still see Helen as Dave unpacked her, and still hear him grasp as he looked her over.

"Man, isn't she a beauty?"

She was beautiful, a dream in plastics and metals, something Keats might have seen dimly as he wrote his sonnet. If Helen of Troy had looked like that, the Greeks must have been pikers when they launched only a thousand ships; at least, that's what I told Dave.

"Helen of Troy, eh?" He looked at her tag. "At least it beats this thing—K2W88. Helen . . . Mmmm . . . Helen of Alloy."

"Not much swing to that, Dave, too many unstressed syllables in the middle. How about Helen O'Loy?"

"Helen O'Loy she is, Phil." And that's how it began—one part beauty, one part dream, one part science; add a stereo broadcast, stir mechanically, and the result is chaos.

Dave and I hadn't gone to college together, but when I came to Messina to practice medicine, I found him downstairs in a little robot repair shop. After that, we began to pal around, and when I started going with one twin, he found the other equally attractive, so that we made it a foursome.

When our business grew better, we rented a house near the rocket field—noisy but cheap, and the rockets discouraged apartment building. We liked room enough to stretch ourselves. I suppose, if we hadn't quarreled with them, we'd married the twins in time. But Dave wanted to look over the latest Venus-rocket attempt when his twin wanted to see a display stereo starring Larry Ainslee, and they were both stubborn. From then on, we forgot the girls and spent our evenings at home.

But it wasn't until "Lena" put vanilla on our steak instead of salt that we got off on the subject of

103

emotions and robots. While Dave was dissecting Lena to find the trouble, we naturally mulled over the future of the mechs. He was sure that robots would beat men some day, and I couldn't see it.

"Look here, Dave," I argued. "You know Lena doesn't think—not really. When those wires crossed, she could have corrected herself. But she didn't bother; she followed the mechanical impulse. A man might have reached for the vanilla, but when he saw it in his hand, he'd have stopped. Lena has sense enough, but she has no emotions, no consciousness of self."

"All right, that's the big trouble with mechs now. But we'll get around it, put in mechanical emotions, or something." He screwed Lena's head back on, turned on her juice. "Go back to work, Lena, it's nineteen o'clock."

Now I specialized in endocrinology and related subjects. I wasn't exactly a psychologist, but I did understand the glands, secretions, hormones, and miscellanies that are the physical causes of emotions. It took medical science three hundred years to find out how and why they worked, and I couldn't see men duplicating them mechanically in much less time.

I brought home books and papers to prove it, and Dave quoted the invention of memory coils and veritoid eyes. During that year we swapped knowledge until Dave knew the whole theory of endocrinology, and I could have made Lena from memory. The more we talked, the less sure I grew about the impossibility of *homo mechanensis* as the perfect type.

Poor Lena. Her cuproberyl body spent half its time in scattered pieces. Our first attempts were successful only in getting her to serve fried brushes for breakfast and wash the dishes in oleo oil. Then one day she served a perfect dinner with six wires crossed, and Dave was in ecstasy.

He worked all night on her wiring, put in a new coil, and taught her a fresh set of words. And the next day she flew into a tantrum and swore vigorously at us when we told her she wasn't doing her work right.

"It's a lie," she yelled, shaking a suction brush. "You're all liars. If you so-and-so's would leave me whole long enough, I might get something done around the place."

When we calmed her temper and got her back to work, Dave ushered me into the study. "Not taking any chances with Lena," he explained. "We'll have to cut that adrenal pack out and restore her to normalcy. But we've got to get a better robot. A housemaid mech isn't complex enough.

"How about Dillard's new utility models? They seem to combine everything in one."

"Exactly. Even so, we'll need a special one built to order, with a full range of memory coils. And out of respect to old Lena, let's get a female case for its works."

The result, of course, was Helen. The Dillard people had performed a miracle and put all the works in a girl-modeled case. Even the plastic and rubberite face was designed for flexibility to express emotions, and she was complete with tear glands and taste buds, ready to simulate every human action, from breathing to pulling hair. The bill they sent with her was another miracle, but Dave and I scraped it together; we had to turn Lena over to an exchange to complete it, though, and thereafter we ate out.

I'd performed plenty of delicate operations on living tissues, and some of them had been tricky, but I still felt like a pre-med student as we opened the front plate of her torso and began to sever the leads of her "nerves." Dave's mechanical glands were all prepared, complex little bundles of radio tubes and wires that heterodyned on the electrical thought impulses and distorted them as adrenalin distorts the reactions of the human mind.

Instead of sleeping that night, we pored over the schematic diagrams of her structures, tracing the thoughts through mazes of her wiring, severing the leaders, implanting the heterones, as Dave called them. And while we worked, a mechanical tape fed carefully prepared thoughts of consciousness and awareness of life and feeling into an auxiliary memory coil. Dave believed in leaving nothing to chance.

It was growing light as we finished, exhausted and exultant. All that remained was the starting of her electric power; like all the Dillard mechs, she was equipped with a tiny atomotor instead of batteries, and once started would need no further attention.

Dave refused to turn her on. "Wait until we've slept and rested," he advised. "I'm as eager to try her as you are, but we can't do much studying with our minds half dead. Turn in, and we'll leave Helen until later."

Even though we were both reluctant to follow it, we knew the idea was sound. We turned in, and sleep hit us before the air-conditioner could cut down to sleeping temperature. And then Dave was pounding on my shoulder.

"Phil! Hey, snap out of it!"

I groaned, turned over, and faced him. "Well? . . . Uh! What is it? Did Helen—"

No, it's old Mrs. van Styler. She 'visored to say her son has an infatuation for a servant girl, and she wants you to come out and give counter-hormones. They're at the summer camp in Maine."

Rich Mrs. van Styler! I couldn't afford to let that account down, now that Helen had used up the last of my funds. But it wasn't a job I cared for.

"Counter-hormones! That'll take two weeks! Anyway, I'm no society doctor, messing with glands to keep fools happy. My job's taking care of serious trouble."

"And you want to watch Helen." Dave was grinning, but he was serious, too. "I told her it'd cost her fifty thousand!"

"*Huh?*"

"And she said okay, if you hurried."

Of course, there was only one thing to do, though I could have wrung fat Mrs. van Styler's neck cheerfully. It wouldn't have happened if she'd use robots like everyone else—but she had to be different.

Consequently, while Dave was back home puttering with Helen, I was racking my brain to trick Archy van Styler into getting the counter-hormones, and giving the servant girl the same. Oh, I wasn't supposed to, but the poor kid was crazy about Archy. Dave might have written, I thought, but never a word did I get.

It was three weeks later instead of two when I reported that Archy was "cured" and collected on the line. With that money in my pocket, I hired a personal rocket and was back in Messina in half an hour. I didn't waste time in reaching the house.

As I stepped into the alcove, I heard a light patter of feet, and an eager voice called out, "Dave, dear?" For a minute I couldn't answer, and the voice came again, pleading, "Dave?"

I don't know what I expected, but I didn't expect Helen to meet me that way, stopping and staring at me, obvious disappointment on her face, little hands fluttering up against her breast.

"Oh," she cried. "I thought it was Dave. He hardly comes home to eat now, but I've had supper waiting hours." She dropped her hands and managed a smile. "You're Phil, aren't you? Dave told me about you when . . . at first. I'm so glad to see you home, Phil."

"Glad to see you doing so well, Helen." Now what does one say for light conversation with a robot? "You said something about supper?"

"Oh, yes. I guess Dave ate downtown again, so we might as well go in. It'll be nice having someone to talk to around the house, Phil. You don't mind if I call you Phil, do you? You know, you are sort of a godfather to me."

We ate. I hadn't counted on such behavior, but apparently she considered eating as normal as walking. She didn't do much eating, at that; most of the time she spent staring at the front door.

Dave came in as we were finishing, a frown a yard wide on his face. Helen started to rise, but he ducked toward the stairs, throwing words over his shoulders.

"Hi, Phil. See you up here later."

There was something radically wrong with him. For a moment, I'd thought his eyes were haunted, and as I turned to Helen, hers were filling with tears. She gulped, choked them back, and fell to viciously on her food.

"What's the matter with him . . . and you?" I asked.

"He's sick of me." She pushed her plate away and got up hastily. "You'd better see him while I clean up. And there's nothing wrong with me. And it's not my fault, anyway." She grabbed the dishes and ducked into the kitchen. I could have sworn she was crying.

Maybe all thought is a series of conditioned reflexes—but she certainly had picked up a lot of conditioning while I was gone. Lena in her heyday had been nothing like this. I went up to see if Dave could make any sense out of the hodgepodge.

He was squirting soda into a large glass of apple brandy, and I saw that the bottle was nearly empty. "Join me?" he asked.

It seemed like a good idea. The roaring blast of an iron rocket overhead was the only familiar thing left in the house. From the look around Dave's eyes, it wasn't the first bottle he'd emptied while I was gone, and there were more left. He dug out a new bottle for his own drink.

"Of course, it's none of my business, Dave, but that stuff won't steady your nerves any. What's gotten into you and Helen? Been seeing ghosts?"

Helen was wrong; he hadn't been eating downtown—nor anywhere else. His muscles collapsed into a chair in a way that spoke of fatigue and nerves, but mostly of hunger. "You noticed it, eh?"

"Noticed it? The two of you jammed it down my throat."

"Uhmmm." He swatted at a nonexistent fly, and slumped further down in the pneumatic. "Guess maybe I should have waited with Helen until you got back. But if that stereo cast hadn't changed . . . anyway, it did. And those mushy books of yours finished the job."

"Thanks. That makes it all clear."

"You know, Phil, I've got a place in the country . . . fruit ranch. My dad left it to me. Think I'll look it over."

And that's the way it went. But finally, by much liquor and more perspiration, I got some of the story out of him before I gave him an amytal and put him to bed. Then I hunted up Helen and dug the rest of the story from her, until it made sense.

Apparently, as soon as I was gone, Dave had turned her on and made preliminary tests, which were entirely satisfactory. She had reacted beautifully—so well that he decided to leave her and go down to work as usual.

Naturally, with all her untried emotions, she was filled with curiosity and wanted him to stay. Then he had an inspiration. After showing her what her duties about the house would be, he set her down in front of the stereo-visor, tuned in a travelogue, and left her to occupy her time with that.

The travelogue held her attention until it was finished, and the station switched over to a current serial with Larry Ainslee, the same cute emoter who'd given us all the trouble with the twins. Incidentally, he looked something like Dave.

Helen took to the serial like a seal to water. This play acting was a perfect outlet for her newly excited emotions. When that particular episode finished, she found a love story on another station, and added still more to her education. The afternoon programs were mostly news and music, but by then she'd found my books; and I do have rather adolescent taste in literature.

Dave came home in the best of spirits. The front alcove was neatly swept, and there was the odor of food in the air that he'd missed around the house for weeks. He had visions of Helen as the super-efficient housekeeper.

So it was a shock to him to feel two strong arms around his neck from behind and hear a voice all a-quiver coo into his ears, "Oh, Dave, darling, I've missed you so, and I'm so *thrilled* that you are back." Helen's technique may have lacked polish, but it had enthusiasm, as he found when he tried to stop her from kissing him. She had learned fast and furiously—also, Helen was powered by an atomotor.

Dave wasn't a prude, but he remembered that she was only a robot, after all. The fact that she felt, acted, and looked like a young goddess in his arms didn't mean much. With some effort, he untangled himself and dragged her off to supper, where he made her eat with him to divert her attention.

After her evening work, he called her into the study and gave her a thorough lecture on the folly of her ways. It must have been good, for it lasted three solid hours, and covered her station in life, the idiocy of stereos, and various other miscellanies. When he finished, Helen looked up with dewy eyes and said wistfully, "I know, Dave, but I still love you."

That's when Dave started drinking.

It grew worse each day. If he stayed downtown, she was crying when he came home. If he returned on time, she fussed over him and threw herself at him. In his room, with the door locked, he could hear her downstairs pacing up and down and muttering; and when he went down, she stared at him reproachfully until he had to go back up.

I sent Helen out on a fake errand in the morning and got Dave up. With her gone, I made him eat a decent breakfast and gave him a tonic for his nerves. He was still listless and moody.

"Look here, Dave," I broke in on his brooding, "Helen isn't human, after all. Why not cut off her power and change a few memory coils? Then we can convince her that she never was in love and couldn't get that way."

"You try it. I had the idea, but she put up a wail that would wake Homer. She says it would be murder—and the hell of it is that I can't help feeling the same way about it. Maybe she isn't human, but you wouldn't guess it when she puts on that martyred look and tells you to go ahead and kill her."

"We never put in substitutes for some of the secretions present in man during the love period."

"I don't know what we put in.

Maybe the heterones backfired, or something. Anyway, she's made this idea so much a part of her thoughts that we'd have to put in a whole new set of coils."

"Well, why not?"

"Go ahead. You're the surgeon of this family. I'm not used to fussing with emotions. Matter of fact, since she's been acting this way, I'm beginning to hate work on any robot. My business is going to blazes."

He saw Helen coming up the walk and ducked out of the back door for the monorail express. I'd intended to put him back in bed, but let him go. Maybe he'd be better off at his shop than at home.

"Dave's gone?" Helen did have that martyred look now.

"Yeah. I got him to eat, and he's gone to work."

"I'm glad he ate." She slumped down in a chair as if she were worn out, though how a mech could be tired beat me. "Phil?"

"Well, what is it?"

"Do you think I'm bad for him? I mean, do you think he'd be happier if I weren't here?"

"He'll go crazy if you keep acting this way around him."

She winced. Those little hands were twisting about pleadingly, and I felt like an inhuman brute. But I'd started, and I went ahead. "Even if I cut out your power and changed your coils, he'd probably still be haunted by you."

"I know. But I can't help it. And I'd make him a good wife, really I would, Phil."

I gulped; this was getting a little too far. "And give him strapping sons to boot, I suppose. A man wants flesh and blood, not rubber and metal."

"Don't, please! I can't think of myself that way; to me, I'm a woman. And you know how perfectly I'm made to imitate a real woman . . . in all ways. I couldn't give him sons, but in every other way . . . I'd try so hard, I know I'd make him a good wife."

I gave up.

Dave didn't come home that night, nor the next day. Helen was fussing and fuming, wanting me to call the hospitals and the police, but I knew nothing had happened to him. He always carried identifications. Still, when he didn't come on the third day, I began to worry. And when Helen started out for his shop, I agreed to go with her.

Dave was there with another man I didn't know. I parked Helen where he couldn't see her, but where she could hear, and went in as soon as the other fellow left.

Dave looked a little better and seemed gad to see me. "Hi, Phil —just closing up. Let's go eat."

Helen couldn't hold back any longer, but came trooping in. "Come on home, Dave. I've got roast duck with spice stuffing, and you know you love that."

"Scat!" said Dave. She shrank back, turned to go. "Oh, all right, stay. You might as well hear it, too. I've sold the shop. The fellow you saw just bought it, and I'm going up to the old fruit ranch I told you about, Phil. I can't stand the mechs any more."

"You'll starve to death at that," I told him.

"No, there's a growing demand for old-fashioned fruit, raised out-of-doors. People are tired of this water-culture stuff. Dad always made a living out of it. I'm leaving as soon as I can get home and pack."

Helen clung to her idea. "I'll pack, Dave, while you eat. I've got apple cobbler for dessert." The world was toppling under her feet, but she still remembered how crazy he was for apple cobbler.

Helen was a good cook; in fact, she was a genius, with all the good points of a woman and a mech combined. Dave ate well enough, after he got started. By the time supper was over, he'd thawed out enough to admit he liked the duck and cobbler, and to thank her for packing. In fact, he even let her kiss him good-bye, though he firmly refused to let her go to the rocket field with him.

Helen was trying to be brave when I got back, and we carried on a stumbling conversation about Mrs. van Styler's servants for a while. But the talk began to lull, and she sat staring out of the window at nothing most of the time. Even the stereo comedy lacked interest for her, and I was glad to have her go off to her room. She could cut her power down to simulate sleep when she chose.

As the days slipped by, I began to realize why she couldn't believe herself a robot. I got to thinking of her as a girl and companion myself. Except for odd intervals when she went off by herself to brood, or when she kept going to the telescript for a letter that never came, she was as good a companion as a man could ask. There was something homey about the place that Lena had never put there.

I took Helen on a shopping trip to Hudson and she giggled and purred over wisps of silk and glassheen as any normal girl might. We went trout fishing for a day, where she proved to be as good a sport and as sensibly silent as a man. I thoroughly enjoyed myself and thought she was forgetting Dave. That was before I came home unexpectedly and found her doubled up on the couch, threshing her legs up and down and crying to the high heavens.

It was then I called Dave. They seemed to have trouble in reaching him, and Helen came over beside me while I waited. She was tense and fidgety as an old maid trying to propose. But finally they located Dave.

"What's up, Phil?" he asked as his face came on the view-plate. "I was just getting my things together to—"

I broke him off. "Things can't go on the way they are, Dave. I've made up my mind. I'm yanking Helen's coils tonight. It won't be worse than what she's going through now."

Helen reached up and touched

my shoulder. "Maybe that's best, Phil. I don't blame you."

Dave's voice cut in. "Phil, you don't know what you're doing!"

"Of course I do. It'll all be over by the time you get here. As you heard, she's agreeing."

There was a black cloud sweeping over Dave's face. "I won't have it, Phil. She's half mine and I forbid it!"

"Of all the—"

"Go ahead, call me anything you want. I've changed my mind. I was packing to come home when you called."

Helen jerked around me, her eyes glued to the panel. "Dave, do you . . . are you—"

"I'm just waking up to what a fool I've been, Helen. Phil, I'll be home in a couple of hours, so if there's anything—"

He didn't have to chase me out. But I heard Helen cooing something about loving to be a rancher's wife before I could shut the door.

Well, I wasn't as surprised as they thought. I think I knew when I called Dave what would happen. No man acts the way Dave had been acting because he hates a girl; only because he thinks he does—and thinks wrong.

No woman ever made a lovelier bride or a sweeter wife. Helen never lost her flair for cooking and making a home. With her gone, the old house seemed empty, and I began to drop out to the ranch once or twice a week. I suppose they had troubles at times, but I never saw it, and I know the neighbors never suspected they were anything but normal man and wife.

Dave grew older, and Helen didn't, of course. But between us, we put lines in her face and grayed her hair without letting Dave know that she wasn't growing old with him; he'd forgotten that she wasn't human, I guess.

I practically forgot, myself. It wasn't until a letter came from Helen this morning that I woke up to reality. There, in her beautiful script, just a trifle shaky in places, was the inevitable that neither Dave nor I had seen.

Dear Phil,

As you know, Dave has had heart trouble for several years now. We expected him to live on just the same, but it seems that wasn't to be. He died in my arms just before sunrise. He sent you his greetings and farewell.

I've one last favor to ask of you, Phil. There is only one thing for me to do when this is finished. Acid will burn out metal as well as flesh, and I'll be dead with Dave. Please see that we are buried together, and that the morticians do not find my secret. Dave wanted it that way, too.

Poor, dear Phil. I know you loved Dave as a brother, and how you felt about me. Please don't grieve too much for us, for we have had a happy life together, and both feel that we should cross this last bridge side by side.

With love and thanks from,
Helen.

It had to come sooner or later, I suppose, and the first shock has worn off now. I'll be leaving in a few minutes to carry out Helen's last instructions.

Dave was a lucky man, and the best friend I ever had. And Helen —Well, as I said, I'm an old man now, and can view things more sanely; I should have married and raised a family, I suppose. But... there was only one Helen O'Loy.

SUGGESTIONS FOR DISCUSSION AND WRITING

1. That Dave and Phil should have named their robot after Helen of Troy is not as incongruous as it may seem: both Helens came into the world in rather odd fashions. Helen O'Loy came out of a crate. Helen of Troy (in Greek legend, the most beautiful of all women) was born from an egg. Can you explain how that happened?

2. The following reference to Helen of Troy is a familiar quotation from *Doctor Faustus*, an English play written in about 1588.
"Was this the face that launch'd a thousand ships,
And burnt the topless towers of Ilium?"
Do you know what mythological event involved a thousand ships, and can you name the author of the play?

3. "Helen O'Loy" was written in 1938—about ten years before television became a home fixture. With amazing foresight, the author describes the afternoon soap operas on the "stereo-viser" and their drastic effect on Helen's behavioral and emotional patterns. Do you feel that, to some extent, you have been "programmed" in the same way?

4. The introduction to this chapter refers to the year 1938 as a time of harsh realities—of transition from depression to war. Today, we find a new generation moved by a great feeling of nostalgia for those "good old days"! A car of the 1930s vintage is now a collector's item; the plays of Noel Coward are being revived—and people flock to see them. Art Deco is a new fad: any item of house furnishings about forty years old is in great demand and worth its weight in gold. Old songs are heard again. Why?

Write an essay giving your personal definition of "the good old days," together with your evaluation of their advantages and drawbacks.

A Bad Day for Sales

FRITZ LEIBER

THE BIG bright doors of the office building parted with a pneumatic *whoosh* and Robie glided onto Times Square. The crowd that had been watching the fifty-foot-tall girl on clothing billboard get dressed, or reading the latest news about the hot truce scrawl itself in yard-high script, hurried to look.

Robie was still a novelty. Robie was fun. For a little while yet, he could steal the show. But the attention did not make Robie proud. He had no more emotions than the pink plastic giantess, who dressed and undressed endlessly whether there was a crowd or the street was empty, and who never once blinked her blue mechanical eyes. But she merely drew business while Robie went out after it.

For Robie was the logical conclusion of the development of vending machines. All the earlier ones had stood in one place, on a floor or hanging on a wall, and blankly delivered merchandise in return for coins, whereas Robie searched for customers. He was the demonstration model of a line of sales robots to be manufactured by Shuler Vending Machines, provided the public invested enough in stocks to give the company capital to go into mass production.

The publicity Robie drew stimulated investments handsomely. It was amusing to see the TV and newspaper coverage of Robie selling, but not a fraction as much fun as being approached personally by him. Those who were usually bought anywhere from one to five hundred shares, if they had any money and foresight enough to see that sales robots would eventually be on every street and highway in the country.

Robie radared the crowd, found that it surrounded him solidly and stopped. With a carefully built-in sense of timing, he waited for the tension and expectation to mount before he began talking.

113

"Say, Ma, he doesn't look like a robot at all," a child said. "He looks like a turtle."

Which was not completely inaccurate. The lower part of Robie's body was a metal hemisphere hemmed with sponge rubber and not quite touching the sidewalk. The upper was a metal box with black holes in it. The box could swivel and duck.

A chromium-bright hoopskirt with a turret on top.

"Reminds me too much of the Little Joe Paratanks," a legless veteran of the Persian War muttered, and rapidly rolled himself away on wheels rather like Robie's.

His departure made it easier for some of those who knew about Robie to open a path in the crowd. Robie headed straight for the gap. The crowd whooped.

Robie glided very slowly down the path, deftly jogging aside whenever he got too close to ankles in skylon or sockassins. The rubber buffer on his hoopskirt was merely an added safeguard.

The boy who had called Robie a turtle jumped in the middle of the path and stood his ground, grinning foxily.

Robie stopped two feet short of him. The turret ducked. The crowd got quiet.

"Hello, youngster," Robie said in a voice that was smooth as that of a TV star, and was, in fact, a recording of one.

The boy stopped smiling. "Hello," he whispered.

"How old are you?" Robie asked.

"Nine. No, eight."

"That's nice," Robie observed. A metal arm shot down from his neck, stopped just short of the boy.

The boy jerked back.

"For you," Robie said.

The boy gingerly took the red polly-lop from the neatly fashioned metal claws, and began to unwrap it.

"Nothing to say?" Robie asked.

"Uh—thank you."

After a suitable pause, Robie continued, "And how about a nice refreshing drink of Poppy Pop to go with your polly-lop?" The boy lifted his eyes, but didn't stop licking the candy. Robie waggled his claws slightly. "Just give me a quarter and within five seconds—"

A little girl wriggled out of the forest of legs. "Give me a polly-lop, too, Robie," she demanded.

"Rita, come back here!" a woman in the third rank of the crowd called angrily.

Robbie scanned the newcomer gravely. His reference silhouettes were not good enough to let him distinguish the sex of children, so he merely repeated, "Hello, youngster."

"Rita!"

"Give me a polly-lop!"

Disregarding both remarks, for a good salesman is single-minded and does not waste bait, Robie said winningly, "I'll bet you read *Junior Space Killers*. Now I have here—"

"Uh-uh, I'm a girl. *He* got a polly-lop."

At the word "girl," Robie broke

off. Rather ponderously, he said, "I'll bet you read *Gee-Gee Jones, Space Stripper*. Now I have here the latest issue of that thrilling comic, not yet in the stationary vending machines. Just give me fifty cents and within five—"

"Please let me get through. I'm her mother."

A young woman in the front rank drawled over her powder-sprayed shoulder, "I'll get her for you," and slithered out on six-inch platform shoes. "Run away, children," she said nonchalantly. Lifting her arms behind her head, she pirouetted slowly before Robie to show how much she did for her bolero half-jacket and her form-fitting slacks that melted into skylon just above the knees. The little girl glared at her. She ended the pirouette in profile.

At this age level, Robie's reference silhouettes permitted him to distinguish sex, though with occasional amusing and embarrassing miscalls. He whistled admiringly. The crowd cheered.

Someone remarked critically to a friend, "It would go over better if he was built more like a real robot. You know, like a man."

The friend shook his head. "This way, it's subtler."

No one in the crowd was watching the newscript overhead as it scribbled, "Ice pack for hot truce? Vanadin hints Russ may yield on Pakistan."

Robie was saying, ". . . in the savage new glamor-tint we have christened Mars Blood, complete with spray applicator and fit-all fingernails that mask each finger completely except for the nail. Just give me five dollars—uncrumpled bills may be fed into the revolving rollers you see beside my arm—and within five seconds—"

"No, thanks, Robie," the young woman yawned.

"Remember," Robie persisted, "for three more weeks, seductivizing Mars Blood will be unobtainable from any other robot or human vendor."

"No thanks."

Robie scanned the crowd resourcefully. "Is there any gentleman here . . ." he began just as a woman elbowed her way through the front rank.

"I told you to come back!" she snapped at the little girl.

"But I didn't get my polly-lop!"

". . . who would care to . . ."

"Rita!"

"Robie cheated, Ow!"

Meanwhile, the young woman in the half-bolero had scanned the nearby gentlemen on her own. Deciding that there was less than a fifty-per-cent chance of any of them accepting the proposition Robie seemed about to make, she took advantage of the scuffle to slither gracefully back into the ranks. Once again the path was clear before Robie.

He paused, however, for a brief recapitulation of the more magical properties of Mars Blood, including a telling phrase about "the passionate claws of a Martian sunrise."

But no one bought. It wasn't quite time. Soon enough silver coins would be clinking, bills going through the rollers faster than laundry, and five hundred people struggling for the privilege of having their money taken away from them by America's first mobile sales robot.

But there were still some tricks that Robie had to do free, and one certainly should enjoy those before starting the more expensive fun.

So Robie moved on until he reached the curb. The variation in level was instantly sensed by his under-scanners. He stopped. His head began to swivel. The crowd watched in eager silence. This was Robie's best trick.

Robie's head stopped swiveling. His scanners had found the traffic light. It was green. Robie edged forward. But then the light turned red. Robie stopped again, still on the curb. The crowd softly *ahhed* its delight.

It was wonderful to be alive and watching Robie on such an exciting day. Alive and amused in the fresh, weather-controlled air between the lines of bright skyscrapers with their winking windows and under a sky so blue you could almost call it dark.

(But way, way up, where the crowd could not see, the sky was darker still. Purple-dark, with stars showing. And in that purple-dark, a silver-green something, the color of a bud, plunged down at better than three miles a second. The silver-green was a newly developed paint that foiled radar.)

Robie was saying, "While we wait for the light, there's time for you youngsters to enjoy a nice refreshing Poppy Pop. Or for you adults—only those over five feet tall are eligible to buy—to enjoy an exciting Poppy Pop fizz. Just give me a quarter, or—in the case of adults, one dollar and a quarter; I'm licensed to dispense intoxicating liquors—and within five seconds . . ."

But that was not cutting it quite fine enough. Just three seconds later, the silver-green bud bloomed above Manhattan into a globular orange flower. The skyscrapers grew brighter and still, the brightness of the inside of the Sun. The windows winked blossoming white fire-flowers.

The crowd around Robie bloomed, too. Their clothes puffed into petals of flame. Their heads of hair were torches.

The orange flower grew, stem and blossom. The blast came. The winking windows shattered tier by tier, became black holes. The walls bent, rocked, cracked. A stony dandruff flaked from their cornices. The flaming flowers on the sidewalk were all leveled at once. Robie was shoved ten feet. His metal hoopskirt dimpled, regained its shape.

The blast ended. The orange flower, grown vast, vanished overhead on its huge, magic beanstalk. It grew dark and very still. The cornice-dandruff pattered down. A few small fragments rebounded from the metal hoopskirt.

Robie made some small, uncertain movements, as if feeling for broken bones. He was hunting for the traffic light, but it no longer shone either red or green.

He slowly scanned a full circle. There was nothing anywhere to interest his reference silhouettes. Yet whenever he tried to move, his under-scanners warned him of low obstructions. It was very puzzling.

The silence was disturbed by moans and a crackling sound, as faint at first as the scampering of distant rats.

A seared man, his charred clothes fuming where the blast had blown out the fire, rose from the curb. Robie scanned him.

"Good day, sir," Robie said. "Would you care for a smoke? A truly cool smoke? Now I have here a yet-unmarketed brand . . ."

But the customer had run away, screaming, and Robie never ran after customers, though he could follow them at a medium-brisk roll. He worked his way along the curb where the man had sprawled, carefully keeping his distance from the low obstructions, some of which writhed now and then, forcing him to jog. Shortly he reached a fire hydrant. He scanned it. His electronic vision, though it still worked, had been somewhat blurred by the blast.

"Hello, youngster," Robie said. Then, after a long pause, "Cat got your tongue? Well, I have a little present for you. Have a nice, lovely polly-lop."

"Take it, youngster," he said after another pause. "It's for you. Don't be afraid."

His attention was distracted by other customers, who began to rise up oddly here and there, twisting forms that confused his reference silhouettes, and would not stay to be scanned properly. One cried, "Water," but no quarter clinked in Robie's claws when he caught the word and suggested, "How about a nice refreshing drink of Poppy Pop?"

The rat-crackling of the flames had become a jungle muttering. The blind windows began to wink fire again.

A little girl marched, stepping neatly over arms and legs she did not look at. A white dress and the once taller bodies around her had shielded her from the brilliance and the blast. Her eyes were fixed on Robie. In them was the same imperious confidence, though none of the delight, with which she had watched him earlier.

"Help me, Robie," she said. "I want my mother."

"Hello youngster," Robie said. "What would you like? Comics? Candy?"

"Where is she, Robie? Take me to her."

"Balloons? Would you like to watch me blow up a balloon?"

The little girl began to cry. The sound triggered off another of Robie's novelty circuits, a service feature that had brought in a lot of favorable publicity.

"Is something wrong?" he asked. "Are you in trouble? Are you lost?"

"Yes, Robie. Take me to my mother."

"Stay right here," Robie said reassuringly, "and don't be frightened. I will call a policeman." He whistled shrilly, twice.

Time passed. Robie whistled again. The windows flared and roared. The little girl begged, "Take me away, Robie," and jumped onto a little step in his hoopskirt.

"Give me a dime," Robie said.

The little girl found one in her pocket and put it in his claws.

"Your weight," Robie said, "is fifty-four and one-half pounds."

"Have you seen my daughter, have you seen her?" a woman was crying somewhere. "I left her watching that thing while I stepped inside—*Rita!*"

"Robie helped me," the little girl began babbling at her. "He knew I was lost. He even called the police, but they didn't come. He weighed me, too. Didn't you, Robie?"

But Robie had gone off to peddle Poppy Pop to the members of a rescue squad which had just come around the corner, more robot-like in their asbestos suits than he in his metal skin.

SUGGESTIONS FOR DISCUSSION AND WRITING

We were toying for a moment with the temptation of renaming the story "The Almost Death of a Salesman!" But this would have entailed discussing the miraculous escapes of Robie, Rita, and her mother. Without a clue —except for the little girl's white dress—we felt unprepared for the questions you were bound to ask. Let us conclude that miracles do happen when needed to make a good story.

1. Robie was a Salesman . . . and the Salesman is the most intricate, the most versatile, the most indispensable cog in that huge machine we call "business." He displays many of the attributes of good salesmanship: a smooth voice, for instance. Can you find six more such attributes in Robie?

2. In the chaos of the atomic blast, Robie's continued "sales pitch" becomes ludicrous because the purpose of his activity is now useless, even callous. But, could not Robie's unique ability to "carry on" in times of emergency be directed towards useful tasks and functions in such fields as public order and public safety? Think it over seriously, and give some examples that are not too farfetched.

Men Are Different

ALAN BLOCH

I'M AN archaeologist, and Men are my business. Just the same, I wonder if we'll ever find out about Men—I mean *really* find out what made Men different from us Robots—by digging around on the dead planets. You see, I lived with a Man once, and I know it isn't as simple as they told us back in school.

We have a few records, of course, and Robots like me are filling in some gaps, but I think now that we aren't really getting anywhere. We know, or at least the historians say we know, that Men came from a planet called Earth. We know, too, that they rode out bravely from star to star; and wherever they stopped, they left colonies—Men, Robots, and sometimes both—against their return. But they never came back.

Those were the shining days of the world. But are we so old now? Men had a bright flame—the old word is "divine," I think—that flung them across the night skies, and we have lost the strands of the web they wove.

Our scientists tell us that Men were very much like us—and the skeleton of a Man is, to be sure, almost the same as the skeleton of a Robot, except that it's made of some calcium compound instead of titanium. They speak learnedly of "population pressure" as a "driving force toward the stars." Just the same, there are other differences.

It was on my last field trip, to one of the inner plants, that I met the Man. He must have been the last Man in this system and he'd forgotten how to talk—he'd been alone so long. Once he learned our language we got along fine together, and I planned to bring him back with me. Something happened to him, though.

One day, for no reason at all, he complained of the heat. I checked his temperature and decided that his thermostat circuits were shot. I had a kit of field spares with me, and he was obviously out of order, so I went to work. I turned him off without any trouble. I pushed the needle into his neck to operate the cut-off switch, and he stopped moving, just like a Robot. But when I opened him up he wasn't the same inside. And when I put him back together I couldn't get him running again. Then he sort of weathered away—and by the time I was ready to come home, about a year later, there was nothing left of him but bones. Yes, Men are indeed different.

SUGGESTIONS FOR DISCUSSION AND WRITING

1. At first reading, the impact of the story seems to be in the last paragraph. We do not think that it is. Do you agree, and if so, why?

2. What change has taken place in the usual relationship between Man and Robot?

3. From the very first sentence and right on through, the author's apparent design seems to be diminishing, blurring, and belittling the image of Man in the reader's mind. Point out sentences that carry out that design, and explain their effect.

4. One paragraph is quite exceptional in that it contains a complimentary reference to "us." Can you find it?

5. The facts and conditions assumed in this extremely well-written story are not likely ever to occur; the author knew that. What reasons could he possibly have had to write the story?

Some Fun With Space Jargon

Most special activities or groups have their own special language out of necessity. At times, however, such esoteric language begins to feed upon itself; its perpetrators form complex-sounding phrases where plain English would be more appropriate. Unfortunately, the language of government, business, science, and even the arts is often designed to impress the general public, rather than to communicate clearly.

Space science, too, has its share of language manglers. See if you can make up some impressive-sounding phrases from the Puffal Grid below by applying random three-digit numbers. Take *123*, for example; it translates as "quasi-logarithmic satellite," a term that would earn respect from the most doubting outsider. Try *456*: "universally galvanic mass." Try your age plus the number of people in your family, or the first three digits of your telephone number.

PUFFAL GRID

0. CRITICALLY	0. COSMIC	0. LASER
1. QUASI-	1. CATACLYSMIC	1. RADAR
2. CELESTIALLY	2. LOGARITHMIC	2. TIME-PHASE
3. STATICALLY	3. GALACTIC	3. SATELLITE
4. UNIVERSALLY	4. STELLAR	4. VACUUM
5. ORBITALLY	5. GALVANIC	5. METEORITE
6. DIURNALLY	6. CALCULATING	6. MASS
7. HERMETICALLY	7. GRAVITATIONAL	7. RETRO-ROCKET
8. SPATIALLY	8. SYNCHRONIZED	8. ROBOT
9. UNILATERALLY	9. ATOMIC	9. SEMI-CONDUCTOR

SCIENCE FICTION AND FANTASY

When you have selected enough phrases to satisfy yourself for the time being, try to answer this question: What parts of speech occur in each column? Why?

Taken alone, the words used in the Puffal Grid are essential parts of the science fiction vernacular. They also include some of the most interesting words in the English language:

1. ANDROID—a living being that has been created partly or wholly through processes other than human birth. (from Greek *andro*, "man.")

2. ASTRONAUT—a traveler in interplanetary space. (from Greek *aster*, "star," and Latin *nauticus*, "sailor.")

3. ATOM—the smallest particle of an element that can exist. (from Greek *a*, "not," and *tomas*, "cut," *not able to be cut.*)

4. CALCULATE—compute. (from the Latin *calculi*, "pebbles," which Roman merchants used to add bills. *Calculi* is also the root of calculus, a form of modern mathematics essential to the advent of the space age.)

5. CATACLYSM—overwhelming destruction, upheaval, and change. (from Greek *klyzo*, "wash," and *kata*, "wholly," to wash out completely.)

6. CELESTIAL—heavenly, of the heavens. (from Latin *caelum*, "sky.")

7. COBALT—now an important element in atomic reactions, cobalt was once considered a useless, dangerous discovery in mines because of the arsenic and sulphur it often contains. (It was thus named after the German *kobalt*, "goblin," or "devil.")

8. COSMOS—the universe. (from the Greek *kosmeo*, "to order or arrange.")

9. DATA—bits of information given as a basis for reasoning or inference. (from *dat*, a form of the Latin verb *do*, "to give.")

10. DIURNAL—having a daily cycle, rotation of the heavens. (from Latin *diurnalis*, "of the day.")

Some Fun With Space Jargon

11. ELECTRIC—of, or pertaining to, or operated by electricity. (from Greek *elektor*, "the beginning sun," probably a reference to the sparks given off by friction.)

12. ERG—a unit of force important in space measurements and calculations. (from Greek *ergon*, "work.")

13. FANTASY—the free play of creative imagination. (literally a "coming before," from the Greek *phantasia* which referred to the mind's ability to visualize things of the imagination.)

14. GALAXY—one of the billions of systems, each including stars, star clusters, nebulae, and interstellar matter that make up the universe. (from Greek *gala*, "milk.")

15. GALVANIC—related to a direct current of electricity. (named after Luigi Galvani, an Italian scientist who discovered electrical currents in animal tissue.)

16. GRAVITY—the attraction of a planet's mass for bodies at or near its surface. (from Latin *gravis*, "heavy.")

17. HERMETICALLY—airtight. (When we read of a hermetically sealed space lock, we do not think of the Greek god *Hermes*. Yet, the process is named after this god of magic and alchemy, who sealed many a mortal wound in battle.)

18. HOLOCAUST—a thorough destruction, essentially by fire. (from Greek *holos*, "whole," and *kaustos*, "burned." Literally, "a burnt offering.")

19. HUMANOID—having human characteristics. (combined form, *human*, and *oid*, "resembling.")

20. LASER—a device that amplifies electromagnetic waves by means of the natural oscillations of atoms. (from initial letters of the words: *l*ight *a*mplification by *s*timulated *e*mission of *r*adiation.)

21. MACH—a number representing the ratio of the speed of a body to the speed of sound. (named after Ernst Mach, Austrian physicist.)

22. MASS—a fundamental physical measurement, that of the amount of space a body occupies that causes it to have weight in a gravitational field. (from Greek *maza*, "to knead.")

SCIENCE FICTION AND FANTASY

23. MICROCOSM—a little world. (from Greek *micro*, "small," and *kosmos*, "world.")

24. ORBIT—a path described by one body in its revolutions around another. (from Latin *orbita*, "track.")

25. QUASAR—very distant objects that emit unusual light signals. (from *quasi*, "somewhat," and stell*ar* radio source.)

26. QUINTESSENCE—the most concentrated part. (from Greek *quinta*, "fifth essence," of which the philosopher Aristotle thought the stars and planets were composed.)

27. RADAR—a device for locating a distant object by means of high frequency radio waves. (from initial letters of the words: *r*adio *d*etecting *a*nd *r*anging.)

28. RAY—a beam of light or other energy of a limited cross section. (from Latin *radius*, "rod.")

29. RETRO-ROCKET—an auxiliary rocket on a space vehicle that produces opposite thrust. (from Greek *retro*, "back," and German *rocca*, "distaff," a reference to the shape of this spinning tool.)

30. ROBOT—a machine that looks like a human being and performs complex tasks. (from the Czech *robotnik*, "'worker" or "slave," made famous by Karel Capek in his play *R. U. R.*)

31. SATELLITE—a celestial or man-made body orbiting another of larger size. (from Latin *satelles*, "attendant.")

32. STAR—any natural luminous body visible in the sky. (from Greek *aster*, "star.")

33. STATIC—relating to bodies at rest, or forces in equilibrium. (from the Latin *sto*, "to stand.")

34. URANIUM—In 1889 a German chemist named Klopoth discovered element 92, which he named *uranium* in honor of the English-German astronomer Sir William Herschel, who had discovered the planet Uranus eight years earlier.

35. UTOPIA—a dreamed-of state where all things are perfect. (Em-

ployed by English philosopher Sir Thomas More in a work about a perfect state, the word is derived from the Greek *utopia*, "the land of nowhere.")

36. VACUUM—empty space. (from Latin *vacare*, "to be empty.")

37. X-RAY—the "X" meaning "unknown," the ray was named by German physicist Wilhelm von Roentgen, who discovered it accidentally.

38. ZENITH—point in the sky directly overhead. (from the Arabic *samt arras*, "way overhead.")

Chapter 4

TRAFFIC WITH THE PLANETS

In the opinion of many, Jules Verne and H. G. Wells are the two giants of science fiction. Herbert George Wells (1866–1946) taught science for a few years, which may account for his accurate prophecies: *The Land Ironclads* (1903) suggested the armored tanks first used by the British in World War I, and *War in the Air* (1907) foresaw the potential value of the airplane as a fighting machine.

The selections from *The War of the Worlds*, which you are about to read, are but an inkling of the dire events that threatened to be "the beginning of the rout of civilization, of the massacre of mankind."

Published in 1898, the novel was a best-seller and helped popularize science fiction. Forty years later, on the night of October 30, 1938, a New Jersey radio station broadcast a dramatized version of the story. It was done so realistically that listeners soon began to think that they were hearing a "Special News Bulletin," and that the Martian invasion was actually taking place all around them, and at that very moment! . . . This memorable broadcast was the brainchild of a 23-year-old actor who, as one would expect, was also the "star" of the show: Mr. Orson Welles.

The reaction to that spectacular false alarm was a big boost for science fiction: if "that kind of a book" was capable of scaring two or three million people, it was worth looking into.

"Of Course" is a gem of a story—and a total, absolute contrast to *The War of the Worlds*. In each story, the subject is exactly the same: the unexpected visit from the inhabitants of one planet to the inhabitants of another. In each case, Earth is the "host" planet, but there the similarity ends. "Of Course" is an example, rare in science fiction, of masterful satire.

Selections from

WAR OF THE WORLDS

H. G. WELLS

THE STORM burst upon us six years ago now. As Mars approached opposition, Lavelle of Java set the wires of the astronomical exchange palpitating with the amazing intelligence of a huge outbreak of incandescent gas upon the planet. It had occurred towards midnight of the 12th; and the spectroscope, to which he had at once resorted, indicated a mass of flaming gas, chiefly hydrogen, moving with an enormous velocity towards this earth. This jet of fire had become invisible about a quarter past twelve. He compared it to a colossal puff of flame suddenly and violently squirted out of the planet, "as flaming gases rushed out of a gun."

A singularly appropriate phrase it proved. Yet the next day there was nothing of this in the papers except a little note in the *Daily Telegraph*, and the world went in ignorance of one of the gravest dangers that ever threatened the human race. I might not have heard of the eruption at all had I not met Ogilvy, the well-known astronomer, at Ottershaw. He was immensely excited at the news, and in the excess of his feelings invited me up to take a turn with him that night in a scrutiny of the red planet.

. . . As I watched, the planet seemed to grow larger and smaller and to advance and recede, but that was simply that my eye was tired. Forty millions of miles it was from us—more than forty millions of miles of void. Few people realise the immensity of vacancy in which the dust of the material universe swims.

Near it in the field, I remember, were three faint points of light, three telescopic stars infinitely remote, and all around it was the unfathomable darkness of empty space. You know how that blackness looks on a frosty starlight night. In a telescope it seems far profounder. And invisible to me because it was so remote and small, flying swiftly and steadily towards me across that incredible distance, drawing nearer every minute by so many thousands of miles, came the Thing they were sending us, the Thing that was to bring so much struggle and calamity and death to the earth. I never dreamed of it then as I watched; no one on earth dreamed of that unerring missile.

THE FALLING STAR

Then came the night of the first falling-star. It was seen early in the morning rushing over Winchester eastward, a line of flame high in the atmosphere. Hundreds must have seen it, and taken it for an ordinary falling-star. Albin described it as leaving a greenish streak behind it that glowed for some seconds. Denning, our greatest authority on meteorites, stated that the height of its first appearance was about ninety or one hundred miles. It seemed to him that it fell to earth about one hundred miles east of him.

I was at home at that hour and writing in my study; and although my French windows face towards Ottershaw and the blind was up (for I loved in those days to look up at the night sky), I saw nothing of it. Yet this strangest of all things that ever came to earth from outer space must have fallen while I was sitting there, visible to me had I only looked up as it passed. Some of those who saw its flight say it travelled with a hissing sound. I myself heard nothing of that. Many people in Berkshire, Surrey, and Middlesex must have seen the fall of it, and, at most, have thought that another meteorite had descended. No one seems to have troubled to look for the falling mass that night.

But very early in the morning poor Ogilvy, who had seen the shooting-star and who was persuaded that a meteorite lay somewhere on the common between Horsell, Ottershaw, and Woking, rose early with the idea of finding it. Find it he did, soon after dawn, and not far from the sand-pits. An enormous hole had been made by the impact of the projectile, and the sand and gravel had been flung violently in every direction over the heath, forming heaps visible a mile and a half away. The heather was on fire eastward, and a thin blue smoke rose against the dawn.

The Thing itself lay almost entirely buried on sand, amidst the scattered splinters of a fir-tree it had shivered to fragments in its descent. The uncovered part had the appearance of a huge cylinder, caked over and its outline softened by a thick scaly dun-coloured incrustation. It had a diameter of about thirty yards. He approached the mass, surprised at the size and more so at the shape, since most meteorites are rounded more or less completely. It was, however, still so hot from its flight through the air as to forbid his near approach. A stirring noise within its cylinder he ascribed to the unequal cooling of its surface; for at that time it had not occurred to him that it might be hollow.

He remained standing at the edge of the pit that the Thing had made for itself, staring at its strange appearance, astonished chiefly at its unusual shape and colour, and dimly perceiving even then some evidence of design in its arrival. The early morning was wonderfully still, and the sun, just clearing the pine-trees towards Weybridge, was already warm. He did not remember hearing any birds that morning, there was certainly no breeze stirring, and the only sounds were the faint movements from within the cindery cylinder. He was all alone on the common.

Then suddenly he noticed with a start that some of the grey clinker, the ashy incrustation that covered the meteorite, was falling off the circular edge of the end. It was dropping off in flakes and raining down upon the sand. A large piece suddenly came off and fell with a sharp noise that brought his heart into his mouth.

For a minute he scarcely realized what this meant, and, although the heat was excessive, he clambered down into the pit close to the bulk to see the Thing more clearly. He fancied even then that the cooling of the body might account for this, but what disturbed that idea was the fact that the ash was falling only from the end of the cylinder.

And then he perceived that, very slowly, the circular top of the cylinder was rotating on its body. It was such a gradual movement that he discovered it only through noticing that a black mark that had been near him five minutes ago was now at the other side of the circumference. Even then he scarcely understood what this indicated, until he heard a muffled grating sound and saw the black mark jerk forward an inch or so. Then the thing came upon him in a flash. The cylinder was artificial—hollow—with an end that screwed out! Something within the cylinder was unscrewing the top!

"Good heavens!" said Ogilvy. "There's a man in it!—Men in it! Half roasted to death! Trying to escape!"

At once, with a quick mental leap, he linked the Thing with the flash upon Mars.

The thought of the confined creature was so dreadful to him that he forgot the heat, and went forward to the cylinder to help turn. But luckily the dull radiation arrested him before he could burn his hands on the still glowing metal. At that he stood irresolute for a moment, then turned, scrambled out of the pit, and set off running wildly into Woking. The time then must have been somewhere about six o'clock. He met a waggoner and tried to make him understand, but the tale he told and his appearance were so wild—his hat had fallen off in the pit—that the man simply drove on. He was equally unsuccessful with the potman who was just unlocking the doors of the public-house by Horsell Bridge. The fellow thought he was a lunatic at large and made an unsuccessful attempt to shut him into the tap-room. That sobered him a little; and when he saw Henderson, the London journalist, in his garden, he called over the palings and made himself understood.

"Henderson," he called, "you saw that shooting-star last night?"

"Well?" said Henderson.

"It's out on Horsell Common now."

"Good Lord!" said Henderson. "Fallen meteorite! That's good."

"But it's something more than a meteorite. It's a cylinder—an artificial cylinder, man! And there's something inside."

Henderson stood up with a spade in his hand.

"What's that?" he said. He was deaf in one ear.

Ogilvy told him all that he had seen. Henderson was a minute or so in taking it in. Then he dropped his spade, snatched up his packet, and came out into the road. The two men hurried back at once to the common, and found the cylinder still lying in the same position. But now the sounds inside had ceased, and a thin circle of bright metal showed between the top and the body of the cylinder. Air was either entering or escaping at the rim with a thin, sizzling sound.

They listened, rapped on the scaly burnt metal with a stick, and, meeting with no response, they both concluded the man or men inside must be insensible or dead.

Of course the two were quite unable to do anything. They shouted consolations and promises, and went off back to the town again to get help. One can imagine them, covered with sand, excited and disordered, running up the little street in the bright sunlight just as the shop folks were taking down their shutters and people were opening their bedroom windows. Henderson went into the railway station at once, in order to telegraph the news to London. The newspaper articles had prepared men's minds for the reception of the idea.

By eight o'clock a number of boys and unemployed men had already started for the common to see the "dead men from Mars."

— THE CYLINDER OPENS

When I returned to the common the sun was setting. Scattered groups were hurrying from the direction of Woking, and one or two persons were returning. The crowd about the pit had increased, and stood out black against the lemon-yellow of the sky—a couple of hundred people, perhaps. There were raised voices, and some sort of struggle appeared to be going on about the pit. Strange imaginings passed through my mind. As I drew nearer I heard Stent's voice:

"Keep back! Keep back!"

A boy came running towards me.

"It's a-movin' " he said to me as he passed.—"a-screwin' and a-screwin' out. I don't like it. I'm a-goin' 'ome, I am."

I went on to the crowd. There were really, I shouldn't think, two or three hundred people elbowing and jostling one another, the one or two ladies there being by no means the least active.

"He's fallen in the pit!" cried someone.

"Keep back!" said several.

The crowd swayed a little, and I elbowed my way through. Everyone seemed greatly excited. I heard a peculiar humming sound from the pit.

"I say!" said Ogilvy; "Help keep these idiots back. We don't know what's in the confounded thing, you know!"

I saw a young man, a shop assistant in Woking I believe he was, standing on the cylinder and trying to scramble out of the hole again. The crowd had pushed him in.

The end of the cylinder was being screwed out from within. Nearly two feet of shining screw projected. Somebody blundered against me, and I narrowly missed being pitched on to the top of the screw. I turned, and as I did so the screw must have come out, for the lid of the cylinder fell upon the gravel with a ringing concussion. I stuck my elbow into the person behind me, and turned my head towards the Thing again. For a moment that circular cavity seemed perfectly black. I had the sunset in my eyes.

I think everyone expected to see a man emerge—possibly something a little unlike us terrestrial men, but in all essentials a man. I know I did. But, looking, I presently saw something stirring within the shadow: greyish billowy movements, one above another, and then two luminous disks—like eyes. Then something resembling a little grey snake, about the thickness of a walking-stick, coiled up out of the writhing middle, and wriggling in the air towards me—and then another.

A sudden chill came over me. There was a loud shriek from a woman behind. I half turned, keeping my eyes fixed upon the cylinder still, from which other tentacles were now projecting, and began pushing my way back from the edge of the pit. I saw astonishment giving place to horror on the faces of the people about me. I heard inarticulate exclamations on all sides. There was a general movement backwards. I saw the shopman struggling still on the edge of the pit. I found myself alone, and saw the people on the other side of the pit running off, Stent among them. I looked again at the cylinder, and ungovernable terror gripped me. I stood petrified and staring.

A big greyish rounded bulk, the size, perhaps, of a bear, was rising slowly and painfully out of the cylinder. As it bulged up and caught the light, it glistened like wet leather.

Two large dark-colored eyes were regarding me steadfastly. The mass that framed them, the head of the Thing, it was rounded, and had, one might say, a face. There was a mouth under the eyes, the lipless brim of which quivered and panted, and dropped saliva. The whole creature heaved and pulsated convulsively. A lank tentacular appendage gripped the edge of the cylinder, another swayed in the air.

Those who have never seen a living Martian can scarcely imagine the strange horror of its appearance. The peculiar V-shaped mouth with its pointed upper lip, the absence of a chin beneath the wedgelike lower lip, the incessant quivering of this mouth, the Gorgon groups of tentacles, the tumultuous breathing of the lungs in a strange atmosphere, the evident heaviness and painfulness of movement due to the greater gravitational energy of the earth—above all, the extraordinary intensity of the immense eyes—were at once vital, intense, inhuman, crippled and monstrous. There was something fungoid in the oily brown skin, something in the clumsy deliberation of the tedious movements unspeakably nasty. Even at this first encounter, this first glimpse, I was overcome with disgust and dread.

Suddenly the monster vanished. It had toppled over the brim of the cylinder and fallen into the pit, with a thud like the fall of a great mass of leather. I heard it give a peculiar thick cry, and forthwith another of these creatures appeared darkly in the deep shadow of the aperture.

I turned and, running madly, made for the first group of trees, perhaps a hundred yards away; but I ran slantingly and stumbling, for I could not avert my face from these things.

THE HEAT-RAY

. . . After the glimpse I had of the Martians emerging from the cylinder in which they had come to the earth from their planet, a kind of fascination paralyzed my actions. I remained standing knee-deep in the heather, staring at the mound that hid them. I was a battle-ground of fear and curiosity.

. . . The sunset faded to twilight before anything further happened. The crowd far away on the left, towards Woking, seemed to grow, and I heard now a faint murmur from it. The little knot of people towards Chobham dispersed. There was scarcely an intimation of movement from the pit.

It was this, as much as anything, that gave people courage, and I suppose the new arrivals from Woking also helped to restore confidence. At any rate, as the dusk came on a slow, intermittent movement upon the sand-pits began, a movement that seemed to gather force as the stillness of the evening about the cylinder remained unbroken. Vertical black figures in twos and threes would advance stop, watch and advance again, spreading out as they did so in a thin irregular crescent that promised to enclose the pit in its attenuated horns. I, too, on my side began to move towards the pit.

Then I saw some cabmen and others had walked boldly into the sand-pits, and heard the clatter of hoofs and the gride of wheels. I saw a lad trundling off a barrow of apples. And then, within thirty yards of the pit, advancing from the direction of Horsell, I noted a little black knot of men, the foremost of whom was waving a white flag.

This was the Deputation. There had been a hasty consultation, and since the Martians were evidently, in spite of their repulsive forms, intelligent creatures, it had been resolved to show them, by approaching them with signals, that we too were intelligent.

Flutter, flutter, went the flag, first to the right, then to the left. It was too far for me to recognize any one there, but afterwards I learned that Ogilvy, Stent, and Henderson were with others in this attempt at communication. This little group had in its advance dragged inward, so to speak, the circumference of the now almost complete circle of people, and a number of dim black figures followed it at discreet distances.

Suddenly there was a flash of light, and a quantity of luminous greenish smoke came out of the pit in three distinct puffs, which drove up, one after the other, straight into the still air.

This smoke (or flame, perhaps, would be the better word for it) was so bright that the deep blue sky overhead and the hazy stretches of brown common towards Chertsey, set with black pine-trees, seemed to darken abruptly as these puffs arose, and to remain the darker after their dispersal. At the same time a faint hissing sound became audible.

Beyond the pit stood the little wedge of people with the white flag at its apex, arrested by these phenomena, a little knot of small vertical black shapes upon the black ground. As the green smoke arose, their faces flashed out pallid green, and faded again as it vanished. Then slowly the hissing passed into a humming, into a long, loud, droning noise. Slowly a humped shade rose out of the pit, and the ghost of a beam of light seemed to flicker out from it.

Forthwith flashes of actual flame, a bright glare leaping from one to another, sprang from the scattered group of men. It was as if some invisible jet impinged upon them and flashed into white flame. It was as if each man were suddenly and momentarily turned to fire.

Then, by the light of their own destruction, I saw them staggering and falling, and the supporters turning to run.

I stood staring, not as yet realizing that this was death leaping from man to man in that little distant crowd. All I felt was that it was something very strange. An almost noiseless and blinding flash of light, and a man fell headlong and lay still; and as the unseen shaft of heat passed over them, pine-trees burst into fire, and every dry furze-brush became with one dull thud a mass of flames.

. . . All this had happened with such swiftness that I had stood motionless, dumbfounded and dazzled by the flashes of light. Had that death swept through a full circle, it must inevitably have slain me in my surprise. But it passed and spared me, and left the night about me suddenly dark and unfamiliar.

. . . Then suddenly the trees in the pine-wood ahead of me were parted, as brittle reeds are parted by a man thrusting through them; they were snapped off and driven headlong, and a huge tripod appeared, rushing, as it seemed, headlong towards me . . .

Seen nearer, the Thing was incredibly strange, for it was no mere insensate machine driving on its way. Machine it was, with a ringing metallic pace, and long, flexible, glittering tentacles (one of which gripped a young pine-tree) swinging and rattling about its strange body. It picked its road as it went striding along, and the brazen hood that surmounted it moved to and fro with the inevitable suggestion of a head looking about. Behind the main body was a huge mass of white metal like a gigantic fisherman's basket, and puffs of green smoke squirted out from the joints of the limbs as the monster swept by me. And in an instant it was gone.

As it passed it set up an exultant deafening howl that drowned the thunder—"Aloo! Aloo"—and in another minute it was with its companions, half a mile away, stooping over something in the field. I have no doubt this Thing in the field was another of the cylinders they had fired at us from Mars.

VOCABULARY STUDY

VOCABULARY QUIZ 4-A

Words to Learn

scrutiny *terrestrial* *insensate*
irresolute *appendage*

Match each italicized word with the appropriate choice from the right.

Words in Context

1. "in a *scrutiny* of the red planet," p. 129.
2. "he stood *irresolute* for a moment," p. 131.
3. "unlike us *terrestrial* men," p. 133.
4. "a lank tentacular *appendage*," p. 134.
5. "no mere *insensate* machine," p. 136.

Definitions

a. a limb or subordinate part
b. an investigation, examination
c. lacking awareness or sensation
d. of or relating to earth
e. undecided, hesitant

VOCABULARY PRACTICE 4-A

Add a suitable selection from the above list to the sentences below.
low.

1. Most cats are _____ creatures, having little to do with water.

2. He considered the people in commune-oriented societies to be too much like ants, too machine-like, too _____.

3. A close _____ of the footprints proved that they were not those of the suspect.

4. Those people heard to say, "I would give my right arm for . . . ," actually would not give up an _____ for any reason!

5. The _____ behavior of Parliament caused inflation to become progressively worse.

SUGGESTIONS FOR DISCUSSION AND WRITING

1. What impelled monstrous creatures from Mars to descend upon Earth with the sole and implacable purpose of destroying humanity?

2. The spaceships which brought the Martians to Earth, and their awesome weapons, demonstrate a high level of technology. May we not, therefore, assume that they could have devised some means of communicating with us, if only to offer us their terms for surrender—and survival? Yet, they did not. Why?

3. The story has a happy ending: about three weeks after their arrival—but not until they had devastated the English countryside and most of London—the "visitors" began to droop, to wither, and to die . . . just like that! Mr. Wells explains that we humans have become immune to the effects of most of the bacterial diseases ever present in the air we breathe and in the things we eat and touch. But, in his own words, "there are no bacteria on Mars, and directly these invaders arrived, directly they drank and fed, our microscopic allies began their overthrow—They were irrevocably doomed, dying and rotting even as they went to and fro." H. G. Wells was a social reformer who had abandoned socialism to work for a better world, but with methods and ideas of his own. In view of this fact, can you *sense* a message in this fantastic and terrifying story? If so, what is it?

4. While none of us has ever seen a Martian, we tend to believe the author's vivid picture of the revolting creature (page 139). The single effect he achieves helps unify all the specific details in his gripping picture. What single effect was Wells trying to convey? What part of the Martian does he focus upon? Why does he omit detailed description of the creature's body?

OF COURSE

CHAD OLIVER

IN BERN, Switzerland, quite early in the morning, the President woke up with a splitting headache. He hadn't been sleeping well for the past three weeks, and last night had been worse than usual. He stayed in bed for a few minutes, frowning at the ceiling. It was an unpleasant situation to be in; there was no denying that. The President, however, had confidence. Surely, with its record since the Congress of Vienna in 1815, the outlook was good for his country. The President managed a smile. Switzerland would be the one, of course.

In Moscow, Russia, seated at the end of a long table, the Premier listened intently to his chief military advisors. He didn't like the position in which he found himself, but he wasn't really worried. There could be no doubt whatever that the Supreme Soviet would be the one chosen. Of course!

In London, England, the Prime Minister stepped out of 10 Downing Street, his pipe smoking determinedly. He climbed into his car for the drive to the Palace, and folded his strong hands. Things might be a bit touch-and-go for a short time, but the Prime Minister was undismayed. England with its glorious history, was the only possible choice. Of course it would be England!

To the east of Lake Victoria in Africa, the tall, slender priest-chief of the Masai, the Laibon, looked out upon the humped cattle grazing on the grassland and smiled. There was but one true God, Em-Gai, and the pastoral Masai were proud. At long last, ancient wrongs would be corrected! The Masai would rise again. They were the only logical choice. Of course . . .

And so it went around the world.

The somewhat dumpy gentleman in the rimless spectacles and the double-breasted suit had a name:

Morton Hillford. He had a title to go with the name: presidential advisor.

Right now, he was pacing the floor.

"You say you've investigated *all* the possibilities, General?" he demanded. "All the . . . um-m-m . . . angles?"

The general, whose name was Larsen, had an erect bearing and iron-gray hair, both of which were very useful when senators had to be impressed. He was a general who knew his business. Naturally, he was upset.

He said: "Every possible line of action has been explored, Mr. Hillford. Every angle has been studied thoroughly."

Morton Hillford stopped pacing. He aimed a forefinger at the general as though it were a .45. His expression indicated strongly that if there had been a trigger he might have pulled it. "Do you mean to tell me, sir, that the United States Army is impotent?"

The general frowned. He coughed briefly. "Well," he said, "let's say that the United States Army is *helpless* in this matter."

"I don't care what words you use! Can you *do* anything?"

"No," said the general, "we can't. And neither, may I point out, can the Navy, the Air Force, or the Marines."

"Or the Coast Guard," mimicked Morton Hillford. He resumed his pacing. "Why *can't* you do anything? That's your job, isn't it?"

General Larsen flushed. "I'm sorry, Mr. Hillford. Our job, as you point out, is to defend the country. We are prepared to do that to the best of our ability, no matter what the odds—"

"Oh, forget it, Larsen. I didn't mean to get under your hide. I guess my breakfast just didn't agree with me this morning. I understand your position in this matter. It's . . . embarrassing, that's all."

"To say the least," agreed General Larsen. "But I venture to say that we've thought of everything from hydrogen bombs to psychological warfare. We have absolutely nothing that stands the ghost of a chance of working. A hostile move on our part would be suicide for all of us, Mr. Hillford. I deplore melodrama, but facts are facts. It wouldn't do to let the people know just how much in their power we are, but nevertheless we *are* on the hook and there isn't any way that I know of to get them off again. We'll keep trying, naturally, but the President must have the correct facts at his disposal. There isn't a thing we can do at the present time.

"Well, General, I appreciate your candor, even if you have little else to offer. It looks as though we will have to keep our fingers crossed and a great big smile on our collective face. The President isn't going to like it though, Larsen."

"I don't like it either," Larsen said.

Morton Hillford paused long enough to look out of the window at the streets of Washington. It was summer, and the sun had driven most people indoors, although there were a few helicopters and cars visible. The old familiar buildings and monuments were there, however, and they imparted to him a certain sense of stability, if not of security.

It's not the heat, his mind punned silently, *it's the humility.*

"We'll just have to trust to their good judgment, I suppose," Morton Hillford said aloud. "It could be worse."

"Much worse," the general agreed. "The position of the United States in the world today—"

Hillford brushed the words aside impatiently. "There isn't the slightest doubt of it! That isn't our problem. Of *course* the United States will be chosen."

"Of course," echoed the general.

"And then everything will be all right, won't it, Larsen?"

"Of course!"

"Just the same," said Morton Hillford pointedly, "you find us a weapon that will work, and do it in a hurry."

"We'll try, Mr. Hillford."

"You *do* it, General. That's all for today."

The general left, keeping his thoughts to himself.

Morton Hillford, presidential advisor, resumed his pacing. Fourteen steps to the window, fourteen steps back. Pause. Light a cigarette. Fourteen steps to the window—

"Of course," he said aloud, "it will be the United States."

And his mind added a postscript: It had BETTER be the United States.

Three weeks ago, the ship had come out of space.

It was a big ship, at least as far as Earth was concerned. It was a good half-mile long, fat and sleek and polished, like a well-fed silver fish in the shallows of a deep and lonely sea. It didn't do much of anything. It just hung high in the air directly above the United Nations building in New York.

Waiting.

Like a huge trick cigar about to blow up in your face.

Simultaneously with its appearance, every government on Earth got a message. Every government got the same message. The ship wasn't fussy about defining "government," either. It contacted every sort of political division. In certain instances where the recipients were illiterate, or nonliterate, the message was delivered vocally.

Every message was sent in the native language. In itself, that was enough to give a man food for thought. There were a lot of languages on Earth, and many of them had never been written down.

The people who came in the ship, what was seen of them, looked quite human.

There was a great deal of talk and frenzied activity when the spaceship and the messages appeared. For one thing, no one had ever seen a spaceship before. However, the novelty of that soon wore off. People had been more or less expecting a spaceship, and they tended to accept it philosophically, as they had accepted electricity and airplanes and telephones and atom bombs. Fine stuff, naturally. What's next?

The message was something else again.

The United Nations and the United States greeted the ship from space with about one and a half cheers. Contact with other worlds was very dramatic and important and all that, but it *did* pose a number of unpleasant questions.

It is difficult to negotiate unless you have something to offer, or else are strong enough so that you don't have to dicker.

Suppose the ship wasn't friendly?

The United States dug into its bag of military tricks and investigated. They weren't fools about it, either. No one went off and tried to drop a hydrogen bomb on an unknown quantity. It was recognized at once that dropping a bomb on the ship might be like hunting a tiger with a cap pistol.

The military looked into the matter, subtly.

They probed, gently, and checked instruments.

The results were not encouraging.

The ship had some sort of a field around it. For want of a better name, it was called a force field. Definitely, it was an energy screen of some sort—and nothing could get through it. It was absolutely impregnable. It was the ultimate armor.

If a man has really foolproof armor and you don't, then you're out of luck.

The military couldn't fight.

After digesting the message, there didn't seem to be much for the diplomats to do either.

The message contained no explicit threat; it was simply a statement of intentions. If anything, it suffered from a certain annoying vagueness that made it difficult to figure out exactly *what* the ship was going to do.

The message read:

"PLEASE DO NOT BE ALARMED. WE HAVE COME IN PEACE ON A MISSION OF GOOD WILL. OUR TASK HERE IS TO DETERMINE TO OUR SATISFACTION WHICH ONE AMONG YOU HAS THE MOST ADVANCED CULTURE ON YOUR PLANET. IT WILL BE NECESSARY TO TAKE ONE REPRESENTATIVE FROM YOUR MOST ADVANCED CULTURE BACK WITH US FOR STUDY. HE WILL NOT BE HARMED IN ANY WAY. IN RETURN FOR HIM, WE WILL UNDERTAKE TO SUPPLY HIS CULTURE WITH WHATEVER IT MOST DESIRES, TO THE BEST OF OUR ABILITIES. WE SINCERELY HOPE THAT WE WILL CAUSE YOU NO INCONVENIENCE AS WE WORK. IT IS SUGGESTED THAT YOU DO NOT ATTEMPT TO COMMUNICATE WITH THIS SHIP UNTIL OUR CHOICE HAS BEEN ANNOUNCED. IT IS ALSO SUGGESTED THAT HOSTILE ACTION ON YOUR PART SHOULD BE CAREFULLY AVOIDED. WE HAVE COME IN PEACE AND WISH TO LEAVE THE SAME WAY WHEN OUR JOB IS DONE.

THANK YOU FOR YOUR COURTESY. WE ARE ENJOYING YOUR PLANET."

That was all.

On the face of it, the message was not too alarming, however unprecedented it may have been. However, second thoughts came fast.

Suppose, thought the United States, that Russia is chosen. Suppose, further, that what Russia most desired was an unbeatable weapon to use against the United States—what then? And suppose, thought Russia, that the United States is chosen—

The situation was somewhat uncomfortable.

It was made decidedly worse by the complete helplessness of the contestants.

There wasn't a thing they could do except to wait and see.

Of course, every single government involved was quite sure that it would be the one chosen. That being the case, the more discerning among them realized that no matter *who* was selected it would come as a shocking surprise to all the rest.

It did.

Morton Hillford, advisor to the President, got the news from the chief American delegate to the United Nations. The delegate hadn't trusted anyone with *this* hot potato; he had come in person, and at full speed.

When he got the news, Morton Hillford sat down, hard.

"That's ridiculous," he said.

"I know it," said the delegate. The shock had partially worn off for him, and he kept on his feet.

"I don't believe it," said Morton Hillford. "I'm sorry, Charlie, but I just don't believe it."

"Here," said the delegate, handing him the message, "you read it."

Hillford read it. His first impulse was to laugh. "Why, they're crazy!"

"Hardly."

Hillford managed to get to his feet and resume his pacing. His rimless spectacles were getting fogged from the heat, so he wiped them off with his handerchief.

"I feel like a fool," he said finally. He shook the message, almost angrily. "It's such a terrific anticlimax, Charlie!" Then, "are you sure they're not joking?"

"They're dead serious. They're going to exhibit the man in New York tomorrow. After that, they're going to show him off in every other capital on Earth. After *that*—"

He shrugged.

Morton Hillford felt a sick sinking in the pit of his stomach. "Do you want to tell the Boss, Charlie?"

"No," said the delegate. "A thousand times no. I've got to get back to the U. N., Mort. *You* tell him."

"Me?"

"Who else?"

Morton Hillford accepted his burden with what stoicism he could muster. His not to reason why—

"Let's have a drink first, Charlie," he said wearily. "Just a small one."

As it turned out, they both told him.

The President eyed them intently, hands on his hips, and demanded to see the message. They showed it to him.

The President was not a handsome man, but he had strength in his features. His rather cold blue eyes were alert and intelligent, and they seldom followed his mouth's lead when he smiled.

He wasn't smiling now, anywhere.

"Well, Boss," asked Morton Hillford, "what do we do now?"

The President frowned. "We'll have to go on with a telecast as soon as possible," he said, speaking with authority. "We'll have to tell the people *something*. Get Doyle and Blatski on that right away, Mort—and tell them to write it up with some sort of a positive slant if they can. Soothe their pride, indicate we're not unwilling to learn, throw in something about unknown science and mysterious factors . . . you know. After that, we'll have to get a project set up to study this whole affair." He consulted the message again. "Hm-m-m. I see they're coming back in one hundred of our years to check up on us. Fine! By then we may have something to argue with in case they mean trouble, although I doubt it. I pity the man in office when they come back—I hope he's a member of the Loyal Opposition. Now! We've got to find out what this is all about."

The United Nations delegate ventured one word: "How?"

The President sat down at his desk and lit a cigarette. He blew smoke out through his compressed lips, slowly. It was a good pose, and he liked it. As a matter of fact, he was a man who relished difficult problems—even this one. He liked action, and routine bored him.

"We need a scientist," he announced. "And not a nuclear physicist this time. We need someone in here who can tell us something about these people. The fact is, we need a *social* scientist."

Morton Hillford warned: "Don't let the *Tribune* find out. They'll crucify you."

The President shrugged. "We'll keep it quiet," he said. "Now! As I said, we need a social scientist. The question is, which kind?"

"Not a psychologist," mused Morton Hillford. "Not yet, anyway. I'm afraid we need a sociologist. If the *Tribune* ever finds out—"

"Forget the papers, man! This is important."

The President got to work on his private telephone. "Hello . . . Henry? Something has come up. I want you to get over here right away, and I want you to bring a sociologist with you. That's right, a *sociologist*. What that? Yes, I KNOW about the *Tribune*! Bring him in the back door."

In due course of time, Henry—who was Secretary of State—arrived. He brought a sociologist with him. The sociologist was unexpectedly normal-looking, and he listened respectfully to what the President had to say. He was naturally surprised when he heard about the ship's choice, but he recovered himself quickly.

The sociologist was an honest man. "I'm terribly sorry, Mr. President," he said. "I could take a stab at it if you like, but what you really need is an anthropologist over here, and hurry."

Henry hurried.

Four hours later, the anthropologist was shown into the President's office. His name was Edgar Vincent, he had a beard, and he smoked a foreign-looking pipe. Well, that couldn't be helped.

Introductions were hastily made. "You are an anthropologist?" asked the President.

"That's right, sir," said Dr. Vincent.

"Fine!" said the President. He leaned back in his chair and folded his hands. "Now we're getting somewhere."

Dr. Vincent looked blank.

"Tell me, Doctor," said the President, "what do you know about the Eskimos?"

The anthropologist stared.

"You don't mean—"

To save time, the President handed him the message that had been sent by the ship to the United Nations. "You might as well read this, Doctor," he said. "It will be released to the papers within an hour anyway, and then everybody will know."

Edgar Vincent puffed on his pipe and read the message:

"WE BRING YOU GREETINGS AND FAREWELL. OUR WORK AMONG YOU HAS NOW BEEN COMPLETED. WE HAVE FOUND THE MOST ADVANCED CULTURE AMONG YOU TO BE THAT OF THE CENTRAL ESKIMO OF BAFFIN LAND. WE HAVE SELECTED ONE MEMBER OF THAT CULTURE TO GO BACK WITH US FOR STUDY. AS INDICATED EARLIER, WE WILL UNDERTAKE TO PROVIDE HIS CULTURE WITH WHATEVER IT MOST DESIRES, BY WAY OF PAYMENT. THE REPRESENTATIVE OF THE HIGHEST CULTURE ON YOUR PLANET WILL BE EXHIBITED IN ALL YOUR POLITICAL CENTERS, AT TIMES WHICH WILL BE INDICATED IN A SEPARATE COMMUNICATION, TO PROVE TO YOU THAT HE HAS NOT BEEN HARMED. WE WILL RETURN TO YOUR WORLD IN ONE HUNDRED EARTH-YEARS, AT WHICH TIME WE HOPE TO DISCUSS MUTUAL PROBLEMS WITH YOU AT GREATER LENGTH. THANK YOU AGAIN FOR YOUR COURTESY. WE HAVE ENJOYED YOUR PLANET."

"Well?" asked the President.

"I hardly know what to say," said the anthropologist. "It's fantastic."

"We already know that, Doctor. say *something*.

Edgar Vincent found a chair and sat down. He stroked his beard thoughtfully. "In the first place," he said, 'I'm not really the man you want."

Henry groaned. "You're an anthropologist, aren't you?"

"Yes, yes, of course. But I'm a *physical* anthropologist. You know —bones and evolution and blood types and all that. I'm afraid that isn't quite what you are after here."

He held up his hand, holding off a wave of protest. "What you need is an ethnologist or social anthropologist, and the man you ought to get is Irvington; he's the Central Eskimo man." He held up his hand again. "Just a moment, please, gentlemen! As I say, you need Irvington. You won't be able to get him for some time, however. I suggest you put in a call for him—he's in Boston now—and in the meantime I'll fill you in as best I can. I do know a *little* cultural anthropology; we're not as specialized as all that."

Henry left to put in the call, and then hurried back. Vincent permitted himself a faint smile. It had been a long time since he had an audience *this* attentive!

"Can you think of any possible reason why an Eskimo might have been chosen?" asked Morton Hillford.

"Frankly, no."

"A secret civilization?" suggested the United Nations delegate. "A lost tribe? Something like that?"

Vincent snorted. "Nonsense," he said. "Sir," he added.

"Look," said the President. "We know they live in igloos. Go on from there."

Vincent smiled. "Even that isn't quite correct, I'm afraid," he said. "Begging your pardon, sir, but the Eskimos don't *live* in igloos, at least not most of the time. They live in skin tents in the summer, stone and earth houses in early winter—"

"Never mind that," the President said. "That's not important."

Vincent puffed on his pipe. "How do you know it isn't?"

"What? Oh . . . yes. Yes, I see what you mean." The President was nobody's fool. It was hardly his fault that he knew nothing about Eskimos. Who did?

"That's the catch, as you are beginning to understand, sir," Vincent said.

"But look here," put in Morton Hillford. "I don't mean to belittle your field of learning, Doctor, but the Eskimos simply aren't the most advanced civilization on this planet! Why, we've got a technology hundreds of years ahead of theirs, science they can't even guess at, a Bill of Rights, a political system centuries in the making—thousands of things! The Eskimos just don't rate."

Vincent shrugged. "To you they don't," he corrected. "But you're not doing the evaluation."

Morton Hillford persisted. "Suppose you were making the choice, Doctor. Would *you* choose an Eskimo?"

"No," admitted the anthropologist. "Probably not. But then, I'm looking at it from roughly the same values that you are. I'm an American too, you know."

"I think I see the problem," the President said slowly. "The people on that ship are far ahead of us— they must be, or they wouldn't *have* that ship. Therefore, their standards aren't the same as our standards. They're not adding up the points the same way we are. Is that right, Doctor?"

Vincent nodded. "That's what I would say, at a guess. It stands to reason. Maybe our culture has overlooked something important—something that outweighs all the big buildings and mass production and voting and all the rest of it. How do we know?"

The President drummed his fingers on his desk. "Let's look at it this way," he suggested. "Could it be that spiritual values are more important than technological progress—something like that?"

Vincent considered. "I don't think so," he said finally. "It might be *something* like that, but then why choose the Eskimos? There are plenty of people worse off in a technological sense than they are—the Eskimos are quite skilled mechanically. They've invented a number of things, such as snow goggles and hunting techniques and intricate harpoon heads. They're quite good at gadgetry, as a matter of fact. I don't think we can throw technology out of the window; it isn't that simple. And as for 'spiritual values,' they're apt to be tricky to handle. Offhand, I wouldn't say that Eskimos had any more than other people, and it's even possible that they have less. Look at India, say—they have *really* put the emphasis on religion. I think you're headed in the right direction, maybe, but you're not on the right track yet."

The delegate from the United Nations wiped his brow. "Well then, what *have* the Eskimos got?"

"More money," sighed the President, a trifle grimly. "Doctor, can't you give us something to go on, just provisionally? I've got a cabinet meeting in an hour, and I have to go in there and say something. And after that, there'll be a television address, and the newspapers, and the foreign diplomats, and Congress, and God knows what all. This won't be so funny a few years from now. Any ideas, Doctor?"

Vincent did his best. "The Eskimos have made a remarkable adjustment to their environment at their technological level," he said slowly. "They're often used as examples of that. I recall one anthropologist who mentioned that they have no word for war, and no conception of it. That might be a good angle to work on. For the rest, you'll have to talk to Irvington. I'm out of my element."

"Well, thanks very much, Dr. Vincent," the President said. "I appreciate your help. And now, let's *all* have a small drink."

They adjourned to another room, all talking furiously, to get ready for the cabinet meeting to come.

Morton Hillford was the last to leave the President's office.

"Eskimos," he said sadly, shaking his head. *"Eskimos."*

Next morning, strictly according to schedule, a smaller ship detached itself from the huge spaceship that hovered high in the sky above the United Nations building in New York.

For the onlooking millions, in person and via television, it was difficult to avoid the impression of a cigarette emerging from a large silver cigar.

The little ship landed, as gently as a falling leaf, in the area that had been cleared for it. A small bubble of force, glinting slightly in the morning sun, surrounded the ship. A circular portal slid open and the exhibition began.

It was simplicity itself.

Two tall, pleasant-looking men stepped out of the ship, staying within the energy shield. Their dress was unique, but rather on the conservative side. They leaned back into the portal and appeared to be speaking to someone.

A bit reluctantly, the Eskimo stepped outside and stood with them. He was dressed in new clothes and looked uncomfortable. He was short, a little on the plump side, and his hair was uncombed.

He gaped at New York City in frank astonishment.

He smiled with shy pleasure.

With only a trace of prompting from the two men, he waved cheerfully to the crowd that had gathered to see him. He stood there, smiling, for two minutes, and then he was escorted back into the ship.

The ship floated soundlessly into the air, and curved up to rejoin the larger ship above.

That was all there was.

The exhibition was over.

Right on schedule, it was repeated elsewhere.

In Bern, Switzerland.
In Moscow, Russia.
In London, England.
In the land of the Masai, in East Africa.
In China, Sweden, Australia, Mexico, Finland, Brazil, Samoa, Turkey, Greece, Japan, Tibet—
All around the world.

And, of course, everywhere the ship went it raised some highly annoying questions. Of course, every government *knew* that a mistake had somehow been made.

But just the same—

As suddenly as it had come, the great spaceship was gone. Its jets flickered with atomic flame, its outlines blurred, and it flashed back into the dark sea from which it had come.

It was headed for Procyon, eleven light-years distant, to check up on the results of a previous experiment that had taken place roughly a century ago.

The Eskimo wandered about the ship, munching on a fish, and tried to figure out what was going on.

Two men watched him, amused but not impressed.

"Well, anyhow," observed the first man, "his people will have plenty of seals from now on."

"Right enough," agreed the second man. "And we can put *him* down on Armiqe—he should be right at home there, and no harm done."

"It's high time we got around to Earth, if you ask me," said the first. "That planet is getting to be the eyesore of our sector."

"Oh, Earth will come along," said the second. "They really *are* making some progress down there, finally."

The Eskimo selected another fish out of his private bucket and watched the two men without interest.

"It must have been something of a shock when we selected *him*. An awfully nice chap, but he *is* a bit on the primitive side."

"A slight stimulus never hurt anyone, my friend. By the time they get through worrying about Eskimo, they ought to have a *real* science down there."

The first man yawned and stretched. "And when we come back in a hundred years," he said, "you know which one of them we'll find with a culture *really* advanced enough so that we can offer them a place in Civilization."

The second man nodded. "Of course," he said, and smiled.

The Eskimo helped himself to another fish out of the bucket and wandered over to the window.

VOCABULARY STUDY

VOCABULARY QUIZ 4-B

Words to Learn

melodrama *sleek* *stoicism*
candor *impregnable*

Match each italicized word with the appropriate choice from the right.

Words in Context

1. "I deplore *melodrama*," p. 140.
2. "I appreciate your *candor*," p. 140.
3. "fat and *sleek* and polished," p. 141.
4. "absolutely *impregnable*," p. 142.
5. "accepted the burden . . . with *stoicism*," p. 143.

Definitions

a. unconquerable
b. smooth, glossy
c. indifference to pleasure or pain
d. fairness, sincerity
e. a sensational or romantic play

VOCABULARY PRACTICE 4-B

Add a suitable selection from the above vocabulary list to the sentences below.

1. Because it was at the summit of a very steep mountain, the fortress was considered _____.
2. The Doberman pinscher has a _____ black and tan coat.

3. _____ is a virtue which brave men share with dumb animals.

4. An opera is nothing but a _____ set to music.

5. When he was told that he had no chance of passing, Jimmy thanked his instructors for their _____.

SUGGESTIONS FOR DISCUSSION AND WRITING

1. Sometimes it is possible to gain a richer interpretation of a story if we compare it (find likenesses) or contrast it (find differences) with another, somewhat similar story. Write a short essay in which you *contrast* the two initially similar selections, *The War of the Worlds* and "Of Course." Use the following introductory statement if you wish, or write one of your own:

> Both *The War of the Worlds* by H. G. Wells and "Of Course" by Chad Oliver begin with a visit to earth by an alien space vehicle. But there the similarity ends.

Continue with an orderly discussion of differences between the two stories. In which is there warning of the visit, for example; in which not? In which is the city of London and its surrounding countryside involved, and in which the entire world? How did each visitor "land"? How did their intentions differ? And so on.

2. Write a brief explanation of the space visitors' purpose in naming the Eskimos the most advanced civilization on Earth. What repercussions did they expect on Earth?

CHAPTER 4   CUMULATIVE VOCABULARY LIST

1. *adroitly*—skillfully
2. *apparition*—appearance, ghost
3. *appendage*—a limb or subordinate part
4. *ardent*—eager, driven
5. *askew*—sideways
6. *assailed*—attacked, assaulted
7. *assiduously*—steadily, attentively
8. *attenuated*—made thin or weak
9. *austere*—somber, stern
10. *Babel*—a noisy scene
11. *banal*—wanting originality or freshness
12. *candor*—fairness, sincerity
13. *catatonic*—in a stupor
14. *cerebral*—of the brain
15. *correlation*—interdependence
16. *countenance*—face, expression
17. *debility*—weakness
18. *denizens*—inhabitants, those who frequent a place
19. *derangement*—disturbance
20. *diorama*—a spectacular, three-dimensional scene
21. *efficacy*—effectiveness
22. *enigmas*—puzzles
23. *execrable*—very bad, detestable
24. *exhilaration*—animation, joy, liveliness
25. *explicit*—plain, direct
26. *facilitate*—make easier
27. *fragrance*—odor, scent
28. *hindrance*—impediment
29. *hypertension*—high blood pressure
30. *imminent*—impending, threatening
31. *immutable*—not changeable
32. *impregnable*—unconquerable
33. *incontinently*—without control
34. *indolence*—laziness, sloth
35. *insensate*—lacking awareness or sensation
36. *interminable*—endless
37. *intermittent*—returning at intervals
38. *intrepid*—fearless

39. *irresolute*—undecided, hesitant
40. *lassitude*—weariness, fatigue
41. *latitude*—distance in degrees from the equator
42. *ludicrous*—laughable, absurd
43. *melodrama*—a sensational or romantic play
44. *meridian*—an imaginary circle passing through both poles
45. *morbid*—despondent, diseased
46. *palpitation*—rapid beating
47. *patriarchs*—fathers or founders
48. *piqued*—challenged or angered
49. *poignant*—pathetic, heart-rending
50. *prodigious*—enormous, extraordinary
51. *progeny*—offspring
52. *protagonist*—main character
53. *provincial*—sectional
54. *purports*—means, intends
55. *rapacious*—excessively grasping or consuming
56. *resuscitation*—revival
57. *retorted*—replied sharply
58. *rudimentary*—undeveloped
59. *schizophrenia*—mental disorder, split personality
60. *scrutiny*—an investigation, examination
61. *sleek*—smooth, glossy
62. *stocism*—indifference to pleasure or pain
63. *sumptuously*—in luxury
64. *surly*—gloomy, rough
65. *symmetry*—balance, harmony
66. *synthesized*—artificially manufactured
67. *tenets*—beliefs
68. *terrestrial*—of or relating to earth
69. *traverse*—to pass through, to cross
70. *undulating*—swaying, moving in waves
71. *vociferations*—outcries

Portrait of Sir Thomas More by Hans Holbein. Copyright The Frick Collection, New York.

Chapter 5

CHANGING THE WORLD FOR BETTER OR WORSE

One of the most conspicuous accomplishments of science fiction writers is the projection of social history, particularly as it prognosticates the quality of life we might expect in our futures . . . or, at least, in the futures of our children. Writers such as Aldous Huxley or George Orwell make the chilling observation that impersonal forces like ecology, scarcity, overpopulation, overmechanization, and overpersuasion by private enterprise and government alike are even now effecting changes in our thoughts and habits. More and more, they suggest, we are becoming a common people, a people of unified thought, a consuming mass, a suggestible herd. *Nineteen Eighty-Four* and *Brave New World* are books which should be read as warnings that we must resist the threats to humanity which continue to grip us.

Isaac Asimov's story "The Fun They Had" and Ray Bradbury's "August 2026: There Will Come Soft Rains" both allude to our technological resourcefulness as a threat to our humanity.

Not all writers have been so pessimistic about man's future. Recurrently throughout literary history, authors have dreamed of better futures for us all. In a time of war and social upheaval (1516), Sir Thomas More wrote his *Utopia* (the word means "no place" in Greek), an essay romance describing an imaginary commonwealth in which political organization, education, religion, and industry approach perfection. Similarly, Edward Bellamy wrote *Looking Backward* in 1888, another era of spiritual and social disruption. *Looking Backward* envisions a cooperative commonwealth in which all people work and share alike, in happiness, culture, and health. William Harben's "In the Year Ten-Thousand" (in Chapter 1) also describes an ideal state, as do Francis Bacon's *New Atlantis* (1626), Thomas Hobbes' *Leviathan* (1651), Bulwer-Lytton's *The Coming Race* (1871), William Morris's *News from Nowhere* (1891), W. D. Howells' *A Traveler from Altruria* (1894), and H. G. Wells' *A Modern Utopia* (1905).

Thus, it is not true that science fiction has always found it necessary to depict the future with a bleak and somber brush. It is a fact, however, that most contemporary projections of social history seem to be anti-utopian in nature . . . possibly in reaction to the unattractive aspects of the "utopian-like" regimes now prevailing in the Soviet Union and mainland China.

A Selection from

Utopia

SIR THOMAS MORE

THEREFORE THEY have accumulated an inestimable amount of gold and silver, but they do not keep it in the form of treasure. I am reluctant to tell you how they keep it, for fear you will not believe me. I would not have believed it myself if anyone had told me about it—not unless I had seen it with my own eyes. It is almost always true that the more different anything is from what people are used to, the harder it is to believe. In view of the fact that the Utopians' customs are so different from ours, a shrewd judge will not be surprised to find that they do not use gold and silver at all as we do. Since they keep gold and silver only for grave contingencies, they take care that in the meantime no one shall value these metals more than they deserve. Iron is obviously greatly superior to either. Men can no more do without iron than without fire or water. But gold and silver have no indispensable qualities. Human folly has made them precious only because of their scarcity. Nature, like a wise and generous parent, has placed the best things everywhere and in the open, such as air and water and the earth itself, but she has hidden vain and useless things in remote and faraway places.

If they kept their gold and silver guarded in a tower, foolish people might suspect the prince and senate of deceiving the citizens and aiming at some advantage for themselves. If they made plate and wrought-metal work out of them, they would not want to give up such articles and melt them down to pay mercenaries. To solve the problem, they have thought out a plan as much in accord with their institutions as it is contrary to ours. The plan seems incredible to us (except to those of us who are very wise), because we regard gold as of great value and hoard it carefully. While their eating and drinking utensils are made of china and glass, beautiful but inexpensive, their chamber pots and stools both in their public halls and their homes are made of gold and silver. They also use these metals for the chains and fetters of their bondmen. They hang gold rings from the ears of criminals, place gold rings on their fingers, gold collars around their necks, and gold crowns on their heads. Thus they hold gold and silver up to scorn in every way.

The result is that when there is need to part with these metals, which others give up as painfully as if their vitals were being torn out, none of the Utopians regard it as any more than the loss of a penny, so to speak. They find pearls on their shores and diamonds and carbuncles on certain rocks, but they do not search for them. If they find them by chance, they polish them and adorn their younger children with them. As children they take pride and pleasure in such ornaments, and consequently put them aside when they are older and observe that only children use such baubles. This results from their own sense of propriety and not from their parents' commands, just as our children throw away their nuts, amulets, and dolls, when they grow up.

VOCABULARY STUDY

VOCABULARY QUIZ 5-A

Words to Learn

prognosticates *indispensable*
utopian *remote*
contingencies

Match each italicized word with the appropriate choice from the right.

Words in Context

1. "it *prognosticates* the quality," p. 155.
2. "*utopian*-like regimes," p. 155.
3. "for grave *contingencies*," p. 157.
4. "no *indispensable* qualities," p. 157.
5. "in *remote* and faraway places," p. 157.

Definitions

a. possibilities
b. absolutely necessary
c. far off, distant
d. foretells, predicts
e. idealistic, impractical

VOCABULARY PRACTICE 5-A

Add a suitable selection from the above vocabulary list to the sentences below.

1. The Alaskan oil deposits are located in the _____ reaches of the frozen northern tundra.

2. The gloomy leader of a strange cult regularly _____ the end of the world in the near future.

3. Our city has an emergency water supply adequate for all the _____ _____ which might arise.

4. The football team soon found out that its starting quarterback was _____; without him, the team was unable to score all afternoon against the tough Tiger defense.

5. Many consider the United Nations a _____ dream, not able to solve the complex political problems of our time.

SUGGESTIONS FOR DISCUSSION AND WRITING

1. Sir Thomas More is the only author in this volume who is a major figure in English history, as well as a martyr in the Roman Catholic Church. Lord chancellor for King Henry VIII in 1529, he incurred the king's wrath when he disapproved of Henry's divorce from Katherine of Aragon, and was eventually beheaded. By describing how a superior people disposes of "vain and useless things" like gold, silver, and precious stones, Sir Thomas More is, of course, commenting upon our habits here on the real globe. *Utopia*, in fact, is a series of interesting discourses on such human concerns as war, international bad faith, education, religion, art, and so on, all more important in what they say about us than about the ideal society. You might want to read more of *Utopia* yourself, but meanwhile, draw up a series of "idealized" visions of a better world that also pointedly criticizes your own world.

2. A typical American household does not contain very much gold or precious jewelry, but there are possessions—material possessions—that might be labeled "vain and useless things." Name some of them and try to find "better" uses for them in the spirit of the Utopians. What values might we substitute for material ones?

A Selection from

Looking Backward

EDWARD BELLAMY

"HE IS going to open his eyes. He had better see but one of us at first."

"Promise me, then, that you will not tell him."

The first voice was a man's, the second a woman's, and both spoke in whispers.

"I will see how he seems," replied the man.

"No, no, promise me," persisted the other.

"Let her have her way," whispered a third voice, also a woman.

"Well, well, I promise, then," answered the man. "Quick, go! He is coming out of it."

There was a rustle of garments and I opened my eyes. A fine looking man of perhaps sixty was bending over me, an expression of much benevolence mingled with great curiosity upon his features. He was an utter stranger. I raised myself on an elbow and looked around. The room was empty. I certainly had never been in it before, or one furnished like it. I looked back at my companion. He smiled.

"How do you feel?" he inquired.

"Where am I?" I demanded.

"You are in my house," was the reply.

"How came I here?"

"We will talk about that when you are stronger. Meanwhile, I beg you will feel no anxiety. You are among friends and in good hands. How do you feel?"

"A bit queerly," I replied, "but I am well, I suppose. Will you tell me how I came to be indebted to your hospitality? What has happened to me? How came I here? It was in my own house that I went to sleep."

"There will be time enough for explanations later," my unknown host replied, with a reassuring smile. "It will be better to avoid agitating talk until you are a little more yourself. Will you oblige me by taking a couple of swallows of this mixture? It will do you good. I am a physician."

I repelled the glass with my hand and sat up on the couch,

161

although with an effort, for my head was strangely light.

"I insist upon knowing at once where I am and what you have been doing with me," I said.

"My dear sir," responded my companion, "let me beg that you will not agitate yourself. I would rather you did not insist upon explanations so soon, but if you do, I will try to satisfy you, provided you will first take this draught, which will strengthen you somewhat."

I thereupon drank what he offered me. Then he said, "It is not so simple a matter as you evidently suppose to tell you how you came here. You can tell me quite as much on that point as I can tell you. You have just been roused from a deep sleep, or, more properly, trance. So much I can tell you. You say you were in your own house when you fell into that sleep. May I ask you when that was?"

"When?" I replied, "when? Why, last evening, of course, at about ten o'clock. I left my man Sawyer orders to call me at nine o'clock. What has become of Sawyer?"

"I can't precisely tell you that," replied my companion, regarding me with a curious expression, "but I am sure that he is excusable for not being here. And now can you tell me a little more explicitly when it was that you fell into that sleep, the date, I mean?"

"Why, last night, of course; I said so, didn't I? That is, unless I have overslept an entire day. Great heavens! that cannot be possible; and yet I have an odd sensation of having slept a long time. It was Decoration Day that I went to sleep."

"Decoration Day?"

"Yes, Monday, the 30th."

"Pardon me, the 30th of what?"

"Why, of this month, of course, unless I have slept into June, but that can't be."

"This month is September."

"September! You don't mean that I've slept since May! God in heaven! Why, it is incredible."

"We shall see," replied my companion; "you say that it was May 30th when you went to sleep?"

"Yes."

"May I ask of what year?"

I stared blankly at him, incapable of speech, for some moments.

"Of what year?" I feebly echoed at last.

"Yes, of what year, if you please? After you have told me that I shall be able to tell you how long you have slept."

"It was the year 1887," I said.

My companion insisted that I should take another draught from the glass, and felt my pulse.

"My dear sir," he said, "your manner indicates that you are a man of culture, which I am aware was by no means the matter of course in your day it now is. No doubt, then, you have yourself made the observation that nothing in this world can be truly said to be more wonderful than anything else. The causes of all phenomena are equally adequate, and the results equally matters of course. That you should be startled by what I shall tell you is to be expected; but I am confident that you will not permit it to affect your equanimity unduly. Your appearance is that of a young man of barely thirty, and your bodily condition seems not greatly different from that of one just roused from a somewhat too long and profound sleep, and yet this is the tenth day of September in the year 2000, and you have slept exactly one hundred and thirteen years, three months, and eleven days."

Feeling partially dazed, I drank a cup of some sort of broth at my companion's suggestion, and, immediately afterward becoming very drowsy, went off into a deep sleep.

When I awoke it was broad daylight in the room, which had been lighted artificially when I was awake before. My mysterious host was sitting near. He was not looking at me when I opened my eyes, and I had a good opportunity to study him and meditate upon my extraordinary situation, before he observed that I was awake. My giddiness was all gone, and my mind perfectly clear. The story that I had been asleep one hundred and thirteen years, which, in my former weak and bewildered condition, I had accepted without question, recurred to me now only to be rejected as a preposterous attempt at an imposture, the motive of which it was impossible remotely to surmise.

Something extraordinary had certainly happened to account for my waking up in this strange house with this unknown companion, but my fancy was utterly impotent to suggest more than the wildest guess as to what that something might have been. Could it be that I was the victim of some sort of conspiracy? It looked so, certainly; and yet, if human lineaments ever gave true evidence, it was certain that this man by my side, with a face so refined and ingenuous, was no party to any scheme of crime or outrage. Then it occurred to me to question if I might not be the butt of some elaborate practical joke on the part of friends who had somehow learned the secret of my underground chamber and taken this means of impressing me with the peril of mesmeric experiments. There were great difficulties in the way of this theory; Sawyer would never have betrayed me, nor had I any friends at all likely to undertake such an enterprise; nevertheless the supposition that I was the victim of a practical joke seemed on the whole the only one tenable. Half expecting to catch a glimpse of some familiar face grinning from behind a chair or curtain, I looked carefully about the room. When my eyes next rested on my companion, he was looking at me.

"You have had a fine nap of twelve hours," he said briskly, "and I can see that it has done you good. You look much better. Your color is good and your eyes are bright. How do you feel?"

"I never felt better," I said, sitting up.

"You remember your first waking, no doubt," he pursued, "and your surprise when I told you how long you had been asleep?"

"You said, I believe, that I had slept one hundred and thirteen years."

"Exactly."

"You will admit," I said, with an ironical smile, "that the story was rather an improbable one."

"Extraordinary, I admit," he responded, "but given the proper conditions, not improbably nor inconsistent with what we know of the trance state. When complete, as in your case, the vital functions are absolutely suspended, and there is no waste of the tissues. No limit can be set to the possible duration of a trance when the external conditions protect the body from physical injury. This trance of yours is indeed the longest of which there is any positive record, but there is no known reason wherefore, had you not been discovered and had the chamber in which we found you continued intact, you might not have remained in a state of suspended animation till, at the end of indefinite ages, the gradual refrigeration of the earth had destroyed the bodily tissues and set the spirit free."

I had to admit that, if I were indeed the victim of a practical joke, its authors had chosen an admirable agent for carrying out their imposition. The impressive and even eloquent manner of this man would have lent dignity to an argument that the moon was made of cheese. The smile with which I had regarded him as he advanced his trance hypothesis did not appear to confuse him in the slightest degree.

"Perhaps," I said, "you will go on and favor me with some particulars as to the circumstances under which you discovered this chamber of which you speak, and its contents. I enjoy good fiction."

"In this case," was the grave reply, "no fiction could be so strange as the truth. You must know that these many years I have been cherishing the idea of building a laboratory in the large garden beside this house, for the purpose of chemical experiments for which I have a taste. Last Thursday the excavation for the cellar was at last begun. It was completed by that night, and Friday the masons were to have come. Thursday night we had a tremendous deluge of rain, and Friday morning I found my cellar a frog-pond and the walls quite washed down. My daughter, who had come out to view the disaster with me, called my attention to a corner of masonry laid bare by the crumbling away of one of the walls. I cleared a little earth from it, and, finding that it seemed part of a large mass, determined to investigate it. The workmen I sent for unearthed an oblong vault some eight feet below the surface, and set in the corner of what had evidently been the foundation walls of an ancient house. A layer of ashes and charcoal on the top of the vault showed that the house above had perished by fire. The vault itself was perfectly intact, the cement being as good as when first applied. It had a door, but this we could not force, and found entrance by removing one of the flagstones which formed the roof. The air which came up was stagnant but pure, dry and not cold. Descending with a lantern, I found myself in an apartment fitted up as a bedroom in the style of the nineteenth century. On the bed lay a young man. That he was dead and must have been dead a century was of course to be taken for granted; but the extraordinary state of preservation of the body struck me and the medical colleagues whom I had summoned with amazement. That the art of such embalming as this had ever been known we should not have believed, yet here seemed conclusive testimony that our immediate ancestors had possessed it. My medical colleagues, whose curiosity was highly excited, were at once for undertaking experiments to test the nature of the progress employed, but I withheld them. My motive in so doing, at least the only motive I now need speak of, was the recollection of something I once had read about the extent to which your contemporaries had cultivated the subject of animal magnetism. It had occurred to me as just conceivable that you might be in a trance, and that the secret of your bodily integrity after so long a time was not the craft of an embalmer, but life. So extremely fanciful did this idea seem, even to me, that I did not risk the ridicule of my fellow physicians by mentioning it, but gave some other reason for postponing their experiments. No sooner, however, had they left me, than I set on foot a systematic attempt at resuscitation, of which you know the result."

Had its theme been yet more incredible, the circumstantiality of this narrative, as well as the impressive manner and personality of the narrator, might have staggered a listener, and I had begun to feel very strangely, when, as he closed, I chanced to catch a glimpse of my reflection in a mirror hanging on the wall of the room. I rose and went up to it. The face I saw was the face to a hair and a line and not a day older than the one I had looked at as I tied my cravat before going to Edith that Decoration Day, which, as this man would have me believe, was celebrated one hundred and thirteen years before. At this, the colossal character of the fraud which was being attempted on me, came over me afresh. Indignation mastered my mind as I realized the outrageous liberty that had been taken.

"You are probably surprised," said my companion, "to see that, although you are a century older than when you lay down to sleep in that underground chamber, your appearance is unchanged. That should not amaze you. It is by virtue of the total arrest of the vital functions that you have survived this great period of time. If your body could have undergone any change during your trance, it would long ago have suffered dissolution."

"Sir," I replied, turning to him, "what your motive can be in reciting to me with a serious face this remarkable farrago, I am utterly unable to guess; but you are surely yourself too intelligent to suppose that anybody but an imbecile could be deceived by it. Spare me any more of this elaborate nonsense and once for all tell me whether you refuse to give me an intelligible account of where I am and how I came here. If so, I shall proceed to ascertain my whereabouts for myself, whoever may hinder."

"You do not, then, believe that this is the year 2000?"

"Do you really think it necessary to ask me that?" I returned.

"Very well," replied my extraordinary host. "Since I cannot convince you, you shall convince yourself. Are you strong enough to follow me upstairs?"

"I am as strong as I ever was," I replied angrily, "as I may have to prove if this jest is carried much farther."

"I beg, sir," was my companion's response, "that you will not allow yourself to be too fully persuaded that you are the victim of a trick, lest the reaction, when you are convinced of the truth of my statements, should be too great."

The tone of concern, mingled with commiseration, with which he said this, and the entire absence of any sign of resentment at my hot words, strangely daunted me, and I followed him from the room with an extraordinary mixture of emotions. He led the way up two flights of stairs and then up a shorter one, which landed us upon a belvedere on the house-top. "Be pleased to look around you," he said, as we reached the platform, "and tell me if this is the Boston of the nineteenth century."

At my feet lay a great city. Miles of broad streets, shaded by trees and lined with fine buildings, for the most part not in continuous blocks but set in larger or smaller inclosures, stretched in every direction. Every quarter contained large open squares filled with trees, among which statues glistened and fountains flashed in the late afternoon sun. Public buildings of a colossal size and an architectural grandeur unparalleled in my day raised their stately piles on every side. Surely I had never seen this city nor one comparable to it before. Raising my eyes at last towards the horizon, I looked westward. That blue ribbon winding away to the sunset, was it not the sinuous Charles? I looked east; Boston harbor stretched before me within its headlands, not one of its green islets missing.

I knew then that I had been told the truth concerning the prodigious thing which had befallen me.

VOCABULARY STUDY

VOCABULARY QUIZ 5-B

Words to Learn

equanimity *ingenuous* *commiseration*
preposterous *tenable* *sinuous*
surmise *ironical*
impotent *farrago*

Match each italicized word with the appropriate choice from the right.

Words in Context

1. "to affect your *equanimity*," p. 163.
2. "a *preposterous* attempt," p. 163.
3. "it was impossible . . . to *surmise*," p. 163.
4. "my fancy was utterly *impotent*," p. 163.
5. "a face so refined and *ingenuous*," p. 163.
6. "the only one *tenable*," p. 163.
7. "an *ironical* smile," p. 164.
8. "this remarkable *farrago*," p. 166.
9. "mingled with *commiseration*," p. 166.
10. "the *sinuous* Charles," p. 166.

Definitions

a. guess
b. powerless
c. absurd
d. frank, honest, noble
e. capable of being maintained
f. the expression of sorrow or compassion
g. winding, twisting
h. composure
i. a confused collection
j. saying one thing and meaning another

VOCABULARY PRACTICE 5-B

Add an appropriate choice from the above vocabulary list to the sentences below.

1. The _____ behavior and manners of the newcomer soon earned him the respect of the community.

2. War widows and orphans deserve the _____ of their countrymen.

3. They soon found that their position above the rocks was not _____; it was vulnerable to the arrows of Indian scouts hiding in the trees.

4. The _____ Grande Corniche road in the French Riviera is world famous for its hairpin turns and breath-taking curves.

5. The congratulations which the poor loser extends to the winner are often _____ in tone.

6. Bad news does not upset a strong man's _____.

7. The suspect's story was a _____ of conflicting lies and hastily contrived alibis.

8. _____ claims are often found in commercial advertisements.

9. One can only _____ at the existence or absence of life on other planets.

10. Even the rescue services of the world's mightiest navies are _____ in the face of a hurricane at sea.

SUGGESTIONS FOR DISCUSSION AND WRITING

1. In *Looking Backward: 2000–1887*, Edward Bellamy goes on, from the selection reproduced here, to detail the world of 2000, concentrating on the items and subjects listed below. If you have not yet read the novel, see if you can approximate his predictions by writing a brief paragraph for each particular; after all, you have a ninety-five year advantage! Be sure to check the accuracy of your predictions by referring to the book itself.

- a. clothing
- b. capitalism
- c. labor unions
- d. politics
- e. welfare
- f. unemployment
- g. wages
- h. shopping
- i. money
- j. musical reproduction
- k. restaurants
- l. libraries
- m. law and justice
- n. prisons
- o. education
- p. women's liberation

2. There are many stylistic and contextual clues to apprise the reader that *Looking Backward* was written nearly a century ago. List at least a dozen of these giveaways.

A selection from

Brave New World

ALDOUS HUXLEY

MR. FOSTER was left in the Decanting Room. The D. H. C. and his students stepped into the nearest lift and were carried up to the fifth floor.

INFANT NURSERIES. NEO-PAVLOVIAN CONDITIONING ROOMS, announced the notice board.

The Director opened a door. They were in a large bare room, very bright and sunny; for the whole of the southern wall was a single window. Half a dozen nurses, trousered and jacketed in the regulation white viscose-linen uniform, their hair aseptically hidden under white caps, were engaged in setting out bowls of roses in a long row across the floor. Big bowls, packed tight with blossom. Thousands of petals, ripe-blown and silkily smooth, like the cheeks of innumerable little cherubs, but of cherubs, in that bright light, not exclusively pink and Aryan, but also luminously Chinese, also Mexican, also apoplectic with too much blowing of celestial trumpets, also pale as death, pale with the posthumous whiteness of marble.

The nurses stiffened to attention as the D. H. C. came in.

"Set out the books," he said curtly.

In silence the nurses obeyed his command. Between the rose bowls the books were duly set out—a row of nursery quartos opened invitingly each at some gaily coloured image of beast or fish or bird.

"Now bring in the children."

They hurried out of the room and returned in a minute or two, each pushing a kind of tall dumb-waiter laden, on all its four wire-netted shelves, with eight-month-old babies, all exactly alike (a Bokanovisky Group, it was evident) and all (since their caste was Delta) dressed in khaki.

"Put them down on the floor."

The infants were unloaded.

"Now turn them so that they can see the flowers and books."

Turned, the babies at once fell silent, then began to crawl towards those clusters of sleek colours, those shapes so gay and brilliant on the white pages. As they approached, the sun came out of a momentary eclipse behind a cloud. The roses flamed up as though with a sudden passion from within; a new and profound significance seemed to suffuse the shining pages of the books. From the ranks of the crawling babies came little squeals of excitement, gurgles and twitterings of pleasure.

The Director rubbed his hands. "Excellent!" he said. "It might almost have been done on purpose."

The swiftest crawlers were already at their goal. Small hands reached out uncertainly, touched, grasped, unpetaling the transfigured roses, crumpling the illuminated pages of the books. The Director waited until all were happily busy. Then, "Watch carefully," he said. And, lifting his hand, he gave the signal.

The Head Nurse, who was standing by a switchboard at the other end of the room, pressed down a little lever.

There was a violent explosion. Shriller and ever shriller, a siren shrieked. Alarm bells maddeningly sounded.

The children started, screamed; their faces were distorted with terror.

"And now," the Director shouted (for the noise was deafening), "now we proceed to rub in the lesson with a mild electric shock."

He waved his hand again, and the Head Nurse pressed a second lever. The screaming of the babies suddenly changed its tone. There was something desperate, almost insane, about the sharp spasmodic yelps to which they now gave utterance. Their little bodies twitched and stiffened; their limbs moved jerkily as if to the tug of unseen wires.

"We can electrify that whole strip of floor," bawled the Director in explanation. "But that's enough," he signalled to the nurse.

The explosions ceased, the bells stopped ringing, the shriek of the siren died down from tone to tone into silence. The stiffly twitching bodies relaxed, and what had become the sob and yelp of infant maniacs broadened out once more into a normal howl of ordinary terror.

"Offer them the flowers and the books again."

The nurses obeyed; but at the approach of the roses, at the mere sight of those gaily-coloured images of pussy and cock-a-doodle-doo and baa-baa black sheep, the infants shrank away in horror; the volume of their howling suddenly increased.

"Observe," said the Director triumphantly, "observe."

Books and loud noises, flowers and electric shocks—already in the infant mind these couples were compromisingly linked; and after two hundred repetitions of the same or a similar lesson would be wedded indissolubly. What man has joined, nature is powerless to put asunder.

"They'll grow up with what the psychologists used to call an 'instinctive' hatred of books and flowers. Reflexes unalterably conditioned. They'll be safe from books and botany all their lives." The Director turned to his nurses. "Take them away again."

Still yelling, the khaki babies were loaded on to their dumbwaiters and wheeled out, leaving behind them the smell of sour milk and a most welcome silence.

One of the students held up his hand; and though he could see quite well why you couldn't have lower-caste people wasting the Community's time over books, and that there was always the risk of their reading something which might undesirably decondition one of their reflexes, yet . . . well, he couldn't understand about the flowers. Why go to the trouble of making it psychologically impossible for Deltas to like flowers?

Patiently the D.H.C. explained. If the children were made to scream at the sight of a rose, that was on grounds of high economic policy. Not so very long ago (a century or thereabouts), Gammas, Deltas, even Epsilons, had been conditioned to like flowers—flowers in particular and wild nature in general. The idea was to make them want to be going out into the country at every available opportunity, and so compel them to consume transport.

"And didn't they consume transport?" asked the student.

"Quite a lot," the D.H.C. replied. "But nothing else."

Primroses and landscapes, he pointed out, have one grave defect: they are gratuitous. A love of nature keeps no factories busy. It was decided to abolish the love of nature, at any rate among the lower classes; to abolish the love of nature, but not the tendency to consume transport. For of course, it was essential that they should keep on going to the country, even though they hated it. The problem was to find an economically sounder reason for consuming transport than a mere affection for primroses and landscapes. It was duly found.

"We condition the masses to hate the country," concluded the Director. "But simultaneously we condition them to love all country sports. At the same time, we see to it that all country sports shall entail the use of elaborate apparatus. So that they consume manufactured articles as well as transport. Hence those electric shocks."

"I see," said the student, and was silent, lost in admiration.

There was a silence: then, clearing his throat, "Once upon a time," the Director began, "while our Ford was still on earth, there was a little boy called Reuben Rabinovitch. Reuben was the child of Polish-speaking parents." The Director interrupted himself. "You know what Polish is, I suppose?"

"A dead language."

"Like French and German," added another student, officiously showing off his learning.

"And 'parent'?" questioned the D.H.C.

There was an uneasy silence. Several of the boys blushed. They had not yet learned to draw the significant but often very fine distinction between smut and pure science. One, at last, had the courage to raise a hand.

"Human beings used to be . . ." he hesitated; the blood rushed to his cheeks. "Well, they used to be viviparous."

"Quite right." The Director nodded approvingly. "And when the babies were decanted . . ."

" 'Born,' " came the correction.

"Well, then they were the parents —I mean, not the babies, of course; the other ones." The poor boy was overwhelmed with confusion.

"In brief," the Director summed up, "the parents were the father and the mother." The smut that was really science fell with a crash into the boys' eye-avoiding silence. "Mother," he repeated loudly rubbing in the science; and, leaning back in his chair, "These," he said gravely, "are unpleasant facts; I know it. But then most historical facts *are* unpleasant."

He returned to Little Reuben—to Little Reuben, in whose room, one evening, by an oversight, his father and mother (crash, crash!) happened to leave the radio turned on.

("For you must remember that in those days of gross viviparous reproduction, children were always brought up by their parents and not in State Conditioning Centres.")

While the child was asleep, a broadcast programme from London suddenly started to come through; and the next morning, to the astonishment of his crash and crash (the more daring of the boys ventured to grin at one another), Little Reuben woke up repeating word for word a long lecture by that curious old writer ("one of the very few whose works have been permitted to come down to us"), George Bernard Shaw, who was speaking, according to a well-authenticated tradition, about his own genius. To Little Reuben's wink and snigger, this lecture was, of course, perfectly incomprehensible and, imagining that their child had suddenly gone mad, they sent for a doctor. He, fortunately, understood English, recognized the discourse as that which Shaw had broadcasted the previous evening, realized the significance of what had happened, and sent a letter to the medical press about it.

"The principle of sleep-teaching, or hypnopaedia had been discovered." The D.H.C. made an impressive pause.

The principle had been discovered; but many, many years were to elapse before that principle was usefully applied.

"The case of Little Reuben occurred only twenty-three years after our Ford's first T-Model was put on the market." (Here the Director made a sign of the T on his stomach and all the students reverently followed suit.) "And yet . . ."

Furiously the students scribbled. "*Hypnopaedia, first used officially in A.F. 214. Why not before? Two reasons. (a) . . .*"

"These early experimenters," the D.H.C. was saying, "were on the wrong track. They thought that hypnopaedia could be made an instrument of intellectual education . . ."

(A small boy asleep on his right side, the right arm stuck out, the right hand hanging limp over the edge of his bed. Through a round grating in the side of a box a voice speaks softly.

"The Nile is the longest river in Africa and the second in length of all the rivers of the globe. Although falling short of the length of the Mississippi-Missouri, the Nile is at the head of all rivers as regards the length of its basin, which extends through 35 degrees of latitude . . ."

At breakfast the next morning, "Tommy," someone says, "do you know which is the longest river in Africa?" A shaking of the head. "But don't you remember something that begins: The Nile is the . . ."

"The - Nile - is - the - longest - river - in - Africa - and - the - second - in - length - of - all - the - rivers - of - the - globe . . ." The words come rushing out. "Although - falling - short - of . . ."

"Well, now, which is the longest river in Africa?"

The eyes are blank. "I don't know."

"But the Nile, Tommy."

"The - Nile - is - the - longest - river - in - Africa - and - second . . ."

"Then which river is the longest, Tommy?"

Tommy bursts into tears. "I don't know," he howls.

That howl, the Director made it plain, discouraged the earliest investigators. The experiments were abandoned. No further attempt was made to teach children the length of the Nile in their sleep. Quite rightly. You can't learn a science unless you know what it's all about.

"Whereas, if they'd only started on *moral* education," said the Director, leading the way towards the door. The students followed him, desperately scribbling as they walked and all the way up in the lift. "Moral education, which ought never, in any circumstances, to be rational."

"Silence, silence," whispered a loud speaker as they stepped out of the fourteenth floor, and "Silence, silence," the trumpet mouths indefatigably repeated at intervals down every corridor. The students and even the Director himself rose automatically to the tips of their toes. They were Alphas, of course; but even Alphas have been well conditioned. "Silence, silence." All the air of the fourteenth floor was sibilant with the categorical imperative.

Fifty yards of tiptoeing brought them to a door which the Director cautiously opened. They stepped over the threshold into the twilight of a shuttered dormitory. Eighty cots stood in a row against the wall. There was a sound of light regular breathing and a continuous murmur, as of very faint voices remotely whispering.

A nurse rose as they entered and came to attention before the Director.

"What's the lesson this afternoon?" he asked.

"We had Elementary Sex for the first forty minutes," she answered. "But now it's switched over to Elementary Class Consciousness."

The Director walked slowly down the long line of cots. Rosy and relaxed with sleep, eighty little boys and girls lay softly breathing. There was a whisper under every pillow. The D.H.C. halted and, bending over one of the little beds, listened attentively.

"Elementary Class Consciousness, did you say? Let's have it repeated a little louder by the trumpet."

At the end of the room a loud speaker projected from the wall. The Director walked up to it and pressed a switch.

". . . all wear green," said a soft but very distinct voice, beginning in the middle of a sentence, "and Delta Children wear khaki. Oh no, I *don't* want to play with Delta children. And Epsilons are still worse. They're too stupid to be able to read or write. Besides they wear black, which is such a beastly colour. I'm *so* glad I'm a Beta."

There was a pause; then the voice began again.

"Alpha children wear grey. They work much harder than we do, because they're so frightfully clever. I'm really awfully glad I'm a Beta, because I don't work so hard. And then we are much better than the Gammas and Deltas. Gammas are stupid. They all wear green, and Delta children wear khaki. Oh no, I *don't* want to play with Delta children. And Epsilons are still worse. They're too stupid to be able . . ."

The Director pushed back the switch. The voice was silent. Only its thin ghost continued to mutter from beneath the eighty pillows.

"They'll have that repeated forty or fifty times more before they wake; then again on Thursday, and again on Saturday. A hundred and twenty times three times a week for thirty months. After which they go on to a more advanced lesson."

Roses and electric shocks, the khaki of Deltas and a whiff of asafoetida—wedded indissolubly before the child can speak. But wordless conditioning is crude and wholesale; cannot bring home the finer distinctions, cannot inculcate the more complex courses of behavior. For that there must be words, but words without reason. In brief, hypnopaedia.

"The greatest moralizing and socializing force of all time."

The students took it down in their little books. Straight from the horse's mouth.

Once more the Director touched the switch.

". . . so frightfully clever," the soft, insinuating, indefatigable voice was saying. "I'm really awfully glad I'm a Beta, because . . ."

Not so much like drops of water, though water, it is true, can wear holes in the hardest granite; rather, drops of liquid sealing-wax, drops that adhere, incrust, incorporate themselves with what they fall on, till finally the rock is all one scarlet blob.

"Till at last the child's mind *is* these suggestions, and the sum of the suggestions *is* the child's mind. And not the child's mind only. The adult's mind too—all his life long. The mind that judges and desires and decides—made up of these suggestions. But all these suggestions are *our* suggestions!" The Director almost shouted in his triumph. "Suggestions from the State." He banged the nearest table. "It therefore follows . . ."

A noise made him turn around.

"Oh, Ford!" he said in another tone, "I've gone and woken the children."

SUGGESTIONS FOR DISCUSSION AND WRITING

1. In 1958, some twenty-seven years after the publication of *Brave New World*, Aldous Huxley wrote *Brave New World Revisited*, a short book which seeks to persuade us that our world is rapidly becoming the one he imagined in 1931. It focuses primarily on the science of thought control, and contains detailed commentary on overpopulation, overorganization, propaganda, advertising, brainwashing, chemical and subconscious persuasion, and "hypnopaedia" as it now exists. Obtain a copy of *Brave New World Revisited* and summarize at least one of its chapters, with a brief evaluative comment of your own.

2. It is unsettling to be told that our minds are being manipulated almost as readily as the minds of the masses in *Brave New World*. Yet, many popular books on the recent market offer strong testimonials to that effect. Find one of them and summarize its thesis in a documented essay, adding at least one paragraph in which you express an opinion of your own. Here are some suggestions:

Herman Kahn and Anthony J. Wiener, *The Year 2000*, Macmillan, 1967

Perry London, *Behavior Control*, Harper & Row, 1969

Vance Packard, *The Hidden Persuaders*, McKay, 1959; *The Pyramid Climbers*, Fawcett World, 1964; *The Status Seekers*, McKay, 1959; *The Waste Makers*, McKay, 1960

Maya Pines, *Revolution in Learning: The Years from Birth to Six*, Harper & Row, 1966

Theodore Roszak, *The Making of a Counter Culture*, Doubleday, 1968

Adam Smith, *The Money Game*, Random House, 1967

Gordon R. Taylor, *The Biological Time Bomb*, World, 1968

Tom Wolfe, *The Pump House Gang*, Farrar, Strauss & Giroux, 1968; *The Electric Kool-Aid Acid Test*, Bantam, 1969

A selection from

Nineteen Eighty-Four

GEORGE ORWELL

AS HE put his hand to the doorknob Winston saw that he had left the diary open on the table. DOWN WITH BIG BROTHER was written all over it, in letters almost big enough to be legible across the room. It was an inconceivably stupid thing to have done. But, he realized, even in his panic he had not wanted to smudge the creamy paper by shutting the book while the ink was wet.

He drew in his breath and opened the door. Instantly a warm wave of relief flowed through him. A colorless, crushed-looking woman, with wispy hair and a lined face, was standing outside.

"Oh, comrade," she began in a dreary, whining sort of voice, "I thought I heard you come in. Do you think you could come across and have a look at our kitchen sink? It's got blocked up and—"

It was Mrs. Parsons, the wife of a neighbor on the same floor. ("Mrs." was a word somewhat discountenanced by the Party—you were supposed to call everyone "comrade"—but with some women one used it instinctively.) She was a woman of about thirty, but looking much older. One had the impression that there was dust in the creases of her face. Winston followed her down the passage. These amateur repair jobs were an almost daily irritation. Victory Mansions were old flats, built in 1930 or thereabouts, and were falling to pieces. The plaster flaked constantly from the ceiling and walls, the pipes burst in every hard frost, the roof leaked whenever there was snow, the heating system was usually running at half steam when it was not closed down altogether from motives of economy. Repairs, except what you could do for yourself, had to be sanctioned by remote committees which were liable to hold up even the mending of a window pane for two years.

"Of course it's only because Tom isn't home," said Mrs. Parsons vaguely.

The Parson's flat was bigger than Winston's, and dingy in a different way. Everything had a battered, trampled-on look, as though the place had just been visited by some large violent animal. Games impedimenta—hockey sticks, boxing gloves, a burst football, a pair of sweaty shorts turned inside out—lay all over the floor, and on the table there were books. On the walls were scarlet banners of the Youth League and the Spies, and a full-sized poster of Big Brother. There was the usual boiled cabbage smell, common to the whole building, but it was shot through by a sharper reek of sweat, which—one knew this at the first sniff, though it was hard to say how—was the sweat of some person not present at the moment. In another room someone with a comb and a piece of toilet paper was trying to keep tune with the military music which was still issuing from the telescreen.

"It's the children," said Mrs. Parsons, casting a half-apprehensive glance at the door. "They haven't been out today. And of course—"

She had a habit of breaking off her sentences in the middle. The kitchen sink was full nearly to the brim with filthy greenish water which smelt worse than ever of cabbage. Winston knelt down and examined the angle-joint of the pipe. He hated using his hands, and he hated bending down, which was always liable to start him coughing. Mrs. Parsons looked on helplessly.

"Of course if Tom was home he'd put it right in a moment," she said. "He loves anything like that. He's ever so good with his hands, Tom is."

Parsons was Winston's fellow employee at the Ministry of Truth. He was a fattish but active man of paralyzing stupidity, a mass of imbecile enthusiasms—one of those completely unquestioning, devoted drudges on whom, more even than on the Thought Police, the stability of the Party depended. At thirty-five he had just been unwillingly evicted from the Youth League, and before graduating into the Youth League he had managed to stay on in the Spies for a year beyond the statutory age. At the Ministry he was employed in some subordinate post for which intelligence was not required, but on the other hand he was a leading figure on the Sports Committee and all the other committees engaged in organizing community hikes, spontaneous demonstrations, savings campaigns, and voluntary activities generally. He would inform you with quiet pride, between whiffs of his pipe, that he had put in an appearance at the Community Center every evening for the past four years. An overpowering smell of sweat, a sort of unconscious testimony to the strenuousness of his life, followed him about wherever he went, and even remained behind him after he had gone.

"Have you got a spanner?" said Winston, fiddling with the nut on the angle-joint.

"A spanner," said Mrs. Parsons, immediately becoming invertebrate. "I don't know, I'm sure. Perhaps the children—"

There was a trampling of boots and another blast on the comb as the children charged into the living room. Mrs. Parsons brought the spanner. Winston let out the water and disgustedly removed the clot of human hair that had blocked up the pipe. He cleaned his fingers as best he could in the cold water from the tap and went back into the other room.

"Up with your hands!" yelled a savage voice.

A handsome, tough-looking boy of nine had popped up from behind the table and was menacing him with a toy automatic pistol, while his small sister, about two years younger, made the same gesture with a fragment of wood. Both of them were dressed in the blue shorts, gray shirts, and red neckerchiefs which were the uniform of the Spies. Winston raised his hands above his head, but with an uneasy feeling, so vicious was the boy's demeanor, that it was not altogether a game.

"You're a traitor!" yelled the boy. "You're a thought-criminal! You're a Eurasian spy! I'll shoot you, I'll vaporize you, I'll send you to the salt mines!"

Suddenly they were both leaping round him; shouting "Traitor!" and "Thought-criminal!", the little girl imitating her brother in every movement. It was somehow slightly frightening, like the gamboling of tiger cubs which soon grow up into man-eaters. There was a sort of calculating ferocity in the boy's eye, a quite evident desire to hit or kick Winston and a consciousness of being very nearly big enough to do so. It was a good job it was not a real pistol he was holding, Winston thought.

Mrs. Parson's eyes flitted nervously from Winston to the children, and back again. In the better light of the living room he noticed with interest that there *was* dust in the creases of her face.

"They do get so noisy," she said. "They're disappointed because they couldn't go see the hanging, that's what it is. I'm too busy to take them, and Tom won't be back from work in time.

"Why can't we go and see the hanging?" roared the boy in his huge voice.

"Want to see the hanging! Want to see the hanging!" chanted the little girl, still capering round.

Some Eurasian prisoners, guilty of war crimes, were to be hanged in the Park that evening, Winston remembered. This happened about once a month, and was a popular spectacle. Children always clamored to be taken to see it. He took his leave of Mrs. Parsons and made for the door. But he had not gone six steps down the passage when something hit the back of his neck an agonizingly painful blow. It was as though a redhot wire had been jabbed into him. He spun round just in time to see Mrs. Parsons dragging her son back into the doorway while the boy pocketed a catapult.

"Goldstein!" bellowed the boy as the door closed on him. But what most struck Winston was the look of helpless fright on the woman's grayish face.

Back in the flat he stepped quickly past the telescreen and sat down at the table again, still rubbing his neck. The music from the telescreen had stopped. Instead, a clipped military voice was reading out, with a sort of brutal relish, a description of the armaments of the new Floating Fortress which had just been anchored between Iceland and the Faroe Islands.

With those children, he thought, that wretched woman must lead a life of terror. Another year, or two years, and they would be watching her night and day for symptoms of unorthodoxy. Nearly all children nowadays were horrible. What was worst of all was that by means of such organizations as the Spies they were systematically turned into ungovernable little savages, and yet this produced in them no tendency whatever to rebel against the discipline of the Party. On the contrary, they adored the Party and everything connected with it. The songs, the processions, the banners, the hiking, the drilling with dummy rifles, the yelling of slogans, the worship of Big Brother—it was all a sort of glorious game to them. All their ferocity was turned outwards, against the enemies of the State, against foreigners, traitors, saboteurs, thoughtcriminals. It was almost normal for people over thirty to be frightened of their own children. And with good reason, for hardly a week passed in which the *Times* did not carry a paragraph describing how some evesdropping little sneak— "child hero" was the phrase generally used—had overheard some compromising remark and denounced his parents to the Thought Police.

The sting of the catapult bullet had worn off. He picked up his pen half-heartedly, wondering whether he could find something more to write in the diary. Suddenly he began thinking of O'Brien again.

Years ago—how long was it? Seven years it must be—he had dreamed that he was walking through a pitch-dark room. And someone sitting to one side of him said as he passed: "We shall meet in the place where there is no darkness." It was said very quietly, almost casually—a statement, not a command. He had walked on without pausing. What was curious was that at the time, in the dream, the words had not made much impression on him. It was only later and by degrees that they had seemed to take on significance. He could not now remember whether it was before or after the dream that he had seen O'Brien for the first time; nor could he remember when he had first identified the voice as O'Brien's. But at any rate the identification existed. It was O'Brien who had spoken to him out of the dark.

Winston had never been able to feel sure—even after this morning's flash of the eyes it was still impossible to be sure—whether O'Brien was a friend or an enemy. Nor did it even seem to matter greatly. There was a link of understanding between them more important than affection or partisanship. "We shall meet in the place where there is no darkness," he had said. Winston did not know what it meant, only that in some way or another it would come true.

The voice from the telescreen paused. A trumpet call, clear and beautiful, floated into the stagnant air. The voice continued raspingly: "Attention! Your attention, please! a newsflash has this moment arrived from the Malabar front. Our forces in South India have won a glorious victory. I am authorized to say that the action we are now reporting may well bring the war within measurable distance of its end. Here is the newsflash—"

Bad news coming, thought Winston, and sure enough, following on a gory description of the annihilation of a Eurasian army, with stupendous figures of killed and prisoners, came the announcement that, as from next week, the chocolate ration would be reduced from thirty grams to twenty.

Winston belched again. The gin was wearing off, leaving a deflated feeling. The telescreen—perhaps to celebrate the victory, perhaps to drown the memory of the lost chocolate—crashed into "Oceania, 'tis for thee." You were supposed to stand to attention. However, in his present position he was invisible.

"Oceania, 'tis for thee" gave way to lighter music. Winston walked over to the window, keeping his back to the telescreen. The day was still cold and clear. Somewhere far away a rocket bomb exploded with a dull, reverberating roar. About twenty or thirty of them a week were falling on London at present.

Down in the street the wind flapped the torn poster to and fro, and the word INGSOC fitfully appeared and vanished. Ingsoc. The sacred principles of Ingsoc. Newspeak, doublethink, the mutability of the past. He felt as though he were wandering in the forests of the sea bottom, lost in a monstrous world where he himself was the monster. He was alone. The past was dead, the future was unimaginable. What certainty had he that a single human creature now living was on his side? And what way of knowing that the dominion of the Party would not endure *for ever*? Like an answer, the three slogans on the white face of the Ministry of Truth came back at him:

WAR	IS	PEACE
FREEDOM	IS	SLAVERY
IGNORANCE	IS	STRENGTH

He took a twenty-five-cent piece out of his pocket. There, too, in tiny clear lettering, the same slogans were inscribed, and on the other face of the coin the head of Big Brother. Even from the coin the eyes pursued you. On coins, on stamps, on the covers of books, on banners, on posters, and on the wrapping of a cigarette packet—everywhere. Always the eyes watching you and the voice enveloping you. Asleep or awake, working or eating, indoors or out of doors, in the bath or in bed—no escape. Nothing was your own except the few cubic centimeters inside your skull.

The sun had shifted round, and the myriad windows of the Ministry of Truth, with the light no longer shining on them, looked grim as the loopholes of a fortress. His heart quailed before the enormous pyramidal shape. It was too strong, it could not be stormed. A thousand rocket bombs would not batter it down. He wondered again for whom he was writing the diary. For the future, for the past—for an age that might be imaginary. And in front of him there lay not death but annihilation. The diary would be reduced to ashes and himself to vapor. Only the Thought Police would read what he had written, before they wiped it out of existence and out of memory. How could you make appeal to the future when not a trace of you, not even an anonymous word scribbled on a piece of paper, could physically survive?

The telescreen struck fourteen. He must leave in ten minutes. He had to be back at work by fourteen-thirty.

Curiously, the chiming of the hour seemed to have put new heart into him. He was a lonely ghost uttering a truth that nobody would ever hear. But so long as he uttered it, in some obscure way the continuity was not broken. It was not by making yourself heard but by staying sane that you carried on the human heritage. He went back to the table, dipped his pen, and wrote:

To the future or to the past, to a time when thought is free, when men are different from one another and do not live alone—to a time when truth exists and what is done cannot be undone:

From the age of uniformity, from the age of solitude, from the age of Big Brother, from the age of doublethink—greeting!

He was already dead, he reflected. It seemed to him that it was only now, when he had begun to be able to formulate his thoughts, that he had taken the decisive step. The consequences of every act are included in the act itself. He wrote:

Thoughtcrime does not entail death: thoughtcrime IS death.

Now that he had recognized himself as a dead man it became important to stay alive as long as possible. Two fingers of his right hand were inkstained. It was exactly the kind of detail that might betray you. Some nosing zealot in the Ministry (a woman, probably; someone like the little sandy-haired woman or the dark-haired girl from the Fiction

Department) might start wondering why he had been writing during the lunch interval, why he had used an old-fashioned pen, *what* he had been writing—then drop a hint in the appropriate quarter. He went to the bathroom and carefully scrubbed the ink away with the gritty dark-brown soap which rasped your skin like sandpaper and was therefore well adapted for this purpose.

He put the diary away in the drawer. It was quite useless to think of hiding it, but he could at least make sure whether or not its existence had been discovered. A hair laid across the page-ends was too obvious. With the tip of his finger he picked up an identifiable grain of whitish dust and deposited it on the corner of the cover, where it was bound to be shaken off if the book was moved.

VOCABULARY STUDY

VOCABULARY QUIZ 5-C

Words to Learn

aseptically
suffuse
gratuitous
officiously

rational
indefatigably
discountenanced
statutory

compromising
zealot

Match each italicized word with the appropriate choice from the right.

Words in Context

1. "their hair *aseptically* hidden," p. 171.
2. "to *suffuse* the . . . pages," p. 172.
3. "they are *gratuitous*," p. 173.
4. "*officiously* showing off," p. 174.
5. "which ought never . . . to be *rational*," p. 175.
6. "*indefatigably* repeated at intervals," p. 175.
7. "*discountenanced* by the Party," p. 179.
8. "beyond the *statutory* age," p. 180.
9. "some *compromising* remark," p. 182.
10. "some nosing *zealot*," p. 184.

Definitions

a. untiringly
b. disapproved of, disfavored
c. determined by law
d. exposing to discredit
e. fanatic
f. in a germ-free state
g. spread throughout
h. freely given, voluntary
i. in a meddlesome way, impertinent
j. having reason or understanding

VOCABULARY PRACTICE 5-C

Add a suitable selection from the above vocabulary list to the sentences below.

1. Anyone working in a hospital is expected to be _____ clean.

2. After talking to the mumbling old man, the team of psychiatrists agreed that he was not _____.

3. The election was won not only by the efforts of the candidate, but with the help of dozens of volunteers who campaigned _____ in his behalf.

4. Proposals to abolish summer vacations were _____ by the Board of Education.

5. The magistrate had no alternative but to sentence the young thief to a ten-year prison term, since the penalty for his crime was _____, not subject to the discretion of the court.

6. It is quite possible to find oneself accidentally in a _____ situation without having done anything to create it.

7. The man who attempts to convert his friends to his own political views is a _____ . . . and a bore!

8. The sun will soon rise and _____ the countryside with the glow of early morning.

9. The _____ services of the Red Cross are available to victims of disasters anywhere in the world.

10. The chairman of the Charity Bazaar acted so _____ that he antagonized everybody.

SUGGESTIONS FOR DISCUSSION AND WRITING

1. Both *Nineteen Eighty-Four* and *Brave New World* are stories about state-controlled societies, dictatorships that manipulate the behavior of their citizens absolutely. Each government achieves its success in a markedly different manner: one by brutal punishment and fear, the other by nonviolent manipulation of thought. Briefly describe the manner of control exercised by each of the two tyrannies. Which would be more successful if imposed on us today?

2. What makes the civilization of *Nineteen Eighty-Four* a frightening possibility for each of us is the fact that governments of the world are becoming stronger and more centralized *out of necessity*, necessity born of the population explosion still out of control over most of the globe. As most nations are beginning to discern all too graphically, overpopulation leads to a troubled economy. And whenever the economy of a country is in danger, its central government *must* assume additional responsibilities to assure the welfare of its people. Write a short essay in which you discuss some examples of increased government power and control, not only in this country, but throughout the world. What are the prospects of a "Big Brother" in our future?

August 2026:
There Will Come Soft Rains

RAY BRADBURY

IN THE living room the voice-clock sang, *Tick-tock, seven o'clock, time to get up, time to get up, seven o'clock!* as if it were afraid that nobody would. The morning house lay empty. The clock ticked on, repeating and repeating its sounds into the emptiness. *Seven-nine, breakfast time, seven-nine!*

In the kitchen the breakfast stove gave a hissing sigh and ejected from its warm interior eight pieces of perfectly browned toast, eight eggs sunnyside up, sixteen slices of bacon, two coffees, and two cool glasses of milk.

"Today is August 4, 2026," said a second voice from the kitchen ceiling, "in the city of Allendale, California." It repeated the date three times for memory's sake. "Today is Mr. Featherstone's birthday. Today is the anniversary of Tilita's marriage. Insurance is payable, as are the water, gas, and light bills."

Somewhere in the walls, relays clicked, memory tapes glided under electric eyes.

Eight-one, tick-tock, eight-one o'clock, off to school, off to work, run, run, eight-one! But no doors slammed, no carpets took the soft tread of rubber heels. It was raining outside. The weather box on the front door sang quietly: "Rain, rain, go away; rubbers, raincoats for today . . ." And the rain tapped on the empty house, echoing.

Outside, the garage chimed and lifted its door to reveal the waiting car. After a long wait the door swung down again.

At eight-thirty the eggs were shriveled and the toast was like stone. An aluminum wedge scraped them into the sink, where hot water whirled them down a metal throat which digested and flushed them away to the distant sea. The dirty dishes were dropped into a hot washer and emerged twinkling dry.

Nine-fifteen, sang the clock, *time to clean.*

Out of warrens in the wall, tiny robot mice darted. The rooms were acrawl with the small cleaning animals, all rubber and metal. They thudded against chairs, whirling their mustached runners, kneading the rug nap, sucking gently at hidden dust. Then, like mysterious invaders, they popped into their burrows. Their pink electric eyes faded. The house was clean.

Ten o'clock. The sun came out from behind the rain. The house stood alone in a city of rubble and ashes. This was the one house left standing. At night the ruined city gave off a radioactive glow which could be seen for miles.

Ten-fifteen. The garden sprinklers whirled up in golden founts, filling the soft morning air with scatterings of brightness. The water pelted windowpanes, running down the charred west side where the house had been burned evenly free of its white paint. The entire west face of the house was black, save for five places. Here the silhouette in paint of a man mowing a lawn. Here, as in a photograph, a woman bent to pick flowers. Still farther over, their images burned on wood in one titanic instant, a small boy, hands flung into the air; higher up, the image of a thrown ball, and opposite him a girl, hands raised to catch a ball which never came down.

The five spots of paint—the man, the woman, the children, the ball—remained. The rest was a thin charcoaled layer.

The gentle sprinkler rain filled the garden with falling light.

Until this day, how well the house had kept its peace. How carefully it had inquired, "Who goes there? What's the password?" and, getting no answer from lonely foxes and whining cats, it had shut up its windows and drawn shades in an oldmaidenly preoccupation with self protection which bordered on a mechanical paranoia.

It quivered at each sound, the house did. If a sparrow brushed a window, the shade snapped up. The bird, startled, flew off! No, not even a bird must touch the house!

The house was an altar with ten thousand attendants, big, small, servicing, attending, in choirs. But the gods had gone away, and the ritual of the religion continued senselessly, uselessly.

Twelve noon.

A dog whined, shivering, on the front porch.

The front door recognized the dog voice and opened. The dog, once huge and fleshy, but now gone back to bone and covered with sores, moved in and through the house, tracking mud. Behind it whirred angry mice, angry at having to pick up mud, angry at inconvenience.

For not a leaf fragment blew under the door but what the wall panels flipped open and the copper scrap rats flashed swiftly out. The offending dust, hair, or paper, seized in miniature steel jaws, was raced back to the burrows. There, down tubes which fed into the cellar, it was dropped into the sighing vent of an incinerator which sat like evil Baal in a dark corner.

The dog ran up stairs, hysterically yelping to each door, at last realizing, as the house realized, that only silence was here.

It sniffed the air and scratched the kitchen door. Behind the door, the stove was making pancakes which filled the house with a rich baked odor and the scent of maple syrup.

The dog frothed at the mouth, lying at the door, sniffing, its eyes turned to fire. It ran wildly in circles, biting its tail, spun in a frenzy, and died. It lay in the parlor for an hour.

Two o'clock, sang a voice.

Delicately sensing decay at last, the regiments of mice hummed out as softly as blown gray leaves in an electrical wind.

Two-fifteen.

The dog was gone.

In the cellar, the incinerator glowed suddenly and a whirl of sparks leaped up the chimney.

Two thirty-five.

Bridge tables sprouted from patio walls. Playing cards fluttered onto pads in a shower of pips. Martinis manifested on an oaken bench with egg-salad sandwiches. Music played.

But the tables were silent and the cards untouched.

At four o'clock the tables folded like great butterflies back through the paneled walls.

Four-thirty.

The nursery walls glowed.

Animals took shape: yellow giraffes, blue lions, pink antelopes, lilac panthers cavorting in crystal substance. The walls were glass. They looked out upon color and fantasy. Hidden films clocked through well-oiled sprockets, and the walls lived. The nursery floor was woven to resemble a crisp, cereal meadow. Over this ran aluminum roaches and iron crickets, and in the hot still air butterflies of delicate red tissue wavered among the sharp aroma of animal spoors! There was the sound like a great matted yellow hive of bees within a dark bellows, the lazy bumble of a purring lion. And there was the patter of okapi feet and the murmur of a fresh jungle rain, like other hoofs, falling upon the summer-starched grass. Now the walls dissolved into distances of parched weed, mile on mile, and warm endless sky. The animals drew away into thorn brakes and water holes.

It was the children's hour.

Five o'clock. The bath filled with clear hot water.

Six, seven, eight o'clock. The dinner dishes manipulated like magic tricks, and in the study a *click*. In the metal stand opposite the hearth where a fire now blazed up warmly, a cigar popped out, half an inch of soft gray ash on it, smoking, waiting.

Nine o'clock. The beds warmed their hidden circuits, for nights were cool here.

Nine-five. A voice spoke from the study ceiling:

"Mrs. McClellan, which poem would you like this evening?"

The house was silent.

The voice said at last, "Since you express no preference, I shall select a poem at random." Quiet music rose to back the voice. "Sara Teasdale. As I recall, your favorite . . .

"There will come soft rains and the smell of the ground,
And swallows circling with their shimmering sound;
And frogs in the pools singing at night,
And wild plum trees in tremulous white;
Robins will wear their feathery fire,
Whistling their whims on a low fence-wire;
And not one will know of the war, not one
Will care at last when it is done.
Not one would mind, neither bird nor tree,
If mankind perished utterly;
And Spring herself, when she woke at dawn
Would scarcely know that we were gone."

The fire burned on the hearth and the cigar fell away into a mound of quiet ash on its tray. The empty chairs faced each other between the silent walls, and the music played.

At ten o'clock the house began to die.

The wind blew. A falling tree bough crashed through the kitchen window. Cleaning solvent, bottled, shattered over the stove. The room was ablaze in an instant!

"Fire!" screamed a voice. The house lights flashed, water pumps shot water from the ceilings. But the solvent spread on the linoleum, licking, eating, under the kitchen door, while the voices took it up in chorus: "Fire, fire, fire!"

The house tried to save itself. Doors sprang tightly shut, but the windows were broken by the heat and the wind blew and sucked upon the fire.

The house gave ground as the fire in ten billion angry sparks moved with flaming ease from room to room and then up the stairs. While scurrying water rats squeaked from the walls, pistoled their water, and ran for more. And the wall sprays let down showers of mechanical rain.

But too late. Somewhere, sighing, a pump shrugged to a stop. The quenching rain ceased. The reserve water supply which had filled baths and washed dishes for many quiet days was gone.

The fire crackled up the stairs. It fed upon Picassos and Matisses in the upper halls, like delicacies, baking off the oily flesh, tenderly

August 2026: There Will Come Soft Rains

crisping the canvases into black shavings.

Now the fire lay in beds, stood in windows, changed the colors of drapes!

And then, reinforcements.

From attic trap doors, blind robot faces peered down with faucet mouths gushing green chemicals.

The fire backed off, as even an elephant must at the sight of a dead snake. Now there were twenty snakes whipping over the floor, killing the fire with a clear, cold venom of green froth.

But the fire was clever. It had sent flame outside the house, up through the attic to the pumps there. An explosion! The attic brain which directed the pumps was shattered into bronze shrapnel on the beams.

The fire rushed back into every closet and felt of the clothes hung there.

The house shuddered, oak bone on bone, its bared skeleton cringing from the heat, its wire, its nerves revealed as if a surgeon had torn the skin off to let the red veins and capillaries quiver in the scalded air. Help, help! Fire! Run, run! Heat snapped mirrors like the first brittle winter ice. And the voices wailed Fire, fire, run, run, like a tragic nursery rhyme, a dozen voices, high, low, like children dying in a forest alone, alone. And the voices fading as the wires popped their sheathings like hot chestnuts. One, two, three, four, five voices died.

In the nursery the jungle burned. Blue lions roared, purple giraffes bounded off. The panthers ran in circles, changing color, and ten million animals, running before the fire, vanished off toward a distant steaming river . . .

Ten more voices died. In the last instant under the fire avalanche, other choruses, oblivious, could be heard announcing the time, playing music, cutting the lawn by remote control mower, or setting an umbrella frantically out and in the slamming and opening front door, a thousand things happening, like a clock shop when each clock strikes the hour insanely before or after the other, a scene of maniac confusion, yet unity; singing, screaming, a few last cleaning mice darting bravely out to carry the horrid ashes away! And one voice, with sublime disregard for the situation, read poetry aloud in the fiery study, until all the film spools burned, until all the wires withered and the circuits cracked.

The fire burst the house and let it slam flat down, puffing out skirts of spark and smoke.

In the kitchen, an instant before the rain of fire and timber, the stove could be seen making breakfasts at a psychopathic rate, ten dozen eggs, six loaves of toast, twenty-dozen bacon strips, which, eaten by fire, started the stove working again, hysterically hissing.

The crash. The attic smashing into kitchen and parlor. The parlor into cellar, cellar into sub-cellar. Deep freeze, armchair, film tapes, circuits, beds, and all like skeletons thrown in a cluttered mound deep under . . .

Smoke and silence. A great quantity of smoke.

Dawn showed faintly in the east. Among the ruins, one wall stood alone. Within the wall, a last voice said, over and over again and again, even as the sun rose to shine upon the heaped rubble and steam:

"Today is August 5, 2026, today is August 5, 2026, today is . . ."

VOCABULARY STUDY

VOCABULARY QUIZ 5-D

Words to Learn

paranoia *manifested* *sublime*
Baal *oblivious*

Match each italicized word with the appropriate choice from the right.

Words in Context

1. "a mechanical *paranoia*," p. 190.
2. "which sat like an evil *Baal*," p. 191.
3. "Martinis *manifested* on an oaken bench," p. 191.
4. "choruses, *oblivious*, could be heard," p. 193.
5. "with *sublime* disregard," p. 193.

Definitions

a. made visible, obvious
b. forgetful, unmindful
c. exalted, majestic
d. a false god, idol
e. mental disorder, persecution complex

VOCABULARY PRACTICE 5-D

Write a mature, thoughtful sentence for each of the words listed below. You may change the word's part of speech or number if you wish.

1. *manifested*   2. *oblivious*   3. *Baal*

SUGGESTIONS FOR DISCUSSION AND WRITING

1. How possible is it that there will be a world like that of "August 2026: There Will Come Soft Rains"? What can you point to today that portends such a future?

2. "August 2026: There Will Come Soft Rains" and "In the Year Ten-Thousand" both depict times in the remote future of humanity. Both describe a world made supremely facile and comfortable by the inventive genius of man. But they differ substantially in the kinds of inventions and in the effects of those inventions on the world. Explain what these differences are with direct references to the stories.

3. Part of this story's effectiveness is due to the author's subtle *personification* of mechanical gadgets that begins on page 189 of the story. Point out a few examples of inanimate objects that seem to acquire human attributes as the story progresses. In your answer be sure to furnish the exact words from the text that give you this impression.

4. Sara Teasdale wrote the title poem of this story in 1920, long before the ecology movement that is so much a part of our thoughts today. Taking advantage of your informed perspective, write a detailed essay about what would happen to the world if, in Teasdale's words, "mankind perished utterly."

The Fun They Had

ISAAC ASIMOV

MARGIE EVEN wrote about it that night in her diary. On the page headed May 17, 2155, she wrote, "Today Tommy found a real book!"

It was a very old book. Margie's grandfather once said that when he was a little boy *his* grandfather told him that there was a time when all stories were printed on paper.

They turned the pages, which were yellow and crinkly, and it was awfully funny to read words that stood still instead of moving the way they were supposed to—on a screen, you know. And then, when they turned back to the page before, it had the same words on it that it had had when they read it the first time.

"Gee," said Tommy, "what a waste. When you're through with the book, you just throw it away, I guess. Our television screen must have had a million books on it and it's good for plenty more. I wouldn't throw *it* away."

"Same with mine," said Margie. She was eleven and hadn't seen as many telebooks as Tommy had. He was thirteen.

She said, "Where did you find it?"

"In my house." He pointed without looking, because he was busy reading. "In the attic."

"What's it about?"

"School."

Margie was scornful. "School? What's there to write about school? I hate school." Margie always hated school, but now she hated it more than ever. The mechanical teacher had been giving her test after test in geography and she had been doing worse and worse until her mother had shaken her head sorrowfully and sent for the County Inspector.

He was a round little man with a red face and a whole box of tools with dials and wires. He smiled at her and gave her an apple, then

197

took the teacher apart. Margie had hoped he wouldn't know how to put it together again, but he knew how all right and, after an hour or so, there it was again, large and black and ugly with a big screen on which all the lessons were shown and the questions were asked. That wasn't so bad. The part she hated most was the slot where she had to put homework and test papers. She always had to write them out in a punch code they made her learn when she was six years old, and the mechanical teacher calculated the mark in no time.

The inspector had smiled after he was finished and patted her head. He said to her mother, "It's not the little girl's fault, Mrs. Jones. I think the geography sector was geared a little too quick. Those things happen sometimes. I've slowed it up to an average ten-year-old level. Actually, the over-all pattern of her progress is quite satisfactory." And he patted Margie's head again.

Margie was disappointed. She had been hoping they would take the teacher away altogether. They had once taken Tommy's teacher away for nearly a month because the history sector had blanked out completely.

So she said to Tommy, "Why would anyone write about school?"

Tommy looked at her with very superior eyes. "Because it's not our kind of school, stupid. This is the old kind of school they had hundreds and hundreds of years ago." He added loftily, pronouncing the word carefully, "*Centuries* ago."

Margie was hurt. "Well, I don't know what kind of school they had all that time ago." She read the book over his shoulder for a while, then said, "Anyway, they had a teacher."

"Sure they had a teacher, but it wasn't a *regular* teacher. It was a man."

"A man? How could a man be a teacher?"

"Well, he just told the boys and girls things and gave them homework and asked questions."

"A man isn't smart enough."

"Sure he is. My father knows as much as a teacher. He knows almost as much, I betcha."

Margie wasn't prepared to dispute that. She said, "I wouldn't want a strange man in my house to teach me."

Tommy screamed with laughter. "You don't know much, Margie. The teachers didn't live in the house. They had a special building and all the kids went there."

"And all the kids learned the same thing?"

"Sure, if they were the same age."

"But my mother says a teacher has to be adjusted to fit the mind of each boy and girl it teaches and that each kid has to be taught differently."

"Just the same, they didn't do it that way then. If you don't like it, you don't have to read the book."

"I didn't say I didn't like it," Margie said quickly. She wanted to read about those funny schools.

They weren't even half finished when Margie's mother called, "Margie! School!"

Margie looked up. "Not yet, mamma."

"Now," said Mrs. Jones. "And it's probably time for Tommy, too."

Margie said to Tommy, "Can I read the book some more with you after school?"

"Maybe," he said nonchalantly. He walked away whistling, the dusty old book tucked beneath his arm.

Margie went into the schoolroom. It was right next to her bedroom, and the mechanical teacher was on and waiting for her. It was always on at the same time every day except Saturday and Sunday, because her mother said little girls learned better if they learned at regular hours.

The screen was lit up, and it said: "Today's arithmetic lesson is on the addition of proper fractions. Please insert yesterday's homework in the proper slot."

Margie did so with a sigh. She was thinking about the old school they had when her grandfather's grandfather was a little boy. All the kids from the whole neighborhood came, laughing and shouting in the schoolyard, sitting together in the schoolroom, going home together at the end of the day. They learned the same things so they could help one another on the homework and talk about it.

And the teachers were people . . . .

The mechanical teacher was flashing on the screen. "When we add the fractions ½ and ¼ . . ."

Margie was thinking about how the kids must have loved it in the old days. She was thinking about the fun they had.

SUGGESTIONS FOR DISCUSSION AND WRITING

1. Isaac Asimov's versatile genius has been felt in many fields, one being that of "robotics." Frequently his stories (like those in *I, Robot* (1950) and *The Rest of the Robots* (1964), and his novels *The Caves of Steel* (1954) and *The Naked Sun* (1954) involve an interplay between human beings and robots. The robots, like Margie's teacher in this story, are so far advanced that we can scarcely find them credible, but the human beings like Margie and Tommy help us relate to that world. Is it logical to assume in the advanced world of 2155 that people would be so homespun and conventional? How do you think the people of the future will differ from us?

2. What is the girl's attitude toward her "teacher"? Describe your own teacher, explaining in what ways he or she differs from Margie's. Have you ever encountered teachers as impersonal?

3. Do you believe Asimov intended the title of "The Fun They Had" to be ironic; that is, meaning the opposite of what it says? How might the attitude many students today possess toward school be improved? How realistic is it to hope for such improvement? How might the school help shift student feelings?

CHAPTER 5 CUMULATIVE VOCABULARY LIST

1. *adroitly*—skillfully
2. *apparition*—appearance, ghost
3. *appendage*—a limb or subordinate part
4. *ardent*—eager, driven
5. *aseptically*—in a germ-free state
6. *askew*—sideways
7. *assailed*—attacked, assaulted
8. *assiduously*—steadily, attentively
9. *attenuated*—made thin or weak
10. *austere*—somber, stern
11. *Baal*—a false god, idol
12. *Babel*—a noisy scene
13. *banal*—wanting originality or freshness
14. *candor*—fairness, sincerity
15. *catatonic*—in a stupor
16. *cerebral*—of the brain

17. *commiseration*—the expression of sorrow or compassion
18. *compromising*—exposing to discredit
19. *contingencies*—possibilities
20. *correlation*—interdependence
21. *countenance*—face, expression
22. *debility*—weakness
23. *denizens*—inhabitants, those who frequent a place
24. *derangement*—disturbance
25. *diorama*—a spectacular, three-dimensional scene
26. *discountenanced*—disapproved of, disfavored
27. *efficacy*—effectiveness
28. *enigmas*—puzzles
29. *equanimity*—composure
30. *execrable*—very bad, detestable
31. *exhilaration*—animation, joy, liveliness
32. *explicit*—plain, direct
33. *facilitate*—make easier
34. *farrago*—a confused collection
35. *fragrance*—odor, scent
36. *gratuitous*—freely given, voluntary
37. *hindrance*—impediment
38. *hypertension*—high blood pressure
39. *imminent*—impending, threatening
40. *immutable*—not changeable
41. *impotent*—powerless
42. *impregnable*—unconquerable
43. *incontinently*—without control
44. *indefatigably*—untiringly
45. *indispensable*—absolutely necessary
46. *indolence*—laziness, sloth
47. *ingenuous*—frank, honest, noble
48. *insensate*—lacking awareness or sensation
49. *interminable*—endless
50. *intermittent*—returning at intervals
51. *intrepid*—fearless
52. *ironical*—saying one thing and meaning another
53. *irresolute*—undecided, hesitant
54. *lassitude*—weariness, fatigue
55. *latitude*—distance in degrees from the equator
56. *ludicrous*—laughable, absurd
57. *manifested*—made visible, obvious
58. *melodrama*—a sensational or romantic play
59. *meridian*—an imaginary circle passing through both poles

60. *morbid*—despondent, diseased
61. *oblivious*—forgetful, unmindful
62. *officiously*—in a meddlesome, impertinent way
63. *palpitation*—rapid beating
64. *paranoia*—mental disorder, persecution complex
65. *patriarchs*—fathers or founders
66. *piqued*—challenged or angered
67. *poignant*—pathetic, heart-rending
68. *preposterous*—absurd
69. *prodigious*—enormous, extraordinary
70. *progeny*—offspring
71. *prognosticates*—foretells, predicts
72. *protagonist*—main character
73. *provincial*—sectional
74. *purports*—means, intends
75. *rapacious*—excessively grasping, consuming
76. *rational*—having reason or understanding
77. *remote*—far off, distant
78. *resuscitation*—revival
79. *retorted*—replied sharply
80. *rudimentary*—undeveloped
81. *schizophrenia*—mental disorder, split personality
82. *scrutiny*—an investigation, examination
83. *sinuous*—winding, curving
84. *sleek*—smooth, glossy
85. *statutory*—determined by law
86. *stoicism*—indifference to pleasure or pain
87. *sublime*—exalted, majestic
88. *suffuse*—to spread throughout
89. *sumptuously*—in luxury
90. *surly*—gloomy, rough
91. *surmise*—guess
92. *symmetry*—balance, harmony
93. *synthesized*—artificially manufactured
94. *tenable*—capable of being maintained
95. *tenets*—beliefs
96. *terrestrial*—of or relating to earth
97. *traverse*—to pass through, to cross
98. *undulating*—swaying, moving in waves
99. *utopian*—idealistic, impractical
100. *vociferations*—outcries
101. *zealot*—fanatic

Chapter 6

EXTENSION? PREDICTION? FANTASY?

Worldwide shortages of food, energy sources, and raw materials that occurred in the early 1970s have resulted in troubling proclamations of disaster to come. Newspaper features, magazine articles, pamphlets, and books have begun predicting in gloomy detail the chaotic world Man will inherit in time. Most of these accounts of future calamity make use of a clever literary device called *extension*, long a mainstay of the science fiction writer. Many of the stories you have encountered so far, in fact, serve as examples of this essential technique.

Extension is the author's preconception that certain social trends today (usually disturbing ones like crime, overpopulation, materialism, or dehumanization) will become worse and worse in scope. To dramatize his belief, the author jumps to some future date, and describes, in discouraging detail, how our present faults have, by extension, become monsters that threaten our very existence. In this respect, science fiction can be considered the shortest distance between two points—the present and the future. *Primarily, criticism of existing conditions lies behind the author's employment of this device.*

On the other hand, some science fiction writers merely *predict* the future, with no intention of criticizing their own world, or of projecting its various ailments. In their stories, enough of the world can be recognized to indicate that the planet and civilization intended are our own, but they have been greatly altered by means of plausible additions and transformations *which do not have origins in the world we know.*

Finally, some science fiction writers neither attempt to project social trends nor predict the world to come. They permit their inventive muse complete freedom, rendering their imaginations sole authority for the stories they spin. They are not bound by the test of plausibility as the predictive science fiction writer is, or by the need to trace projections back to the present. They create stories of *fantasy*.

It should surprise no one that the contemporary stories in this chapter depend as heavily on the modes of science fiction as stories of the past. They are a varied selection, chosen to illustrate each mode. As you read them, try to classify each according to the category you believe appropriate. They are listed here with dates of publication.

"The Great Nebraska Sea" (1963) *Allan Danzig*
"Erem" (1970) *Gleb Anfilov*
"Report from the Planet Proteus" (1972) *Lawrence Sail*
"In the Matter of the Assassin Merefirs" (1972) *Ken W. Purdy*
"Eat, Drink, and Be Merry" (1974) *Dian Crayne*

THE GREAT NEBRASKA SEA

ALLAN DANZIG

EVERYONE—ALL the geologists, at any rate—had known about the Kiowa Fault for years. This was before there was anything very interesting to know about it. The first survey of Colorado traced its course north and south in the narrow valley of Kiowa Creek about twenty miles east of Denver; it extended south to the Arkansas River. And that was about all even the professionals were interested in knowing. There was never so much as a landslide to bring the Fault to the attention of the general public.

It was still a matter of academic interest when in the late 40's geologists speculated on the relationship between the Kiowa Fault and the Conchas Fault farther south, in New Mexico, and which followed the Pecos as far south as Texas.

Nor was there much in the papers a few years later when it was suggested that the Niobrara Fault (just inside and roughly parallel to the eastern border of Wyoming) was a northerly extension of the Kiowa. By the mid-sixties it was definitely established that the three faults were in fact a single line of fissure in the essential rock, stretching almost from the Canadian border well south of the New Mexico-Texas line.

It is not really surprising that it took so long to figure out the connection. The population of the states affected was in places as low as five people per square mile! The land was so dry it seemed impossible that it would ever be used except for sheep farming.

It strikes us today as ironic that from the late 50's there was grave concern about the level of the water table throughout the entire area.

The even more ironic solution to the problem began in the summer of 1973. It had been a particularly hot and dry August, and the For-

205

estry Service was keeping an anxious eye out for the fires it knew it could expect. Dense smoke was reported above a virtually uninhabited area along Black Squirrel Creek, and a plane was sent out for a report.

The report was—no fire at all. The rising cloud was not smoke, but dust. Thousands of cubic feet of dry earth rising lazily on the summer air. Rock slides, they guessed; certainly no fire. The Forestry Service had other worries at the moment, and filed the report.

But after a week had gone by, the town of Edison, a good twenty miles away from the slides, was still complaining of the dust. Springs were going dry, too, apparently from underground disturbances. Not even in the Rockies could anyone remember a series of rock slides as bad as this.

Newspapers in the Mountain states gave it a few inches on the front page; anything is news in late August. And the geologists became interested. Seismologists were reporting unusual activity in the area, tremors too severe to be rock slides. Volcanic activity? Specifically, a dust volcano? Unusual, they knew, but right on the Kiowa fault —could be.

Labor Day crowds read the scientific conjectures with late summer lassitude. Sunday supplements ran four-color artists' conceptions of the possible volcano. "Only Active Volcano in U.S.?" demanded the headlines, and some papers even left off the question mark.

It may seem odd that the simplest explanation was practically not mentioned. Only Joseph Schwartzberg, head geographer of the Department of the Interior, wondered if the disturbance might not be a settling of the Kiowa Fault. His suggestion was mentioned on page nine or ten of the Monday newspapers (page 27 of the *New York Times*). The idea was not clearly as exciting as a volcano, even a lavaless one, and you couldn't draw a very dramatic picture of it.

To excuse the other geologists, it must be said that the Kiowa fault had never acted up before. It never side-stepped, never jiggled, never, never produced the regular shows of its little sister out in California, which almost daily bounced San Francisco or Los Angeles, or some place in between. The dust volcano was on the face of it a more plausible theory.

Still, it was only a theory. It had to be proved. As the tremors grew bigger, along with the affected area, as several towns including Edison were shaken to pieces by incredible earthquakes, whole bus- and planeloads of geologists set out for Colorado, without even waiting for their university and government departments to approve budgets.

They found, of course, that Schwartzberg had been perfectly correct.

They found themselves on the scene of what was fast becoming the most violent and widespread earthquake North America—probably the world—has ever seen in historic times. To describe it in the simplest terms, land east of the Fault was settling, and at a precipitous rate.

Rock scraped rock with a whining roar. Shuddery as a squeaky piece of chalk raked across a blackboard, the noise was deafening. The surfaces of the land east and west of the Fault seemed no longer to have any relation to each other. To the west, tortured rocks reared into cliffs. East, where sharp reports and muffled wheezes told of continued buckling and dropping, the earth trembled downward. Atop the new cliffs, which seemed to grow by sudden inches from heaving rubble, dry earth fissured and trembled, sliding acres at a time to fall, smoking, into the bucking, heaving bottom of the depression.

There the devastation was even more thorough, if less spectacular. Dry earth churned like mud, and rock shards weighing tons bumped and rolled about like pebbles as they shivered and cracked into pebbles themselves. "It looks like sand dancing in a child's sieve," said the normally impassive Schwartzberg in a nationwide broadcast from the scene of disaster. "No one here has ever seen anything like it." And the landslip was growing, north and south along the Fault.

"Get out while you can," Schwartzberg urged the population of the affected area. "When it's over you can come back and pick up the pieces." But the band of scientists who had rallied to his leadership privately wondered if there would be any pieces.

The Arkansas River, at Avondale and North Avondale, was sluggishly backing north into the deepening trough. At the rate things were going, there might be a new lake the entire length of El Paso and Pueblo counties. And, warned Schwartzberg, this might only be the beginning.

By 16 September the landslip had crept down the Huerfano River past Cedarwood. Avondale, North Avondale and Boone had totally disappeared. Land west of the Fault was holding firm, though Denver had recorded several small tremors; everywhere east of the Fault, to almost twenty miles away, the now-familiar lurch and steady fall had already sent several thousand Coloradans scurrying for safety.

All mountain climbing was forbidden on the eastern slope because of the danger of rock slides from minor quakes. The geologists went home to wait.

There wasn't much to wait for. The news got worse and worse. The Platte River, now, was creating a vast puddle where the town of Orchard had been. Just below Masters, Colorado, the river had leaped seventy-foot cliffs to add to the chaos below. And the cliffs were higher every day as the land beneath them groaned downward in mile-square gulps.

As the Fault moved north and south, new areas quivered into unwelcome life. Fields and whole mountainsides moved with deceptive sloth down, down. They danced "like sand in a sieve"; dry, they boiled into rubble. Telephone lines, railroad tracks, roads snapped and simply disappeared. Virtually all east-west land communication was suspended, and the President declared a national emergency.

By 23 September the Fault was active well into Wyoming on the north, and rapidly approaching the border of New Mexico to the south. Trinchera and Branson were totally evacuated, but even so the overall death toll had risen above one thousand.

Away to the east the situation was quiet but even more ominous. Tremendous fissures opened up perpendicular to the Fault, and a general subsidence of the land was noticeable well into Kansas and Nebraska. The western borders of these states, and soon of the Dakotas and Oklahoma as well, were slowly sinking.

On the actual scene of the disaster (or the *scenes*: it is impossible to speak of anything this size in the singular) there was a horrifying confusion. Prairie and hill cracked open under intolerable strains as the land shuddered downward in gasps and leaps. Springs burst to the surface in hot geysers and explosions of steam.

The downtown section of North Platte, Nebraska, dropped eight feet, just like that, on the afternoon of 4 October. "We must remain calm," declared the Governor of Nebraska. "We must sit this thing out. Be assured that everything possible is being done." But what could be done, with his state dropping straight down at a mean rate of a foot a day?

The Fault nicked off the southeast corner of Montana. It worked its way north along the Little Missouri. South, it ripped past Roswell, New Mexico, and tore down the Pecos toward Texas. All the upper reaches of the Missouri were standing puddles by now, and the Red River west of Paris, Texas, had begun to run backward.

Soon the Missouri began slipping slowly away westward over the slowly churning land. Abandoning its bed, the river spread uncertainly across farmland and prairie, becoming a sea of mud beneath the sharp new cliffs which rose in rending line, ever taller as the land continued to sink, almost from Canada to the Mexican border. There were virtually no floods, in the usual sense. The water moved too slowly, spread itself with no real direction or force. But the vast sheets of sluggish water and jelly-like mud formed deathtraps for the countless refugees now streaming east.

Perhaps the North Platte disaster had been more than anyone could take. One hundred ninety-three people had died in that one cave-in. Certainly by 7 October it had to be officially admitted that there was an exodus of epic proportion. Nearly two million people were on the move, and the U.S. was faced with a gigantic wave of refugees. Rails, roads and airlanes were jammed with terrified hordes who had left everything behind to crowd eastward.

All through October hollow-eyed motorists flocked into Tulsa, Topeka, Omaha, Sioux Falls and Fargo. St. Louis was made distributing center for emergency squads which flew everywhere with milk for babies and dog food for evacuated pets. Gasoline trucks boomed west to meet the demand for gas, but once inside the "zone of terror," as the newspapers now called it, they found their routes blocked by eastbound cars on the wrong side of the road. Shops left by their fleeing owners were looted by refugees from further west; an American Airlines plane was wrecked by a mob of would-be passengers in Bismark, North Dakota. Federal and state troops were called out, but moving two million people was not to be done in an orderly way.

And still the landslip grew larger. The new cliffs gleamed in the autumn sunshine, growing higher as the land beneath them continued its inexorable descent.

On 21 October, at Lubbock, Texas, there was a noise variously described as a hollow roar, a shriek, and a deep musical vibration like a church bell. It was simply the tortured rock of the substrata giving way. The second phase of the national disaster was beginning.

The noise traveled due east at better than eighty-five miles per hour. In its wake the earth to the north "just seemed to collapse on itself like a punctured balloon," read one newspaper report. "Like a cake that's failed," said a Texarkana housewife who fortunately lived a block *south* of Thayer Street, where the fissure raced through. There was a sigh and a great cloud of dust, and Oklahoma subsides at the astounding rate of six feet per hour.

At Biloxi, on the Gulf, there had been uneasy shufflings under foot all day. "Not tremors, exactly," said the captain of a fishing boat which was somehow to ride out of the coming flood, "but like as if the land wanted to be somewhere else."

Everyone in doomed Biloxi would have done well to have been somewhere else that evening. At approximately 8:30 P.M. the town shuddered, seemed to rise a little like the edge of a hall carpet caught in a draft, and sank. So did the entire Mississippi and Alabama coast, at about the same moment. The tidal wave which was to gouge the center from the U.S. marched on land.

From the north shore of Lake Ponchartrain to the Appalachicola River in Florida, the Gulf coast simply disappeared. Gulfport, Biloxi, Mobile, Pensacola, Panama City; two hundred miles of shoreline vanished, with over two and a half million people. An hour later a wall of water has swept over every town from Dothan, Alabama, to Bogalusa on the Louisiana-Mississippi border.

"We must keep panic from our minds," said the Governor of Alabama in a radio message delivered from a hastily arranged all station hookup. "We of the gallant southland have faced and withstood invasion before." Then, as ominous creakings and groanings of the earth announced the approach of the tidal wave, he flew out of Montgomery half an hour before the town disappeared forever.

One head of the wave plunged north, eventually to spend itself in the hills south of Birmingham. The main sweep followed the lowest land. Reaching west, it swallowed Vicksburg and nicked the corner of Louisiana. The whole of East Carroll Parish was scoured from the map.

The Mississippi River now ended at about Eudora, Arkansas, and minute by minute the advancing flood bit away miles of riverbed, swelling north. Chicot, Jennie, Lake Village, Arkansas City, Snow Lake, Elaine, Helena and Memphis felt the tremors. The tormented city shuddered through the night. The earth continued its descent, eventually tipping 2½ degrees down to the west. The "Memphis Tilt" is today one of the unique and charming characteristics of the gracious Old Town, but during the night of panic Memphis residents were sure they were doomed.

South and west the waters carved deeply into Arkansas and Oklahoma. By morning it was plain that all of Arkansas was going under. Waves advanced on Little Rock at almost one hundred miles an hour, new crests forming, overtopping the wave's leading edge as towns, hills and the thirst of the soil temporarily broke the furious charge.

Washington announced the official hope that the Ozarks would stop the wild gallop of the unleashed Gulf, for in northwest Arkansas the land rose to over two thousand feet. But nothing could save Oklahoma. By noon the water reached clutching fingers around Mt. Scott and Elk Mountain, deluging Hobart and almost all of Greer County.

Despite hopeful announcements that the wave was slowing, had virtually stopped after inundating Oklahoma City, was being swallowed up in the desert near Amarillo, the wall of water continued its advance. For the land was still sinking, and the floods were constantly replenished from the Gulf. Schwartzberg and his geologists advised the utmost haste in evacuating the entire area between Colorado and Missouri, from Texas to North Dakota.

Lubbock, Texas, went under. On a curling reflex the tidal wave blotted out Sweetwater and Big Spring. The Texas panhandle disappeared in one great swirl.

Whirlpools opened. A great welter of smashed wood and human debris was sucked under, vomited up and pounded to pieces. Gulf water crashed on the cliffs of New Mexico and fell back on itself in foam. Would-be rescuers on the cliffs along what had been the west bank of the Pecos River afterward recalled the hiss and scream like tearing silk as the water broke furiously on the newly exposed rock. It was the most horrible sound they had ever heard.

"We couldn't hear any shouts, of course, not that far away and with all the noise," said Dan Weaver, Mayor of Carlsbad. "But we knew there were people down there. When the water hit the cliffs, it was like a collision between two solid bodies. We couldn't see for over an hour, because of the spray."

Salt spray. The ocean had come to New Mexico.

The cliffs proved to be the only effective barrier against the westward march of the water, which turned north, gouging out lumps of rock and tumbling down blocks of earth onto its own back. In places scoops of granite came out like ice cream. The present fishing town of Rockport, Colorado, is built on a harbor created in such a way.

The water had found its farthest westering. But still it poured north along the line of the original Fault. Irresistible fingers closed on Sterling, Colorado, on Sidney, Nebraska, on Hot Springs, South Dakota. The entire tier of states settled, from south to north, down to its eventual place of stability one thousand feet below the level of the new sea.

Memphis was by now a seaport. The Ozarks, islands in a mad sea, formed precarious havens for half-drowned humanity. Waves bit off a corner of Missouri, flung themselves on Wichita. Topeka, Lawrence and Belleville were the last Kansas towns to disappear. The Governor of Kansas went down with his State.

Daniel Bernd of Lincoln, Nebraska, was washed up half-drowned in a cove of the Wyoming cliffs, having been sucked from one end of vanished Nebraska to the other. Similar hairbreadth escapes were recounted on radio and television.

Virtually the only people saved out of the entire population of Pierre, South Dakota, were the six members of the Creeth family. Plucky Timothy Creeth carried and dragged his aged parents to the loft of their barn on the outskirts of town. His brother Geoffrey brought along the younger children and what provisions they could find— "Mostly a ham and about half a ton of vanilla cookies," he explained to his eventual rescuers. The barn, luckily collapsing in the vibration as the waves bore down on them, became an ark in which they rode out the disaster.

"We must of played cards for four days straight," recalled genial Mrs. Creeth when she afterwards appeared on a popular television spectacular. Her rural good humor undamaged by an ordeal few women can ever have been called on to face, she added, "We sure wondered why flushes never came out right. Jimanettly, we'd left the king of hearts behind, in the rush!"

But such lightheartedness and

such happy endings were by no means typical. The world could only watch aghast as the water raced north under the shadow of the cliffs which occasionally crumbled, roaring, into the roaring waves. Day by day the relentless rush swallowed what had been dusty farmland, cities and towns.

Some people were saved by the helicopters which flew mercy missions just ahead of the advancing waters. Some found safety in the peaks of western Nebraska and the Dakotas. But when the waters came to rest along what is roughly the present shoreline of our inland sea, it was estimated that over fourteen million people had lost their lives.

No one could even estimate the damage to property: almost the entirety of eight states and portions of twelve others, had simply vanished from the heart of the North American continent forever.

It was in such a cataclysmic birth that the now-peaceful Nebraska Sea came to America.

Today, nearly one hundred years after the unprecedented—and happily unrepeated—disaster, it is hard to remember the terror and despair of those weeks in October and November, 1973. It is inconceivable to think of the United States without its beautiful and economically essential curve of interior ocean. Two-thirds as long as the Mediterranean, it graduates from the warm waters of the Gulf of Mexico through the equally blue waves of the Mississippi Bight, becoming cooler and greener north and west of the pleasant fishing isles of the Ozark Archipelago, finally shading into the gray-green chop of the Gulf of Dakota.

What would the United States have become without the 5,600-mile coastline of our inland sea? It is only within the last twenty years that any but the topmost layer of water has cleared sufficiently to permit a really extensive fishing industry. Mud still held in suspension by the restless waves will not precipitate fully even in our lifetimes. Even so, the commercial fisheries of Missouri and Wyoming contribute no small part to the nation's economy.

Who can imagine what the Middle West must have been like before the amelioration of climate brought about by the proximity of a warm sea? The now-temperate state of Minnesota (to say nothing of the submerged Dakotas) must have been Siberian. From contemporary accounts Missouri, our second California, was unbelievably muggy, and almost uninhabitable during the summer months. Our climate today, from Ohio and North Carolina to the rich fields of New Mexico and the orchards of Montana, is directly ameliorated by the marine heart of the continent.

Who today could imagine the United States without the majestic sea cliffs in stately parade from New Mexico to Montana? The beaches of Wyoming, the American Riviera, where fruit trees grow almost to the water's edge? Or incredible Colorado, where the morning skier is the afternoon bather, thanks to the monorail connecting the highest peaks with the glistening white beaches?

Of course there have been losses to balance slightly these strong gains. The Mississippi was, before 1973, one of the great rivers of the world. Taken together with its main tributary, the Missouri, it vied favorably with such giant systems as the Amazon and the Ganges. Now, ending as it does at Memphis and drawing its water chiefly from the Appalachian Mountains, it is only a slight remnant of what it was. And though the Nebraska Sea today carries many times the tonnage of shipping in its ceaseless traffic, we have lost the old romance of river shipping. We may only guess what it was like when we look upon the Ohio and the truncated Mississippi.

And transcontinental shipping is somewhat more difficult, with trucks and the freight-railroads obliged to take the sea ferries across the Nebraska Sea. We shall never know what the United States was like with its numerous coast-to-coast highways busy with trucks and private cars. Still, the ferry ride is certainly a welcome break after days of driving, and for those who wish a glimpse of what it must have been like, there is always the Cross-Canada Throughway and the magnificent U.S. Highway 73 looping north through Minnesota and passing through the giant port of Alexis, North Dakota, shipping center for the wheat of Manitoba and crossroad of a nation.

The political situation has long been a thorny problem. Only tattered remnants of the eight submerged states remained after the flood, but none of them wanted to surrender its autonomy. The tiny fringe of Kansas seemed, for a time, ready to merge with contiguous Missouri, but following the lead of the Arkansas Forever faction, the remaining population decided to retain its political integrity. This has resulted in the continuing anomaly of the seven "fringe states" represented in Congress by the usual two senators each, though the largest of them is barely the size of Connecticut and all are economically indistinguishable from their neighboring states.

Fortunately it was decided some years ago that Oklahoma, only one of the eight to have completely disappeared, could not in any sense be considered to have a continuing political existence. So, though there are still families who proudly call themselves Oklahomans, and the Oklahoma Oil Company continues to pump oil from its submerged real estate, the state has in fact disappeared from the American political scene.

But this is by now no more than a petty annoyance, to raise a smile when the talk gets around to the question of States' rights. Not even the tremendous price the country paid for its new sea—fourteen million dead, untold property destroyed—really offsets the asset we enjoy today. The heart of the continent, now open to the shipping of the world, was once dry and landlocked, cut off from the bustle of trade and the ferment of world culture.

It would indeed seem odd to an American of the '50s or '60s of the last century to imagine sailors from the merchant fleets of every nation walking the streets of Denver, fresh ashore at Newport, only fifteen miles away. Or to imagine Lincoln, Fargo, Kansas City and Dallas as world ports and great manufacturing centers. Utterly beyond their ken would be Roswell, New Mexico; Benton, Wyoming; Westport, Missouri; and the other new ports of over a million inhabitants each which have developed on the new harbors of the inland sea.

Unimaginable too would have been the general growth of population in the states surrounding the new sea. As the water tables rose and manufacturing and trade moved in to take advantage of the just-created axis of world communication, a population explosion was touched off of which we are only now seeing the diminution. This new westering is to be ranked with the first surge of pioneers which created the American west. But what a difference! Vacation paradises bloom, a new fishing industry thrives; her water road is America's main artery of trade, and fleets of all the world sail . . . where once the prairie schooner made its laborious and dusty way west!

VOCABULARY STUDY

VOCABULARY QUIZ 6-A

Words to Learn

conjectures
plausible
shards
subsidence

exodus
inexorable
precarious
cataclysmic

archipelago
amelioration
proximity
anomaly

Match each italicized word with the appropriate choice from the right.

Words in Context

1. "the scientific *conjectures*," p. 206.
2. "a more *plausible* theory," p. 206.
3. "rock *shards* weighing tons," p. 207.
4. "a general *subsidence*," p. 208.
5. "an *exodus* of epic proportions," p. 208.
6. "its *inexorable* descent," p. 209.
7. "formed *precarious* havens," p. 211.
8. "a *cataclysmic* birth," p. 212.

Definitions

a. characterized by sudden and violent change
b. nearness
c. uncertain, insecure
d. betterment, improvement
e. guesses, surmises
f. fragments, broken pieces
g. a chain of islands
h. believable

9. "the Ozark *Archipelago*," p. 212.
10. "the *amelioration* of climate," p. 212.
11. "the *proximity* of a warm sea," p. 212.
12. "in the continuing *anomaly*," p. 221.

i. abnormality, irregularity
j. a migration, departure of a large number
k. lessening, diminution
l. relentless, merciless

VOCABULARY PRACTICE 6-A

Add a suitable selection from the above vocabulary list to the sentences below.

1. Fear of invasion by the Roman legions led to the _____ of most of the women and children of Carthage.

2. Better housing, more jobs, and security usually result in the _____ _____ of social conditions throughout the community.

3. Because the branch supporting it was about to break, the treehouse was in a very _____ position.

4. The _____ of the atomic generating plant to the San Andreas Fault was reason enough for the alarm of the local residents.

5. The creation of the Hawaiian Islands must have been _____, the whole chain being volcanic in origin.

6. The _____ of ancient pottery give archaeologists much information about the eating habits of ancient tribes.

7. What had seemed to be a _____ of the hurricane was only the eye of the storm; soon the winds and rain began to rage again.

8. The passage of time is _____; the years go by, and we all grow older.

9. The alibi of the third suspect seemed to be the most _____, so he was released shortly after arrest.

10. "Suppositions, theories, or _____ are not permitted here," said Mr. Gradgrind. "What we want are facts, facts, facts!"

11. The Galapagos Islands are a famous _____ off the coast of Ecuador.

12. The bumblebee has long been considered an _____ of nature; because of its weight, size, and small wingspread, it should not be able to fly.

SUGGESTIONS FOR DISCUSSION AND WRITING

1. On a map of the United States, plot out the Great Nebraska Sea. What eight states have virtually disappeared? On the basis of what you know about the states, explain what the country has lost in population, natural resources, industries, agriculture, and so on.

2. What other part of the country might Danzig have chosen as the disaster area? What differences would such a transposition have produced in the nature and scope of this disaster?

3. Compare the beginning of the story "The Great Nebraska Sea" to the beginning of *War of the Worlds*. Both deal with impending disaster; in what important ways are they different?

EREM

Anfilov is a young Russian writer; this story was first published in English in 1970.

AT THE sound of the siren, Spassky snatched up the telephone receiver. With his left hand, he dialed the number of the industrial cybernetics expert, and with his right he hurriedly turned the safety switches.

"Nothing I can do here! There's a breach in the wall!" he shouted in the receiver.

"What, what?" They did not understand him at the other end.

"There's been an accident! The wall is breached, the silicon is gushing out!"

"Failure of the blocking system?"

"I tell you, there's a breach in the wall!"

"It must be repaired at once."

"I know that myself. Can I use Erem?"

"Erem?" There was a pause. "I guess it can't be helped . . ."

Spassky put down the receiver and pressed the button for the repair machine. A few seconds later the door opened and Erem rolled into the room. Four quartz lenses stared questionably at Spassky.

"There's a bad leakage of the molten silicon in the southern sector," said Spassky. "I don't know the exact place. The television cable burnt out. Will you remember?"

"Yes," creaked Erem. "What is the temperature inside?"

"A thousand degrees. And it's rising rapidly."

"How much liquid in the crystallizer?" asked Erem.

"A million tons . . . The heat-proofing material is on the left as you enter. Go on, Erem," Spassky said warmly. "Hurry up!"

Erem turned and disappeared. Spassky threw himself back in his chair, sighed, and stretched his hand for a cigarette.

While Spassky was taking the first puff, Erem rolled headlong to the southern sector of the crystallizer, unlocked the door, and burst

219

into the vestibule. Even here it was hot—about five-hundred degrees. Erem checked the rhythms of his logical center. This took a second. To make sure the memory crystals did not crack, he waited another second, then threw open the inner door and found himself in the interior, facing the red-hot ceramic wall. Directly over him, some eight meters from the top, a wide, uneven gap gleamed like a white flame. Streams of molten silicon ran down from the gap, bubbling and shooting sparks.

"The breach is found," said Erem over the radiotelephone.

"Large?" asked Spassky.

"About three meters long."

"Make it fast," said Spassky.

Drippings of the thickening liquid formed a ribbed pattern running down the wall. It would be difficult to reach the gap. Erem thought for a few milliseconds. Then he threw out a horizontal manipulator and seized a large wad of fireproof insulation from the pile near the door. Now he had to climb up. It's very high, he thought. He thrust out his bottom hoist and two side-pieces. The temperature was twelve hundred degrees. The oil in his chamber became liquid like water. Erem knew that it could stand another hundred degrees, and connected the hoist.

A shiny, jointed leg thrust itself out of the white asbestos jacket. The oil was drying, coagulating into a wrinkled crust.

"What are you doing?" Erem heard Spassky's impatient voice.

"Climbing to the breach."

"Faster!" cried Spassky.

Erem knew himself that he must hurry, but there was nothing he could do. The speed of ascent was three meters per minute.

Bracing himself against the wall with his side-pieces, Erem climbed up and up. The stream of molten silicon became wider. The gap spread. Beneath it, a round bulge had formed, and the molten fluid fell from it in large, heavy splashes. One of them struck Erem's side-piece. It bent and slipped off the wall. Erem swayed on the long leg of the hoist. His massive body nearly lost its balance. But he instantly thrust out a reserve piece, pressed it into the overflow, and stopped his fall.

"How is it going?" asked Spassky. "Why are you silent?"

"I am climbing to the breach," answered Erem.

He could not extend the leg of the hoist any farther. The oil was boiling. Erem opened the valves and poured it out. Then he disconnected the inner attachment of the hoist. The leg separated itself and toppled slowly. It was easier now. Some two meters remained between him and the gap, and Erem managed to scale them with the aid of the side-pieces which held him between the walls.

The temperature was already over fifteen hundred degrees.

Despite his internal cooling mechanism and the thick layer of heatproof jackets, his logical scheme began to deviate from normal. There was confusion of visual images. Against the dark crimson background of the wall with its streaming liquid there suddenly appeared Spassky's face with silently moving lips. This interfered with concentration. By an effort of will, Erem banished the image from the wall and turned on the spare sections of his electronic brain.

It was getting still hotter. It would not take long before his logical scheme disintegrated. To delay disintegration, Erem switched on the pain center. And then he felt the incinerating heat directly, with his own indicators. His side-pieces were aching, his asbestos casing was fiery hot, the lenses of his eyes were burning, but his mind began to work clearly and fast. Erem realized that no more than a minute remained before total failure of function unless . . . unless the temperature was reduced. He needed cold, he needed it badly. Just a little of it. And it was so easy to achieve: merely switch on the fans. But cooling was bad for the molten silicon; it was strictly forbidden. Nevertheless, Erem asked uncertainly:

"Is it possible to turn on the cooling for twenty seconds?"

"No," Spassky answered at once. "Under no circumstances! The silicon will be ruined. What are you doing?"

"Starting the repair."

Erem had been almost certain that Spassky would not permit the cooling. And he accepted the refusal as a matter of course. But to him it meant a death sentence. This repair job would destroy him. Evidently, the crystallization of a million tons of silicon was more important than the life of a repair machine. Erem accepted the order and went to work.

He moderated the pains of the burns with his psychocorrector. He brought out his second horizontal manipulator and seized a strip of the heat-resistant insulation with it. He stretched it and aimed it at the uneven, fire-breathing gap, framed in gleaming lips. With a precise movement, he thrust the strip into the fiery ooze. Both manipulators bent, cracked, and fell away.

Erem brought out a second pair of manipulators, separated a second strip, drove it in. Again the tungsten arms broke with a dry, crackling sound and dropped off. Confusion returned to the logical scheme. The memory of his first day came to Erem with sharp clarity. Desperately manipulating his psychocorrector, Erem vainly tried to eliminate from consciousness the uninvited picture of the assembly line where he was born, the smiling human faces, the glints of sunlight on machines . . . Light! It was his first light! . . . The noise of the plant, human speech, someone's merry voice: "I congratulate you with existence, new intelligence!" The gap . . . He must coordinate the movements of his last pair of manipulators. The casing of an essential block of mechanisms was slipping off. Aim it right! Push it in! The third strip of fireproof insulation closed the gap. He leaned back sharply . . .

Someone chattering on the telephone . . . Spassky. Erem no longer understood what he was saying, but he forced out the answer:

"Repair accomplished. That is all . . ."

Then came delirium. The school for training repair machines. The teacher Kallistov, shouting during the efficiency test: "Up! Touch the ceiling, touch the left wall! . . ." His first job, repair of a bridge piling on the Black Sea . . . Stones dropping easily and slowly through the water. And fish . . . A lesson in fearlessness . . . A lesson in mechanics . . . "It's called the Coriolis force . . ." People, machines, fragments of thoughts flashed before him . . . "It was a difficult job, it was the last job, but an important one . . .

Erem did not notice when the entire lower block of his mechanisms dropped off. No more pain. The pulley of the central motor whirled senselessly, irregularly. Stopped. Like a broken phonograph record, two empty signal words, over and over again: "Scheme disintegrated, scheme disintegrated, scheme disintegrated . . ."

Spassky took a last puff and stubbed out the cigarette butt. He picked up the telephone and dialed the number of the industrial cybernetics expert.

"Everything in order," he said. "The crystallizer is O.K."

"What about Erem?" asked the expert.

"The signal is 'Scheme disintegrated.' "

"A pity," said the expert. "A pity . . . I don't know if we can restore him. When the crystallization is finished, call me. I'll come and take a look."

"I will," said Spassky, and put down the receiver.

SUGGESTIONS FOR DISCUSSION AND WRITING

1. People have always personified animals and inanimate objects, giving them human attributes, endowing horses, dogs, and cats with various traits of human character, or even demonstrating warm feelings toward ships, trains, automobiles, and buildings. It is not surprising, then, that fictional people of the future are presented to us with emotional feelings—of amusement, affection, or contempt—toward their robots. Sulla and Marius from *R. U. R.*, Helen O'Loy, Robie from "A Bad Day for Sales," and Erem are cases in point. It is a question of human values, of the basis by which we judge something important to us, worthy of our notice, affection, or respect. Can you define what it is that makes something important to you, so important that you are emotionally attached to it? Is it only familiarity?

2. What details in the story intrude upon the image of Erem as a lifeless machine? At what point does this personification become an important force in the story?

Science fiction, long confined to the written word, in prose, is now availing itself of all media of expression: the theater, radio, movies, television, even POETRY.

As an interesting change of pace, this poem is offered to you for study and comment.

REPORT FROM THE PLANET PROTEUS

LAWRENCE SAIL

They have arrived—at last! and, as we feared,
In nothing better than a brittle box of metal
Crammed with outmoded data. I could hardly believe
The shock transmitted by my regolith,
The rigid impact of their primitive craft
Thudding, juddering down.

I haven't the heart or, come to that, the language
To tell them that their cargo of rattling digits
And slick equations will serve no purpose here.
In the end, of course, they're bound to notice something—
The way their footprints fade, horizons shift,
All measurements misfit.

I've done my best for them, supplied a ledge
Of solid rock, a layer of purple dust,
Even a hillock flared with astroblemes.
I only hope it lasts, because I sense
A growing impulse, in that very region,
Towards a methane sea.

There is, for once, no choice: we must allow
Their stunted minds to glean at least a semblance
Of so-called "facts." They are not ready yet
To do without the security of selection.
Here's hoping that gamma nine can stabilise
Enough to suggest a moon.

Let them return to earth, report their findings.
Distortions protect us; they will not find us again
Or recognize us if they did. One day
They too may learn to live as multiforms—
Till then our possible orbits, fellow planets,
Laughingly ring their science.

SUGGESTIONS FOR DISCUSSION AND WRITING

1. What is the literal meaning of such words as *proteus*, *regolith*, *methane*, and *multiforms*? Do these words clarify the meaning of the poem? Who is the *persona* of the poem?

2. Who are the visitors to Proteus? What clues can you find to support your answer? What sort of life are the visitors accustomed to?

3. Is life on Proteus intelligent? Why do you say so? What seems to be the overriding constant in their lives?

4. What does the fourth stanza tell us about the intellectual development of the visitors? Is there hope for them yet?

5. What might the theme of this poem be, especially as it applies to mortals on earth?

IN THE MATTER OF THE ASSASSIN MEREFIRS

KEN W. PURDY

THE JUDGE enters the courtroom. Think of him as a man of middle age: a hundred and twenty-five or so. Being a judge, he has no name. See him going into the bench. (Nothing in the law is more fascinating than its persistence in looking backward: indeed, is not the law in its entirety based on backward-looking, the search for precedent? So we still call it the bench, although it is only a cube of flexibo big enough for one man, and judges wear around their necks a scrap of black, relic of the robes of ancient times. Such is the nature of things.) So, he enters, he sits, the bench rises soundlessly half way to the ceiling, he stares down upon us, implacable, merciless, and he speaks.

"The matter before this court," he says, "is the trial of the assassin Merefirs. The gavel has fallen."

The persecutor is Dafton, flat-faced as a door, reedy, impalpable, a century of mediocrity behind him. His assignment is a doom-cry for Merefirs: Dafton draws only certainties, and has for years, since a boy barely sixty, a year out of law school, pinned him to the wall in an easy and insignificant first-degree mopery case. Well, legally insignificant, but alas for poor Dafton, a son of the then Regent was a principal, and Dafton's career was forever blighted. Such is the nature of things.

"If the court will but indulge us," Dafton says, "the state will briefly review the crime for which the abominable Merefirs is to be put to maceration.

"Azulno, or perhaps I should say, as all who were living on that tragic day know, the Regional Eminence Fallet was, while in the performance of his public duty, namely and twit, the dedication of the 101st National Euthenic Unit, in this mega, made dead by the assassin Merefirs. Of the commission of the crime, azulno, there is no shred of question: the affidavits of 246,744 actual witnesses have been deposited with this court, and I may say that I myself did see, before the said affidavits were put under seal, a convincing sampling of them. There can be no doubt that they are genuine affidavits in every particular. Further, the Media Communicative Authority has verified that on that day, indeed at the relevant millisecond, 196,593,017 citizens, and a lesser but still weightily significant number of humans, and rather more than a million subhumans, in the categories of slaves, servants, sexers and so on, experienced the tragedy on the telfee. The assassin Merefirs is guilty beyond all question, and it is a mark of the mercy of the present Eminence that the state requires that his punishment be merely the mild one of six-hour maceration. Fibular disintegration would be a more fitting punishment, if I may intrude a personal view, and . . ."

The judge clears his throat, a sound for all the world like the death rattle of a foggus.

"You may intrude nothing, fool," he says. "You should yourself have been macerated decades since. Proceed."

(Here we see the clear thread of modern jurisprudential connection with the ancient Anglo-Saxon law: the judge as impartial arbiter, friend of no one, no one's foe.)

"If it please," Dafton says, "I most humbly agree. The state rests."

The judge speaks.

"We will hear, briefly," he says, "the attorney for the despicable Merefirs."

This is Terravan, the legendary Terravan, savior of lost causes, snatchers from the brink, whose tongue, they say, is gold—and all the rest of him, too. Merefirs, a mere civil servant, could not afford the price of a nod from Terravan, much less a five-minute appointment with him. Terravan has taken the case without fee and out of sheer bravado because no one else in this mega, or any other, would have the temerity. It is a hopeless case, and not only that . . . the assassination of a regional Eminence? Any other lawyer would well know that if by a wild chance he won an acquittal, ex-sanguination within twenty-four hours would be the very best he could expect. Terravan is beyond all that, being famous, rich, and deeply knowledgeable, as we say, as to where the bodies are buried. Such is the nature of things.

So Terravan rises, a short, heavy, feral-looking man, barely a century old, full of fire and ferocity.

"If it please," he says, "I will not contest the statement of Persecutor, uh, hm-m-m, Persecutor, ah, yes, Dafter, Dafton. My client, the assassin Merefirs, did in fact kill, or make dead, the Eminence Fallet. Of course he did, and with premeditation, with every intention. His sole purpose in attending the dedication was to strike down the Regional Eminence, and he did strike him down.

"But that is not the point, as I shall make clear. I call to witness the assassin Merefirs."

Two men in the ruby-red uniforms of warders wheel him in, strapped nude to the witness-stretcher. From the bright life-support box at the head of it the usual wires and tubes lead into him and out of him, serous fluid pump, heart-actuator, oxygen supply, renal filter, waste—exhaust, and so on. When they have him in place at the foot of the bench, they switch the litter to upright, and there he stands, more or less, clamped. The spectators spontaneously applaud, and I must say I myself join in. From head to toe, Merefirs is spectacularly multicolored, and the pattern of the bruises, from the merest blush of pink through mauve and yellow to deep purple, clearly shows, as if he had been signed, the work of the famous chief warder Toddi. Toddi's preliminary witness-beatings are the despair of his competitors, and well they may be. Aesthetics aside, however, Merefirs does not look well. As a human person, he does not look well. He is by no means whole, various parts of him are missing, his head is notably lumpy—he simply does not look well, although I must say I have seen witnesses in much less important cases, matters of mere civic accident, for example, who were worse off. But, to be sure, they had been in hands other than Toddi's. And I knew even before he spoke into the microphone that his voice would be strong and firm. Toddi can spend a day and a night at his work, and yet, the witness will always be able to speak clearly. It's a kind of art, I suppose. But I mustn't digress.

Terravan put his client through the standard preliminaries, age, birth lab, citizen class, and all that.

"Now then, assassin," he says, "when you made dead the Eminence Fallet, your weapon was not a dessicator, a defbro, a B-kel or any other common killing device, is that true?"

"That is true," Merefirs says.

The judge speaks.

"Terravan," he says, "every idiot in the planetis knows he did not use a common weapon. You are wasting my time. I will remind you —once—that my patience is not unlimited."

"I humbly thank you," Terravan says. "And if no common weapon, assassin, what did you use?"

"I used a crossbow," Merefirs says.

"Describe it."

"The crossbow was a weapon of the ancients of the planet Earth," Merefirs says, "a sophistication of the plain bow, which was a piece of wood—a fibrous material that once grew wild—bent by a cord, throwing a second piece of wood called an arrow. The crossbow came to its full flower in the Sixteenth Century, Earth reckoning, so there are few who know of it now."

"Why, assassin, did you choose this obscure weapon?"

"Because I could almost be sure that no one would recognize it as a weapon. Therefore, I could freely carry it, and easily approach the Regional Eminence."

"Tell me," Terravan says, "how could you be sure that this primitive device would be effective in your foul purpose?"

"A crossbow of the ancient Earthians," Merefirs says, "would throw an arrow through a thick piece of strong wood and through a man behind it. Also, it would hit an object as small as the palm of a man's hand at a long distance, say a hundred tontas. It seemed in every way suitable for my purpose, and so I built a crossbow on the patterns of the ancients, known to me through study."

The judge interrupts.

"So you admit, wretch, that you read, you studied, as you say, outside the curricula prescribed for Class II citizens?"

"Yes."

Terravan waits for the judge to speak again. He will not.

"So you made ready your weapon, you approached to within twenty-five tontas of the Eminence and you killed him," Terravan says. "Why?"

"Because he was a heretic," Merefirs says.

A gasp, a rustling of whispers runs through the courtroom.

"Animal!" the judge says. "It is not enough that you assassinated the Regional Eminence, you now defame his memory. This trial is over. The sentence imposed by the persecution is now confirmed. The gavel has . . ."

"If the court please!" Terravan shouts. His voice booms through the room. Clever man! And quick! If the judge had pronounced the word "fallen" the trial would in fact have been over, and no appeal would have been possible.

"I most humbly beg the pardon of the court," Terravan says. "I throw myself upon your mercy, O Judge. But I must, in fulfillment of my obligation of this despicable criminal, say to you that the question of the Regent's orthodoxy or the lack of it does in fact go to the heart of the matter, and I pray leave to develop it. I can cite ample precedent."

"Terravan," the judge says, "one day, you will outrage this court past tolerance. You are a proceduralist. Your obsession with the rights of the accused, as against the rights of the persecution, will eventually, and properly, bring you to the macerator."

"I humbly agree with the court," Terravan says, not being an idiot.

"Against my will, and against all reason," the judge says, "I will be generous. You may attempt to cite precedent."

"I thank you. I cite the case of State versus Hamill, 1186/6V, Archive 29, Volume 617, Page 113, in which the court found that the clearly heretical belief of the defendant in monogamous male-female relationship bore directly upon his crime, even though that crime was most heinous, being in fact arglebub in the first degree."

"You reach a long way for your precedent, Terravan," the judge says. "State versus Hamill . . . that was in the year 2125. You cite ancient history."

"True, O Judge," Terravan says. "But—you will forgive my making an absurdly obvious observation to so learned a jurist as yourself—for the record I must point out that the verdict of the court in State versus Hamill was never overturned, and no counterprecedent was ever established."

"An oversight," the judge says. "However, what you say is true enough. You may proceed. Take heed, however. You have been warned."

"I humbly thank you, O Judge," Terravan says. "Tell me, assassin," he goes on, "in what way did you conceive the Eminence to be heretical?"

Merefirs clears his throat. "I appear to be dying," he says. "Perhaps if the oxygen level could be . . ."

One of the warders fiddles with the life-support system.

"Thank you," Merefirs says. "To answer the question, when the Regional Eminence Fallet came to office he did, azulno, appoint me his Primary Postilion, and in this capacity I was privy to his communication core. On the twelfth day of Hobe, in this subera, I learned of his heresy. I was making a routine run-down of the core when I heard the voice of the Eminence—and, I may say, in synch with his image—dictating what was clearly an entry in his private journal. Obviously, he had forgotten to null the fansponder. I was shocked by what I heard. I was stunned. I reran the core, and I committed the entry to memory."

"Please repeat it," Terravan says.

"The Eminence said: 'Today I took food with that moron Javil. It was all I could do to appear to eat, realizing that this specimen of evolutionary disaster is Secretary to the Planetary Council. He went on at great length about the Venusian war. He wants me, in my subcapacity as Obliterative Authority, to support his resolution to throw Venus out of orbit. This is flaming nonsense: we will lose at least a million useful slaves. And, truly vomitous, I will of course have to go along with him, and he knows it.' "

"That is the end of the quotation?" Terravan asks.

"Yes."

"You were naturally horrified to find that your superior, a trusted official, would entertain, much less record, such evil concepts?"

The dough-faced Dafton rises. "I suggest to the court," he says, "that the learned Terravan is coaching his witness."

"True," the judge says. "Furthermore, I warn you, Terravan, do not outrage this court by attempting to present your bestial client in the role of savior of the state, armed in righteous wrath. I warn you!"

"Not at all," Terravan says, "but I will point out that the Eminence did in fact support the Javil resolution, and that the planet Venus, azulno, was in fact deorbitized. Therefore, the Eminence's private reservations did constitute heresy and he was in fact a heretic."

"Terravan," the judge says, "this has nothing to do with the case before us. Your client, a loathsome sneak who abused his place of privilege by memorizing his superior's journal entries, heretical or not, still acted illegally in assassinating the Eminence. Your point is totally irrelevant."

"I beg to disagree, O Judge," Terravan says. "I will cite further precedent. In the year 1139, Earth Reckoning, the Second Lateran Council, a duly authorized, although secular, governing body of the time, formally outlawed the crossbow as a weapon, forbidding its use except—and this goes to the heart of the matter—except against the infidel. The term 'infidel' was understood to mean one who did not profess the accepted faith, in this case Christianity, one of the ancient religions. To be classified an infidel one did not need to reject the entire faith in its every tenet: the rejection of the smallest part of it would suffice. Clearly, therefore, an infidel was a heretic. And clearly the Eminence Fallet, in rejecting the official policy of this planetis, the deorbiting of Venus, was heretical."

"And what of it?" the judge says. "If the Eminence was a heretic, he should have been brought to trial and duly macerated in the regular way. All this has nothing to do with the assassin Merefirs."

"Ah, but it does," Terravan says. "For, you see, if the weapon my despicable client used was one that might be legally used upon a heretic, then, in using it, he committed no illegal act!"

There is no sound in the courtroom. No one draws breath. The audacity of it! The sheer brilliance of the man! And now, seeing the balance tip, he presses on.

"I can cite further precedent," he says. "While the crossbow passed from general use as a military weapon after the Battle of Marignano, in 1515, E.R., it persisted as a hunting and target weapon, on Earth, well into the Twenty-first Century. And in the Twentieth Century, in one of the American principalities called Usa, it was again outlawed, this time as a hunting weapon. In other words, it was forbidden to be used against animals, but, most significantly, not specifically forbidden against men. I argue that this further strengthens my contention that, in killing the Eminence Fallet with a crossbow, the assassin Merefirs did not act illegally.

Dafton comes to his feet. "I too

have studied the precedents," he says, "and I would point out to Terravan that it is not wholly true that the principality of Usa forbade the use of the crossbow against animals. In its final form, just before World War III, Usa consisted of fifty-two individual subdivisions, called states, and only fifty-one of them forbade the crossbow."

He sits, looking desperately pleased with himself.

The judge looks at him with obvious loathing. "You are a formidable antagonist in a court of law, Dafton," he says. "Terravan is no doubt terrified. But, nevertheless, perhaps he will be able to go on. You have more to say, Terravan?"

"I rest my case, O Judge," Terravan says.

"The court finds as follows," the judge says. "The Regional Eminence Fallet was a heretic. The assassin Merefirs killed him. But by his choice of weapon, Merefirs, standing upon the precedents cited by his counsel, is found not guilty of assassination, although he did assassinate. So much for that.

"Azulno, the common statutes of the planetis forbid disclosure by a civic servant of material made known to him in the course of his duty. To breach this statute is, upon the arguments and precedents here cited by Terravan, clearly heretical. Thus, Merefirs is a heretic. He should therefore be indicted upon that charge, tried and macerated. However, in the light of what we have learned today . . . Warder, do you understand the workings of this weapon, this crossbow?"

"Me, O Judge?" the bigger of the two warders says.

"You, idiot!" the judge says.

"Yes, O Judge, in a way I do understand how the thing works."

"Good. You may demonstrate," the judge says.

The warder takes the crossbow from the exhibition rack. He stands it on the floor, put his right foot into the stirrup and his hands on the string.

"If it please the court," Merefirs says, "may I speak? The warder should put one hand on each side of the string, not both hands on the one side."

The warder changes his grip, pulls up with all his strength until the string falls into its notch.

"Now," Merefirs says, "you lay the arrow—it is properly called a bolt, or a quarrel—into the groove, the blunt end tight against the string."

The warder does that.

"Stand across the room," the judge says, "and let us see if you can strike the assassin Merefirs in the middle of his chest. Have no fear. As Terravan has so convincingly proved to us, you will be committing no crime."

The warder lifts the crossbow, peers down the length of it. Suddenly, almost without a sound, the arrow, short and thick as your thumb, flies across the room, nearly faster than the eye can follow, and buries itself Thump! in Merefirs' gaudy chest. His chin drops.

The violet light on the life-support box winks out. A yellow light comes on briefly, and then, the red. The second warder reaches up and flicks off the switches.

"Well done, Warder," the judge says. "Terravan, I congratulate you. You conducted a brilliant and original defense most successfully. Indeed, there is the mark of your success." He nods toward the body of the assassin Merefirs, still upright, a streak of blood leaking out of the black hole where the arrow has gone. "The gavel has fallen."

The bench drops silently to the floor. The judge stands.

"Terravan," he says, "let us take food together."

The warders trundle Merefirs down the aisle under the admiring eyes of the spectators. The miserable Dafton futilely shuffles his papers. The judge and Terravan go off arm in arm, happy as babes. Such is the nature of things.

VOCABULARY STUDY

VOCABULARY QUIZ 6-B

Words to Learn

implacable   *precedent*   *antagonist*
arbiter   *heinous*   *futilely*
temerity   *heretical*
cite   *bestial*

Match each italicized word with the appropriate choice from the right.

Words in Context   **Definitions**

1. "he stares down upon us, *implacable*," p. 227.   a. hateful, odious

2. "the judge as impartial *arbiter*," p. 228.   b. foolhardiness, boldness

3. "no one . . . would have the *temerity*," p. 228.   c. uselessly, in vain

4. "you may attempt to *cite* precedent," p. 230.   d. beastlike, coarse

5. "you may attempt to cite *precedent*," p. 230.   e. opposed to established beliefs

6. "that crime was most *heinous*," p. 231.   f. not to be appeased, inexorable

7. "to be *heretical*," p. 231.   g. umpire, one who decides

8. "your *bestial* client," p. 232.   h. to refer to or mention

9. "you are a formidable *antagonist*," p. 233.   i. a legal decision justifying a subsequent one

10. "*futilely* shuffles his papers," p. 234.   j. contender, opponent

VOCABULARY PRACTICE 6-B

Add an appropriate choice from the above vocabulary list to the sentences below.

1. I _____ the famous Scopes trial as an example of a judicial controversy evolving from the religious tenets of a community.

2. Centuries ago, criminals found guilty of _____, brutal deeds usually were punished by equally brutal sentences.

3. By the same token, people accused of _____ "crimes," that is, of opposing established beliefs, were punished just as harshly.

4. The man caught in the mud kept spinning his wheels _____ even though his car did not appear to be moving at all.

5. A "landmark decision" by a high court is one which usually changes an existing law, or the interpretation of that law, thereby establishing a new _____

6. The young squire had the _____ to approach the king and throw a glove in his face.

7. No man is the sole _____ of his own fate.

8. The table manners of King Henry VIII were _____; holding whole roasted chickens in his hands, he tore them with his teeth.

9. The great champion Joe Louis wore his _____ down with heavy blows to the body.

10. *Les Misérables*, by Victor Hugo, is the classic story of the lifelong pursuit of one man by an _____ policeman.

SUGGESTIONS FOR DISCUSSION AND WRITING

1. What specific words and phrases in the first two pages of this story enable the reader to determine how far in the future it extends? In what ways do the several "'invented" words scattered on these pages (like "flexibo," "mopery," and "maceration" on page 227; and "mega," "azulno," "sexers," and "telfee" on page 228 aid this determination?

2. What attitude does the judge seem to possess toward the prosecutor, defense attorney, and defendant? Supply specific quotations which support your answers. What does the judge's very opinioned conduct of the trial have to say about the future course of the judicial system? Might this story be considered a "low burlesque" of our present system?

3. What are the chief reasons for Warder Toddi's fame? What do his presence and kind of work suggest about the social milieu of this "mega?"

4. Explain what trends in the world today could point us in the direction of the callous "mega" of Merefirs. What warnings might the story offer us?

5. Who is the *persona* of the story? Is the point of view limited entirely to his perspective, or does Purdy shift to other characters? How does the persona's brief intrusion into the story on page 228 strengthen the reader's view of him? What can you infer about him from his repeated use of the phrase "such is the nature of things"?

EAT, DRINK, AND BE MERRY

DIAN CRAYNE

THE GENTLE purr of the alarm brought her out of a half-remembered dream into the soft gray of morning. A muttered "murmpf!" next to her indicated Logan was at least awake, and Cheryl yawned deliciously as the wall lighting came up to a warm and toasty gold.

"Toasty! Oh, I wish I hadn't thought of that," she mused hungrily. "Well, maybe today will be the day."

A gentle kick with both feet propelled her backsliding spouse into wakefulness. Mock resentful he nibbled at her right ear. "Up," she said. "Up, up, up!"

"Murmpf." Cheryl slid out of bed and padded softly to the bathroom. The ambient temperature of the room was always a good deal warmer than when she had first awakened, and she wondered idly what the temperature was like three stories above in the open air. She paused at the door to check the intercom into the boys' room and the sounds of a healthy—and very loud—argument over ownership of a sweatshirt assured her they were awake.

She turned to consider the shower. "Maybe, just maybe," she muttered, "maybe I could step around it. Or not take a shower at all." She rejected this last as unworkable. Once and only once she'd made that attempt, only to find the bathroom door locked and a gently chiding mechanical voice saying, "Mrs. Harbottle, we've neglected our personal hygiene this morning, haven't we?" Ugh.

She bent to gaze in wrinkle-browed concentration at the large black square on the shower floor. The tubular matrix of the shower stall reached from floor to ceiling and was about four and a half feet in diameter. The black square touched the inside wall at all four corners and its nonskid surface stared at her complacently.

A protesting howl from the bed-

239

room told her that, having had its refrigerator coils ignored, the bed had now administered the first of its electrical shocks. Her tousle-haired husband came into the room looking a trifle wary. "Should have got up when I did!" she gloated.

He slapped her lightly on the fanny and headed for the shower.

"Honey!" she yelped, catching him in midstride. "Let's take a shower together, hmmm?"

"You nuts or sump'n?"

Cheryl put on her very best pout. "People used to take showers together, all sort of snuggly and warm, and I could wash your back or something like that."

"The needle spray does all that, and besides we could never get in there together. There isn't room."

"Sure there is. I'll get in first and sort of scrunch over against the side while you get in."

"Okay, kook. Scrunch if it makes you happy." He kissed her on the nose.

Cheryl stepped into the shower, carefully avoiding the black area and leaning against the far wall with her feet uncomfortably on either side of one black angle, resting her weight mostly on one leg. She moved the other foot to touch the black surface lightly, biting her lower lip in concentration. She watched Logan's right foot as he stepped through the door, and as he stepped down she quickly shifted her weight.

She sighed happily and put her arms around his waist as he slid the door shut. The shower had compensated for his height instead of hers and she got a mouthful of soapsuds, but what the hell, you can't have everything.

Wash, rinse, and warm-air dry. Logan slid the door open and stepped out before she had a chance to yelp. Oh, blast!

Chestnut curls drooping forlornly, Cheryl stared down at her feet planted firmly in the middle of the black square. She sighed.

When she walked into the dining-room, neatly attired in a nonorganic Marsfluf robe with gold frogs, her husband was pulling the first page of the morning paper out of the sender, and the boys were still fighting over the sweatshirt. That there were four more in the drawer didn't seem to matter at all.

"Bob," she said firmly, "you sit over here where you can't fight with your brother."

They both looked at her, mouths agape. They'd been sitting in the same places for as long as either could remember.

"No arguments," she snapped, her heart beating furiously and her hopes rising seventeen points. Bob, who was eight, moved over to his mother's chair and Cheryl sat in his—or pretended to sit as she supported most of her weight above it. "You can dial breakfast too," she said.

This treat removed all objections and he rapidly coded in eggs, bacon, pancakes, and orange juice under the envious eyes of his six-year-old brother. With a flourish he added coffee for his parents and two glasses of milk.

Within two minutes the table panels began to slide back. The trays rose from the bowels of the robot chef. Cheryl, her heart in her mouth and her ankles giving out under the strain, watched with dreadful anticipation as the tray rose toward her. Bob was already busily downing his pancakes and eggs in her usual seat.

The tray stopped and clicked into place.

One half grapefruit. One piece of dry toast. One cup of coffee—black. She felt like crying. She did cry. Also, she let her 132 pounds settle into the chair. The computer had figured it all out anyway.

Two pounds, she thought bitterly. Two lousy pounds. She nibbled at her toast. She'd always hated toast. Dry toast, anyway.

She resented her husband. There he sat, callously consuming thick succulent pancakes, dripping with mouth-watering maple-flavored syrup and golden butter substitute. He even used the final moist, flavorful bite to dab up the last deep yellow drops of vitamin-fortified low cholesterol egg yolk. He crammed the slices of bacon into his unfeeling bestial face, washing them down with coffee and not even pausing to savor the Hickory Smoked Goodness, or the Delectable Crunchy Texture.

Fleeting, satisfying, heart-warming visions of divorce flickered through her tortured head. Freedom, and charming beaux, their features invisible but every detail of their presents plain, her vision included: men with Bonbons. Whitman's Sampler. MacDonald's MacDonaldburgers, yet, for God's sake! Fried Chicken. Pizza. More candy.

She didn't even consider the fate of her orphaned children. She could tell they were unfeeling brutes, true sons of a bestial father, by the very way they guzzled their fresh, vitamin-enriched, golden yellow flavor-fortified orange juice.

Ten minutes later, Bob and Teddy were on the way to school and Logan had been straightened, face-wiped, kissed, and sent off to work. Cheryl watched the table ingest the breakfast plates, puttered around a little, and craftily decided to do her hair and go shopping.

"Logan needs new shirts," she said loudly. "I want to pick them myself. And the boys could use some underwear, and I need a checkup." The machine never answered, but it was watching her. She knew, she knew. She very carefully wrote down all the things she would buy.

But inside, where the machine couldn't see, she watched with rapture: snack shops, coffee shops, tearooms, sandwich bars. Her mind gloated.

Duly machine-coiffed and wearing her newest spring suit, Cheryl took the tube car to the first level, where natural sunlight streamed down through translucent panels into the controlled environment. Trees, grass, and flowers grew in the middle of the Mall just as they did under the artificial sunlight on fourth level, but here popular music replaced the recorded Bird Calls and Rustling Leaves of the residential areas. Cheryl browsed contentedly, making all the purchases she had in mind, buying a few knicknacks besides, and always working her way stealthily toward the Kopper Kornukopia Koffee Korner in the middle of the block.

At eleven-thirty she settled gratefully into a booth, slipped off her shoes, and punched her credit card into the proper slot. A moment of delicious anticipation, and then the serious business of ordering lunch.

She lingered enjoyably over the menu card, and finally dialed a chocolate malt, french fries, a Denver sandwich, and cherry pie à la mode.

The Café-Serv beeped quietly as if in reproach. A suave metallic voice—it seemed to fit well into the Kopper Kornukopia Koffee Korner in the middle of the block—said softly, "Your order exceeds your allowable dietary intake for this day by 2,575 calories, Mrs. Harbottle. Please reorder."

Savagely she punched the Dieter's Special. The wall panel opened and dispensed her tray. One meat patty, small, a scoop of cottage cheese, three tomato slices on a withered lettuce leaf, and a cup of tea. No sugar. Cheryl ate glumly.

Like a starved explorer of some bygone era she paused craftily outside the café and looked up and down the street. Two blocks away the French Chocolate Shop leered at her like the wicked witch. With an apple. With a whole gingerbread house. Which she could eat in one sitting. Cheryl stalked her prey determinedly, her mind racing furiously.

Like most stores, there were no clerks. Mouth-watering assortments of candies were temptingly displayed behind lucite panels. All the adjectival art of the best copysmiths had gone into making the legends on the brass plaques below an adventure in starvation just to be read. Sales machines stood shiningly in the center of the room.

Cheryl chose vanilla cremes at $2.65 a pound, punched for store delivery, inserted her card, and waited expectantly.

This machine had an accepted contralto. "Sorree, madame, but we cannot deliver luxury calorics to someone on caloric limitation. May we hold the order for eventual delivery?"

"But it's a gift!"

"Sorree, madame . . ."

Cheryl punched the CANCEL button and dragged wearily out of the shop. Conspiracy, she thought. And all for two lousy pounds. She felt as if the entire computer intertie system was designed just to thwart her, personally.

A tear stole down Cheryl's cheek. The cashless society had eliminated small change, too. She couldn't even buy that slightly used lollypop from the gluttonous happy-faced kid who wandered past.

The next shop wouldn't even deliver a pizza to her neighbor. As a gift.

Feeling sorry for herself and in a mood to eat five pounds of chocolate divinity with pecans if only to spite the General Health Coordination Plan, she descended a level to the General Services area. Medical checkups were a bore, but every citizen was required to have one twice a year. Besides, she hadn't been feeling well lately. "Probably undernourished," she muttered savagely.

Two hours later she stepped back into the apartment, noting that her morning purchases—minus chocolates—had been delivered. She'd have to start thinking about what to dial for dinner pretty soon. Dinner for Logan and the boys. She knew all too well what *her* dinner would be . . .

Maybe, she thought hopefully, just maybe I've walked enough to lose the two pounds. She went into the bathroom, stripped, and stepped onto the black square in the shower. Standing firmly—there wasn't any point in trying to settle part of her weight on the stall structure she'd found—she touched the eye-level square marked VISUAL.

A small dark square lit up 125 in green. Beneath it, a red 132.5 shone like a death sentence. Two and five tenths above the allowable five-pound deviation above or below optimum weight. No dinner tonight, none at all. No nice fluffy dinner rolls, no crepes for appetizers, no mousse for dessert, no baked potato—an infinite list of "no's" loomed endlessly before her, stretched out in fantastic array, all the forbidden delights across a vast Sahara of food.

Thinking thoughtfully of Danish pastry she dressed in a flowing hostess gown, did her hair in a softer style, and waited for her family to come home. The boys were first, at 4:35, then Logan at 5:03. Washed, combed, and hungry, her men settled to the table while Cheryl began to dial dinner, wondering mournfully what sort of Dieter's Joy she'd get in lieu of the Beef Stroganoff, Egg Noodles with Poppy Seeds, and Chocolate Torte.

The delivery slot across the hall dispensed an orange envelope from Health Services. Bob retrieved it for her as she finished coding in a cucumber and tomato salad.

She opened the letter, read it, and passed it wordlessly to her husband. Her eyes glistened with joyful anticipation. Her tray rose laden with succulent dishes, and the machine's voice noted: "Maternity situations necessitate increased consumption of calcium, Mrs. Harbottle. High Calcium Food has been added to your dessert selection."

Cheryl blissfully dipped a spoon into the vanilla ice cream next to her chocolate torte. "Nyah!" she screamed at the machine. "Nyah, nyah, nyah!"

SUGGESTIONS FOR DISCUSSION AND WRITING

We thought it logical to end this book with a delightful story dealing with a subject that has become one of the major preoccupations of our time: dieting. Now, some questions:

1. Does the author maintain one point of view or does she move the perspective about? Illustrate. What is the point of view of the story? (see page 241).

2. Why does the point of view describe Cheryl's home and family so rapidly and in so cursory a manner in the first few pages?

3. In her comments and behavior, what does Cheryl reveal about her character?

4. The story is essentially about a battle—between Cheryl and the mechanized world in which she must live. What opinion is the reader clearly meant to have toward the mechanized world? Cite specific words, phrases, and quotations that help to form this impression.

5. Describe Cheryl's surprise victory. What is particularly refreshing about her conquest of the "system"? (Hint: Did the "system" have anything to do with her new need for calcium?)

CHAPTER 6 CUMULATIVE VOCABULARY LIST

1. *adroitly*—skillfully
2. *amelioration*—betterment, improvement
3. *anomaly*—abnormality, irregularity
4. *antagonist*—contender, opponent
5. *apparition*—appearance, ghost
6. *appendage*—a limb or subordinate part
7. *arbiter*—umpire, one who decides
8. *archipelago*—a chain of islands
9. *ardent*—eager, driven
10. *aseptically*—in a germ-free state
11. *askew*—sideways
12. *assailed*—attacked, assaulted
13. *assiduously*—steadily, attentively
14. *attenuated*—made thin or weak
15. *austere*—somber, stern
16. *Baal*—a false god, idol
17. *Babel*—a noisy scene
18. *banal*—wanting originality or freshness
19. *Bestial*—beastlike, coarse
20. *candor*—fairness, sincerity
21. *cataclysmic*—characterized by sudden and violent change
22. *catatonic*—in a stupor
23. *cerebral*—of the brain
24. *cite*—refer to or mention
25. *commiseration*—the expression of sorrow or compassion
26. *compromising*—exposing to discredit
27. *conjectures*—guesses, surmises
28. *contingencies*—possibilities
29. *correlation*—interdependence
30. *countenance*—face, expression
31. *debility*—weakness
32. *denizens*—inhabitants, those who frequent a place
33. *derangement*—disturbance
34. *diorama*—a spectacular, three-dimensional scene
35. *discountenanced*—disapproved of, disfavored
36. *efficacy*—effectiveness
37. *enigmas*—puzzles
38. *equanimity*—composure

39. *execrable*—very bad, detestable
40. *exhilaration*—animation, joy, liveliness
41. *exodus*—a migration, departure of a large number
42. *explicit*—plain, direct
43. *facilitate*—make easier
44. *farrago*—a confused collection
45. *fragrance*—odor, scent
46. *futilely*—uselessly, in vain
47. *gratuitous*—freely given, voluntary
48. *heinous*—hateful, odious
49. *heretical*—opposed to established beliefs
50. *hindrance*—impediment
51. *hypertension*—high blood pressure
52. *imminent*—impending, threatening
53. *immutable*—not changeable
54. *implacable*—not to be appeased, inexorable
55. *impotent*—powerless
56. *impregnable*—unconquerable
57. *incontinently*—without control
58. *indefatigably*—untiringly
59. *indispensable*—absolutely necessary
60. *indolence*—laziness, sloth
61. *inexorable*—relentless, merciless
62. *ingenuous*—frank, honest, noble
63. *insensate*—lacking awareness or sensation
64. *interminable*—endless
65. *intermittent*—returning at intervals
66. *intrepid*—fearless
67. *ironical*—saying one thing and meaning another
68. *irresolute*—undecided, hesitant
69. *lassitude*—weariness, fatigue
70. *latitude*—distance in degrees from the equator
71. *ludicrous*—laughable, absurd
72. *manifested*—made visible, obvious
73. *melodrama*—a sensational or romantic play
74. *meridian*—an imaginary circle passing through both poles
75. *morbid*—despondent, diseased
76. *oblivious*—forgetful, unmindful
77. *officiously*—in a meddlesome, impertinent way
78. *palpitation*—rapid beating
79. *paranoia*—mental disorder, persecution complex
80. *patriarchs*—fathers or founders
81. *piqued*—challenged or angered

82. *plausible*—believable
83. *poignant*—pathetic, heart-rending
84. *precarious*—uncertain, insecure
85. *precedent*—a legal decision justifying a subsequent one
86. *preposterous*—absurd
87. *prodigious*—enormous, extraordinary
88. *progeny*—offspring
89. *prognosticates*—foretells, predicts
90. *protagonist*—main character
91. *provincial*—sectional
92. *proximity*—nearness
93. *purports*—means, intends
94. *rapacious*—excessively grasping, consuming
95. *rational*—having reason or understanding
96. *remote*—far off, distant
97. *resuscitation*—revival
98. *retorted*—replied sharply
99. *rudimentary*—undeveloped
100. *schizophrenia*—mental disorder, split personality
101. *scrutiny*—an investigation, examination
102. *shards*—fragments, broken pieces
103. *sinuous*—winding, curving
104. *sleek*—smooth, glossy
105. *statutory*—determined by law
106. *stoicism*—indifference to pleasure or pain
107. *sublime*—exalted, majestic
108. *subsidence*—lessening, diminution
109. *suffuse*—to spread throughout
110. *sumptuously*—in luxury
111. *surly*—gloomy, rough
112. *surmise*—guess
113. *symmetry*—balance, harmony
114. *synthesized*—artificially manufactured
115. *temerity*—foolhardiness, boldness
116. *tenable*—capable of being maintained
117. *tenets*—beliefs
118. *terrestrial*—of or relating to earth
119. *traverse*—to pass through, to cross
120. *undulating*—swaying, moving in waves
121. *utopian*—idealistic, impractical
122. *vociferations*—outcries
123. *zealot*—fanatic

ALTERNATE ARRANGEMENT OF CONTENTS

Plot

The Time Machine (Selections) H. G. Wells 23
War of the Worlds (Selections) H. G. Wells 129
Looking Backward (Selection) Edward Bellamy 161
"August 2026: There Will Come Soft Rains" Ray Bradbury 189
"Erem" Gleb Anfilov 219

Character

Frankenstein (Selections) Mary W. Shelley 51
"The Strange Case of Dr. Jekyll and Mr. Hyde" (Selection)
  Robert Louis Stevenson 57
"Fondly Fahrenheit" Alfred Bester 65
"The Man Inside" Bruce McAllister 83
R. U. R. Karel Capek 91
"Helen O'Loy" Lester Del Rey 103
"Eat, Drink, and Be Merry" Dian Crayne 239

Setting

From the Earth to the Moon (Selections) Jules Verne 3
Twenty Thousand Leagues Under the Sea (Selections)
  Jules Verne 13
"Christmas 200,000 B.C." Stanley Waterloo 31
"The Great Nebraska Sea" Allan Danzig 205

249

Theme

"A Bad Day for Sales" Fritz Leiber 113
"Men Are Different" Alan Bloch 119
Brave New World (Selection) Aldous Huxley 171

Tone

"In the Year Ten Thousand" William Harben 39
"Of Course" Chad Oliver 139
Utopia (Selection) Sir Thomas More 157
Nineteen Eighty-Four (Selection) George Orwell 179
"The Fun They Had" Isaac Asimov 197
"Report from the Planet Proteus" Lawrence Sail 225
"In the Matter of the Assassin Merefirs" Ken W. Purdy 227

APPENDIX 1

Short Story Structure and Point of View

Science fiction, like most literary forms, has as its central purpose the *narration*, a series of movements, actions, and steps taken by characters. If the narration or story is to be a close representation of life itself, if it is to be a story about believable people and events, those actions themselves must be less important than the ideas, fears, or intentions which prompt them. Consequently, the actions which make up a story should always be interpreted as clues to help the reader understand the characters in the story; they are, in fact, one of the ways an author has of developing his characters. In a short story, this action line, which is called *plot*, is particularly important to the author because he does not have a great deal of time to reveal character, as he would if he were writing a novel, for example. Thus, if a young man, at the outset of a short story, is asked by his father whether or not he stole money from the school's petty cash drawer, and responds by throwing a glass of water in his father's face, the reader certainly knows more about him than the fact that he threw a glass of water. By his one action, the young man has revealed a desperate, anxious, explosive state of mind that would require many words of description.

By definition, *plot* is the step-by-step sequence of events in a story, consisting of the *exposition* or *situation*, which introduces the characters and setting, the *conflict*, which presents the problem to be solved, the *climax*, the section of the story in which the conflict reaches the highest point of tension, and finally, the *resolution*, which ends the story. The first part of this series, the *exposition* and *climax*, make up the *rising action* or *complication* of a story; the rest makes up the *falling action*. Without the swift presentation of a *conflict* in a short story, readers will be bound to lose interest quickly, for they will see no complication, and they will be searching for no solution. They will not, in short, see the need for resolution that any narrative must possess. Without a swift *falling action*, readers will again be left without motivation for reading, for the conflict has already been resolved.

No narrative, whether it is a short story, a play, a novel, even a television episode, can exist without this essential structure, although sometimes the structure is disguised and rearranged.

PERSONA. Technically, the *persona* of a story is the voice or speaker that we "listen to" as we read. The author's choice of a persona is particularly important in that it enables him to determine the extent to which the reader becomes involved in the story. The vantage point of the persona is called *point of view*.

OMNISCIENT POINT OF VIEW. The omniscient or "all knowing" point of view is the most traditional of all that we consider in this book. The earliest stories told by man were expressed from the vantage point of a god, a persona who could see all things and all times, past, present, and future.

FIRST PERSON POINT OF VIEW. When the persona speaks in the first person ("I" or "we") and is the main character in the story, the reader is viewing everything through his eyes. The strength of the first person point of view is that it enables the reader to become more closely involved with the main character (*protagonist*) than does any other point of view.

FIRST PERSON LIMITED POINT OF VIEW. As the first person point of view does, the first person limited involves the author directly. But the "I" speaking is limited now; he tells us about someone else who is really the *protagonist*. Probably the most frequently used point of view in modern literature, the limited first person has the advantage of enabling the author to release information about his main character at just the pace he wants to, and from a variety of sources: what the persona himself knows and sees, what he hears others say about the protagonist, and what the protagonist says to the persona.

THIRD PERSON LIMITED POINT OF VIEW. At first, this point of view may seem similar to the omniscient vantage, but it is far more limited. When he employs the third person limited point of view, the author is writing as if he were looking over the shoulder of the protagonist, but without any ability to foresee the future, or to enter any other character's mind. He is only aware of what the protagonist sees, feels, and thinks.

BIBLIOGRAPHY

Criticism

Amis, Kingsley. *New Maps of Hell.* New York: Ballantine Books, Inc., 1961.
Asimov, Isaac, ed. *Where Do We Go From Here?* New York: Doubleday & Co., Inc., 1971.
Bretnor, Reginald, ed. *Science Fiction—Its Meaning and Its Future.* New York: Coward, McCann & Geoghegan, Inc., 1953.
Franklin, H. Bruce. *Future Perfect: American Science Fiction of the 19th Century.* New York: Oxford University Press, Inc., 1966.
Howe, Irving, ed. *Orwell's Nineteen Eighty-Four—Texts, Sources, Criticism.* New York: Harcourt Brace Jovanovich, Inc., 1963.
Lundwall, Sam J. *Science Fiction: What It's All About.* New York: Ace Books, 1971.
Stover, Leon E. and Harry Harrison, eds. *Apeman, Spaceman—Anthropological Science Fiction.* New York: Doubleday & Co., Inc., 1968.

Anthologies

Aldiss, Brian W., ed. *Introducing Science Fiction.* London: Faber and Faber, 1964.
Asimov, Isaac and Groff Conklin, eds. *50 Short Science Fiction Tales.* New York: Collier Books, Macmillan, Inc., 1963.
Clarke, Arthur C. *The Nine Billion Names of God.* New York: Harcourt Brace Jovanovich, Inc., 1967.
_____. *Tales of Ten Worlds.* New York: Harcourt Brace Jovanovich, Inc., 1967.
_____. *Time Probe: The Science in Science Fiction.* New York: Dell Publishing Co., Inc., 1966.
Conklin, Groff, ed. *Science Fiction Omnibus.* New York: Crown Publishers, Inc., 1952.

Del Rey, Lester, ed. *Best Science Fiction Stories of the Year.* New York: E. P. Dutton & Co., Inc., 1972.

Disch, Thomas M., ed. *The Ruins of Earth.* New York: G. P. Putnam's Sons, 1971.

Knight, Damon, ed. *100 Years of Science Fiction.* New York: Simon & Schuster, 1962.

Silverberg, Robert, ed. *The Science Fiction Hall of Fame.* New York: Avon Books, 1971.

SOME RECOMMENDED READING

Isaac Asimov. *Fantastic Voyage*; *I, Robot*; *Pebble in the Sky.*

Edwin Balmer and Philip Wylie. *When Worlds Collide, After Worlds Collide.*

Edward Bellamy. *Looking Backward 2000–1887.*

Alfred Bester. *The Demolished Man.*

Ray Bradbury. *Fahrenheit 451, The Illustrated Man, The Martian Chronicles, R Is for Rocket.*

Edgar Rice Burroughs. *The Gods of Mars, Under the Moons of Mars.*

John Campbell. *Islands in Space.*

Karel Capek. *R. U. R.*

Arthur C. Clarke. *Childhood's End, A Fall of Moondust, 2001: A Space Odyssey.*

Cyrano De Bergerac. *A Voyage to the Moon.*

Samuel R. Delany. *The Einstein Intersection, Nova.*

Arthur Conan Doyle. *The Lost World.*

Robert A. Heinlein. *Double Star, Methuselah's Children, Starship Troopers, Stranger in a Strange Land.*

George Orwell. *1984.*

Robert Sheckley. *Journey Beyond Tomorrow.*

Mary W. Shelley. *Frankenstein.*

Clifford D. Simak. *Strangers in the Universe, They Walked Like Men.*

Theodore Sturgeon. *More Than Human, The Synthetic Man, Venus Plus X, A Way Home.*

A. E. Van Vogt. *The Weapon Shops of Isher, The World of Null-A.*

Jules Verne. *From the Earth to the Moon, Twenty-Thousand Leagues Under the Sea, A Journey to the Centre of the Earth.*

Stanley G. Weinbaum. *A Martian Odyssey, The Worlds of If.*

H. G. Wells. *In the Days of the Comet, The Invisible Man, The Island of Doctor Moreau, The Time Machine, The War of the Worlds.*

Roger Zelazny. *Lord of Light.*

Science Fiction Magazines

Analog Science Fiction and Science Fact
Dimensions
Eternity S. F.
Galaxy
If: Worlds of Science Fiction
Infinity
The Magazine of Fantasy and Science Fiction
Outworlds
Science Fiction Adventures
Science Fiction Quarterly
Thrilling Science Fiction